Hiking Arizona's Superstition and Mazatzal Country

A Guide to the Areas' Greatest Hikes

Second Edition

Bruce Grubbs

GUILFORD, CONNECTICUT
HELENA, MONTANA
AN IMPRINT OF GLOBE PEQUOT PRESS

To buy books in quantity for corporate use
or incentives, call **(800) 962-0973**
or e-mail **premiums@GlobePequot.com.**

FALCONGUIDES®

FalconGuides is an imprint of Globe Pequot Press.
Falcon, FalconGuides, and Outfit Your Mind are registered trademarks of Morris Book Publishing, LLC.
Photos by Bruce Grubbs unless otherwise noted.

Maps by Bruce Grubbs
Acquisitions editor: David Legere
Project editor: Staci Zacharski
Layout artist: Mary Ballachino

Library of Congress Cataloging-in-Publication data is available on file.
ISBN 978-1-4930-0145-3

Printed in the United States of America

Contents

The Hikes

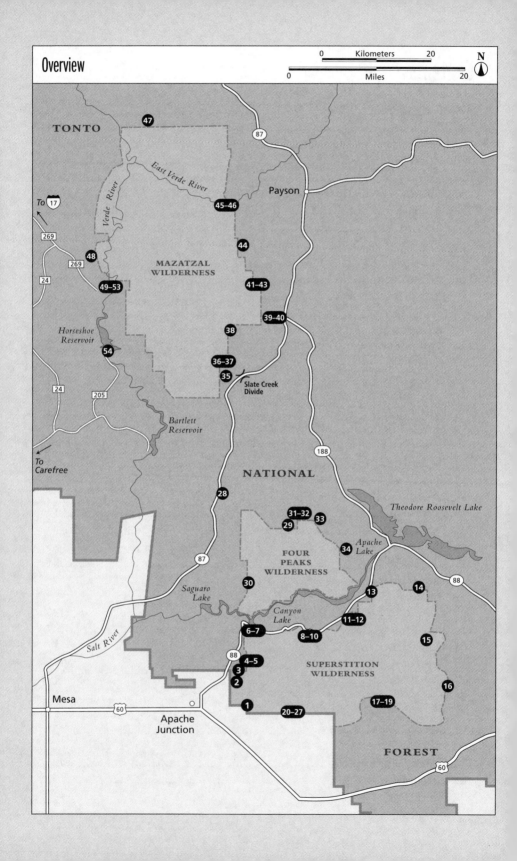

Acknowledgments

I'd like to thank the personnel of the Cave Creek, Mesa, Payson, and Tonto Basin Ranger Districts, Tonto National Forest, who provided me with up-to-date trail information and also reviewed the manuscript and made valuable comments and suggestions. Also, thanks to Rev. David Cooper, who flew while I took the aerial photographs in this book. Thanks to Jean Rukkila for reviewing the manuscript. Thanks to my editor, David Legere, and the production people at Globe Pequot Press for turning my rough manuscript into a finished book. And warm thanks to Duart Martin for encouraging, not to mention aiding and abetting, this project all along the way. It would not have been possible without you.

Introduction

Why hike? Well . . . hiking is enjoyable for people of all ages and abilities. Day hiking requires only a small amount of basic equipment. Wilderness backpacking requires a bit more gear, but a modest investment in high-quality equipment will serve you well for years. Faster hikers can use extra time to explore farther, or indulge in activities such as plant and animal identification, fishing, rockhounding, or loafing. Families and groups can find much to share in the outdoors as long as the hike does not become a competitive event. Hiking is a great way to get exercise. Walking in wild country also promotes self-reliance, a rare enough feeling in a modern civilization that otherwise coddles us from cradle to grave. And, finally, the best argument of all: Roads just don't go to the most interesting places. To get to the unspoiled and undeveloped places in this beautiful region, you have to walk. And getting there is a big chunk of the fun.

This guide covers the Superstition and Mazatzal Mountains in central Arizona. The majority of the hikes are in the Superstition, Four Peaks, and Mazatzal Wildernesses, which include the wildest and most scenic portions of both ranges. This is rugged mountain country—elevations range from about 2,000 feet in the western Superstition foothills to nearly 8,000 feet at the top of Mazatzal Peak. An extensive network of USDA Forest Service trails covers all three wilderness areas. The Superstition Wilderness (160,200 acres) and the Four Peaks Wilderness (60,740 acres) are popular for day hikes and backpack trips from two to four days, though longer trips are possible. The Mazatzal Wilderness, at 252,500 acres, has more than 240 miles of trails suitable for day hikes and short backpack trips and also has some fine extended backpack trips of a week or more that will take you into very remote country. (Mazatzal is an old Indian word meaning "land of the deer" and is pronounced "mah-zaht-zahl.") Because all three areas lie within 50 airline miles of the five million inhabitants of greater Phoenix, the closest and easiest trails can be pretty busy, especially on weekends during the spring and fall. On the other hand, it's also possible to spend a week in one of these wilderness areas without seeing anyone at all.

In this book I present a selection of the best hikes, from easy day hikes to demanding multiday backpack trips. Whenever possible I combine trails into loops or in some other way to make the most interesting hike. I also mention side hikes and other options. Once you have done the routes I present here, you will be well equipped to plan your own hikes. Please regard this guide as an invitation to begin your personal discovery of this wonderful, rugged region.

This second edition has been reviewed and updated throughout. In particular, I've remapped all of the trails and measured distances using digital topo maps. Where possible, I've mapped the trails in the field using GPS.

How to Use This Guide

Hike Descriptions

The hikes are presented in an easy-to-read format with at-a-glance information at the start. Each hike description contains the following information:

Hike number and name: The hike number is also shown on the location map to help you visualize the general location of the hike. I've used the official—or at least the commonly accepted—name for a trail or hike wherever possible. Loop hikes or other routes that use several trails are usually named for the main trail, or for a prominent feature along the way.

Each hike description starts with a general description of the hike, including special attractions, and the name of the wilderness area, if any.

Start: This tells hikers exactly where the trailhead is located.

Distance: The total distance of the hike in miles. Distances were carefully measured using digital topo maps, which is the most accurate method of measuring trail distances short of physically rolling a trail wheel over the route. Both methods are more accurate than measuring distance with the odometer in a GPS receiver because of the 10-meter accuracy limit of GPS. Hikes may be loops, which use a series of trails so that you never retrace your steps; out-and-back routes, which return along the same trails used on the way in; point-to-point hikes, which normally require a car shuttle between trailheads; and lollipops, which include both an out-and-back section and a loop.

Hiking time: This time, in hours or days, is necessarily based on average hiking times for a reasonably fit person. Nonhikers will take longer, and very fit, seasoned hikers will take less.

Difficulty: All the hikes are rated easy, moderate, or strenuous, along with the reason for the rating. This is a subjective rating, but in general, easy hikes can be done by nearly anyone and take a few hours to complete, at most. Moderate hikes take most or all of a day, and require moderate physical abilities and/or wilderness route-finding skills. Strenuous hikes are long, with significant elevation change; they require a full day or several days to accomplish, and may involve cross-country hiking and route finding. These hikes should be attempted only by experienced hikers in good physical condition.

Best seasons: This recommended season to do the hike may be longer or shorter in some years. "Year-round, 24 hours per day" hikes may be hot in summer; you may want to hike early in the morning. And remember that individuals vary in tolerance to heat or cold. A temperature that may be comfortable for one hiker may be unpleasant for another.

Trail surface: Specified as paved, dirt, rocks, sand, cross-country terrain, old roads, etc.

Land status: In this book, you'll be hiking within the Tonto National Forest. All but a few of the hikes are within one of the three wilderness areas—Superstition, Four Peaks, or Mazatzal.

Nearest town: This section lists the nearest town with at least a gas station and a place to acquire basic supplies.

Other users: You may encounter horses in all three wilderness areas. On trails outside the wilderness areas, you may also encounter mountain bikes or all-terrain vehicles.

Water availability: Since this is generally arid country, you should always be aware of water sources along the trail, even for day hikes where you should carry all the water you'll need. Dehydration occurs quickly in the low-humidity conditions that are common in this region, and running out of water can quickly result in a medical emergency, especially during the hotter half of the year. And, of course, backpackers must plan entire trips around water sources. This section lists known sources, including springs, creeks, rivers, and natural water tanks and pockets. Very few water sources in this dry country can be considered absolutely reliable. Don't ever depend on a single water source, no matter how reliable it has been in the past. And remember that all backcountry water should be purified.

Canine compatibility: This section tells you if dogs are permitted or not, and whether they must be on a leash.

Fees and permits: This section lists fees for trailhead parking or backcountry travel, if any, and whether or not a permit is required.

Schedule: This section lists dates that the hike is open.

Maps: The appropriate US Geological Survey (USGS) 7.5-minute topographic quadrangles are always listed, because they are the most detailed maps available. The quadrangle name may also help you find the appropriate area when using digital maps. Hikers planning to follow faint trails or cross-country routes should always carry the 7.5-minute maps and be skilled in reading them. I make note of such hikes in the trail or route description. The USDA Forest Service wilderness map is listed if the hike is shown. Remember that the wilderness maps are detailed enough for hikes on good trails, but lack sufficient detail for hikes on faint trails and for cross-country routes. Nevertheless, the wilderness maps show the official trail systems more accurately than the USGS maps, and I recommend you carry one for any hike in the Mazatzal or Superstition Wilderness. The Tonto National Forest map is listed if it's useful for the hike or the approach road. The trail may not be shown on the map, but it is still useful for general orientation.

Trail contact: The name, address, phone number, and website of the land management agency having jurisdiction over the hike is provided in this section. It's always a good idea to contact the agency before you hike, to learn about trail closures or other unusual conditions.

Finding the trailhead: Driving directions are given in miles from the nearest large town for all of the hikes, followed by the GPS coordinates of the trailhead. To use these coordinates with a map, you must set your GPS to the datum used by your map. For paper USGS topo maps, use NAD27. For most other maps, use WGS84. The coordinates are in latitude and longitude—if you prefer UTM, you can convert from lat/long to UTM at a number of websites, including geodesy.noaa.gov/cgi-bin/utm_getut.prl.

The Hike: In the narrative, I describe the hike in detail, along with interesting natural and human history. The description uses references to landmarks rather than distances wherever possible, since distances are listed in the Miles and Directions. Many summits remain unnamed but are useful as landmarks. I refer to these by their official elevations as shown on the USGS 7.5-minute topo maps; for example, "Peak 1,234."

Miles and Directions: This is a listing of key points along the hike, including trail junctions and important landmarks. You should be able to follow the route by reference to this section; however, the key points are not a substitute for thoroughly reading the hike narrative before taking the trip. Distances are given from the start of the hike in miles.

Wilderness Hiking

Wildlife

The Superstition and Mazatzal country is home to diverse and interesting wildlife. Coyotes are common, as is their prey: small rodents, cottontail rabbits, and jackrabbits. Several species of venomous rattlesnake live here, notably the Mojave and western diamondbacks, as well as nonvenomous racers, bull, and gopher snakes. Rocky Mountain mule deer are very common. Mountain lions still haunt the remotest areas, and black bears are occasionally seen in the Mazatzal Mountains. The raucous call of the crested, blue Steller's jay is common in the ponderosa pine forests at the highest elevations, and you can find the paler blue pinyon jay, appropriately enough, in the pinyon-juniper forests. Ravens scavenge everywhere, and red-tailed hawks and their less common relatives soar in search of unlucky rodents and squirrels. The Verde River, running along the western border of the Mazatzal Wilderness, is the nesting ground for a population of desert bald eagles.

Trail Conditions

Many of the trails in the Superstition and Mazatzal Mountains are infrequently maintained and see little use. Brush grows quickly during wet years and can make a trail very difficult to find. Trails in the western third of the Superstition Mountains are more heavily used and generally in better shape than those in the eastern two-thirds of the range. Much of the Four Peaks area has been burned by a series of large wildfires, and deadfall frequently litters the trails. In the Mazatzal Wilderness, be prepared for faint, overgrown trails nearly everywhere. Only the Mazatzal Divide Trail, the Arizona Trail, the Barnhardt Trail, and the Y Bar Basin Trail receive frequent maintenance.

Weather and Seasons

Because elevations in this area range over nearly 6,000 feet, temperatures and climate vary greatly, not only from season to season but also from place to place. The wet seasons are December through March, when winter storms can be expected, and July through mid-September, when afternoon thunderstorms are common. Fall, winter, and spring are the best hiking seasons, though summer hiking can be enjoyable along the highest trails, above the extreme heat of the deserts.

Autumn is the finest hiking season. The dry, cool weather and changing fall colors make hiking at all elevations an absolute delight from October through November. The first winter storms usually come in late November or early December, and elevations above 5,000 feet often become snowy or muddy. The lower desert areas may experience an occasional snowfall, but most winter precipitation comes in the form of rain. Storms usually last only a day or two, and between storms, the weather is bright and sunny. Winter rain turns normally dry desert into lush terrain with running streams, green grass, and colorful flowers. As a result, the desert can be a very rewarding place to hike in the winter. By mid-March the weather starts to dry out, as the storm track swings farther north. March and April are superb times to hike in this area, and water is usually plentiful because the winter rains and snows have replenished seasonal springs and streams.

By late April, temperatures are rising toward the serious heat of summer, especially in the lowest elevations. Desert temperatures often reach 110°F to 120°F in late May and June. The Superstition Mountains and all but the highest sections of the Mazatzal Mountains are dangerous places for backcountry travel in such heat. Only experts, familiar with water sources and their own limitations, should hike in the desert country during the summer.

Around midsummer, moist air moves in from the Gulf of Mexico, marking the start of Arizona's summer monsoon season. From July through mid-September, afternoon thunderstorms commonly occur over the high country, and then move down into the desert during the evening. You should be off exposed ridges and summits by noon to avoid serious lightning hazard. Flash floods are common during the monsoon, and you should not park vehicles or camp in washes and drainages. Stay out of narrow canyons.

Backcountry Safety

Wilderness is not inherently dangerous, but you must respect it and know your limitations. Once you develop confidence in your technique and equipment, then you'll become comfortable in the backcountry. Hikers should be self-reliant; this capability can be safely developed by starting on easy hikes and progressing to more difficult adventures as your experience broadens. Most wilderness accidents are caused by pushing too hard. Instead, set reasonable goals, allowing for delays caused by weather, deteriorated trails, slow members of your party, unexpectedly rough country, and dry springs. Be flexible enough to eliminate part of a hike if your original plans appear too ambitious. Don't fall into the trap of considering a trip plan cast in stone; rather, take pride in your adaptability. With experience, operating in the backcountry becomes a welcome relief from the complex tangle of civilized living. Wilderness decisions are important, but also basic in nature. While "out there," things that loomed large in civilization lose some of their urgency. In other words, we gain a sense of perspective.

A modest amount of good equipment, along with the skill and technique to use it, make hiking safer and more enjoyable. Experienced hikers with good equipment also have less impact on the backcountry. Good gear is not cheap, but it lasts for decades.

Day hiking is very popular because it can be enjoyed without taking up a lot of time or purchasing specialized equipment. Beginners often find that they already have all the gear needed. For many hikers, the step from day hiking to backpacking is a large one, and often not taken at all. Somehow, the thought of sleeping out in the wild is daunting, as is the additional time, equipment, and skill required. However, the hiker who never stays out overnight is missing as much as the swimmer who only dangles his or her toes in the water. Start out easy, by camping near a trailhead on a familiar trail, then gradually extend your range by camping farther from the road and staying out longer.

Minimum Equipment

On all hikes that are longer and more demanding than a casual stroll, you should carry some minimum equipment: water, food, rain/wind gear, sunglasses, sunscreen, a knife, a lighter or other reliable fire starter, map, compass, a first aid kit, and a flashlight. These items can easily be carried in a small fanny pack, and may save your life if you are delayed or the weather changes.

Footwear

For short easy hikes on good trails, nearly any comfortable footwear, such as tennis shoes or running shoes, will work. It's important the shoes or boots fit snugly but have plenty of toe room. Double-check children's hiking shoes, since they can't determine the proper fit for themselves and won't complain until it is too late.

If you become an avid hiker, you may want to buy a pair of lightweight hiking boots. These are suitable for longer, rougher trails. There are many models available in women's, men's, and children's sizes, usually constructed of synthetic fabrics and leather with molded rubber soles. Some of the more sophisticated and expensive designs use waterproof/breathable fabrics.

For difficult hiking with heavy loads, some hikers prefer all-leather boots with soles that can be replaced when they wear out. Others (including myself) prefer light-weight boots even for difficult cross-country hiking.

Good quality, well-fitting socks are critical to hiking comfort. They provide not only insulation but also padding. A good combination is a light inner sock of cot-ton, wool, or polypropylene, with an outer medium- or heavyweight sock of wool with nylon reinforcing. The outer sock will tend to slide on the inner sock, rather than directly on your skin, reducing the chance of blisters. Inner socks of cotton are comfortable in warm weather, while polypropylene socks will wick moisture away from your skin in cool weather. Wool is the best fiber for the outer, cushioning sock, though small percentages of synthetic fibers make the sock more durable.

Blisters should be treated before they happen! A large or deep blister can be immo-bilizing. At the first sign of a hot spot or other discomfort on your feet, stop and have a look. A hot spot can be protected with a piece of felt moleskin. Often a change of socks will help as well. Once a blister has fully developed, it should be protected by a piece of moleskin with the center cut out around the raised area of skin, like a doughnut.

Clothing

Nearly any durable clothing will do for hiking in good, stable weather. On hot, sunny days, keep your skin covered with long sleeves and long pants, or use a good sun-screen. In the mountains, strong sun and high altitudes can produce painful sunburn in a short time, even on tanned skin; a brimmed sun hat is essential. Long pants also protect your skin from scratches when hiking a brushy trail.

Give a little more thought to your clothing in cool, windy, or changeable weather: Several layers of light, flexible clothing work better than single, heavy layers, such as winter parkas. In cool weather, a warm wool or synthetic watch cap or balaclava makes an amazing difference in comfort because up to half your body's heat is lost through your head. Protect your hands with wool or synthetic gloves or mittens.

The Norwegians have a saying: "There's no such thing as bad weather, just bad clothing." The layer system becomes even more important while backpacking because you'll want to keep your load as light as possible. The "four layer" system can handle nearly any weather condition. The inner layer consists of lightweight, synthetic, moisture-wicking long underwear. A pair of sturdy pants (with shorts or convertible pants as a warm-weather addition) and a sturdy shirt that will hold up to brush and rocks forms the second layer. The third layer consists of an insulating jacket or parka. Down is the lightest and most durable insulation—look for down that has been treated to increase its water resistance. If you expect wet weather, consider a jacket insulated with a synthetic fill. Synthetic pile or fleece is the warmest, driest insulator for very wet conditions. Even when soaked it can be wrung out and worn immediately. Finally, the fourth layer consists of a good set of rain pants and jacket with hood. If this outer layer is constructed from a waterproof and breathable fabric, then it will do double duty as a wind shell.

Don't put up with being overheated or chilled—while hiking, stop to add or subtract layers as necessary to stay comfortable.

Food

You should bring some food on all but the shortest hikes. High calorie food keeps your energy level high. You can make up sandwiches and other picnic items, or bring fruit, cheese, crackers, nuts, and drink mixes. I like to keep an energy bar or two in my pack, just in case.

Although a great deal of dehydrated food is made especially for backpacking and lightweight camping, it's very expensive. You can find many items in supermarkets that make good backpacking food at lower cost. Using just supermarket food, I have done countless backpack trips with 1.5 pounds of food per person per day. Some suggestions:

- For breakfast: low-bulk cold cereals with powdered milk, hot cereals, dried fruit, breakfast bars, hot chocolate, tea and coffee bags.
- For lunch: munchies such as nuts, cheese, crackers, dried fruit, candy bars, energy bars, dried soup, hard candy, beef or turkey jerky, sardines, and fruit-flavored drink mixes.
- For dinner: dried noodle or rice-based dishes, either prepackaged or made up at home, possibly supplemented with margarine and/or a small can of tuna, turkey, or chicken.

Before leaving home, remove excess packaging such as cardboard boxes. Plastic bags with zip closures are excellent for repackaging food. Messy items should be double-bagged. Pack margarine and peanut butter in reliable, wide-mouth plastic jars (available from outdoor suppliers). Put the container in a plastic bag as extra insurance! Extra bags are useful during the trip for double-bagging messy trash. Dedicate one or more nylon stuff sacks to food storage; don't use them for anything else during the trip. The idea is to confine food odors as much as possible, which reduces the attractiveness of your equipment to rodents and other marauding animals. Never cook in your tent or sleeping bag.

To keep your food safe from animals in camp, hang your food sacks from a 10- or 15-foot-high tree limb, if possible. The most foolproof technique is to divide your food into two equal sacks. Use a stone to toss the end of a piece of nylon cord over the limb well out from the trunk, then tie half your food to the end. Pull the food up to the limb, then tie your remaining food sack onto the cord as high as you can reach. Stuff the excess cord into the food sack, then use a stick to push the second sack several feet higher than your head. The first sack will act as a counterweight and descend a few feet, but it should remain at least as high as the second sack. In the morning, use a stick to pull down one of the sacks. This method protects your food from most animals, including bears. In treeless areas, you can make a tripod with three hiking sticks and hang your food sacks from the middle, away from camp. This method is useless against bears but it keeps rodents away from your food.

Water

On day hikes, bring water from home. It's easier and faster than purifying backcountry water sources. Many of the day hikes in the Mazatzal and Superstition Mountains don't have any reliable water sources during the dry season. Remember that each hiker may drink a gallon or more during a long, difficult, hot hike.

Backpackers must plan carefully around springs, streams, rock tanks, and other natural water sources. Many springs and streams are seasonal and dry up during both the summer and fall dry seasons. Never depend on a single water source—always have a backup plan and be prepared to retreat to the last good water source. In the Superstition and Mazatzal Mountains, many drainages are misleadingly named "creeks." If you envision tumbling mountain freshets, think again. Most of these "streams" are bone-dry washes except when they are flooding with a torrent of muddy water. Others contain water only during or after a wet winter. Some of the springs shown on the maps are reliable, even in the hot season; some have water only in wet years; and others have been dry for a long time, if they ever existed at all. Even reliable springs may be small and difficult to find, especially on little-traveled trails and routes. If you are inexperienced in desert hiking, gain some experience by hiking well-traveled trails during the cooler and wetter half of the year before tackling longer, harder trails, and especially before hiking cross-country. If you can find someone experienced to hike with on your first few trips, so much the better.

Backcountry water sources are not safe to drink. Appearance is no indication of safety—even sparkling clear water may contain dangerous parasites. Contamination comes from wild and domestic animals, as well as from careless humans. Infections from contaminated water are uncomfortable and can be disabling. Giardiasis, for example, is a severe gastrointestinal infection caused by small cysts. Giardiasis is spread by all mammals, including humans, and can be disabling to the point where a hiker might need to be evacuated. Purify all backcountry water sources; you have no way of telling if a given source is safe. Chlorine dioxide tablets, available from outdoor shops, are the most effective wilderness water purification system. This treatment will kill nearly every dangerous organisms, including Giardia and Cryptosporidium cysts, within four hours. Carefully read and follow the directions on the bottle to ensure effective use. To retain their potency, the tablets must be kept dry until used.

Water filters are a popular alternative to chemical tablets, but they are heavier and slower. Look for a filter system with a pore diameter of less that 1.0 micron (to removed cysts) and an active iodine element (to kill viruses).

Water can also be purified by bringing it to a rolling boil. The time required to heat the water to a boil is sufficient to kill disease organisms, even at high altitude. The disadvantages of boiling water are that it uses extra fuel and gives the water a flat taste. You can improve the taste by pouring the water back and forth between two containers several times. This restores the dissolved air that boiling removes.

The best water containers are plastic bottles with leak-proof caps carried inside your pack under a layer of insulation to keep the water cool. Another popular arrangement is a fanny pack with external bottle carriers, although the water will get warm in the sun. Some hikers also like the "hydration systems" that are popular with mountain bikers. These consist of a flexible water bladder carried inside a pack and a hose with a valve attached to the pack's shoulder strap, allowing you to get a drink without stopping.

Knife

A knife is necessary for many routine tasks, such as cutting cord, and is vital for emergency fire building. Some hikers prefer the Swiss army or a multipurpose tool with scissors and other implements, while others like a simple, folding, large-bladed knife.

Sunglasses

A good pair of sunglasses is essential when traveling in open areas in bright sunlight. Good glasses are optically correct and remove invisible ultraviolet and infrared light, reducing eyestrain and headaches. Ultraviolet protection is especially important. The tag on the glasses will specify whether ultraviolet and infrared rays are filtered. Cheap sunglasses with no ultraviolet protection are worse than no sunglasses at all. Poor glasses reduce visible light, causing the eye's iris to open and admit more damaging ultraviolet. Excessive ultraviolet exposure causes snowblindness, a temporary but very uncomfortable condition. Hikers who are dependent on prescription glasses or contact lenses should carry a spare pair of glasses. You can protect your expensive lenses with a hard-shell plastic case.

Sunscreen

Sunscreen is another essential. Lotions are rated by their sun protection factor (SPF), which approximates the amount of protection provided by the sunscreen as compared to unprotected skin. For example, a sunscreen rated at SPF 15 gives about 15 times your natural protection. An SPF of 30 is a good minimum for hiking in this area during spring and summer. Few things can ruin a hike more completely than a bad sunburn—and burning ages your skin and increases your risk of skin cancer.

Pack

A well-fitting, well-made day pack goes a long way toward making your hike a pleasant experience. Look for firm foam padding on the back panel and on the shoulder straps. Larger day packs usually have a waist belt, which may or may not be padded, and a reinforced bottom. Fanny packs are another popular alternative. They are especially comfortable in warm weather because your back has free air circulation. Their main drawback is limited capacity, which makes them unsuited for long hikes in remote areas or in changeable weather. Fanny packs work well for young children, because they can carry a token amount of stuff, which helps them feel included in the group.

Packs for backpacking fall into two categories, internal frame and external frame. Internal frame packs have the frame built into the pack; the pack rides closer to your body and balances well when hiking cross-country or on challenging terrain. External frame packs usually have a frame of aluminum tubing with a separately attached pack bag. They are easier to pack for extended trips and give your back better ventilation in hot weather. A good backpack of either type carefully distributes the load between your shoulders, back and hips, with most of the weight on your hips. Make sure you get a good fit by trying out the pack with a load, preferably in the store.

A loaded pack means that you'll walk at a slower pace, especially uphill. Remember to allow for this when planning overnight trips versus day hikes. A walking stick can be helpful, especially at stream crossings, on rough talus, or other places where the footing is uncertain. Walking sticks can also be used to push brush and low branches out of the way, as a prop to turn a pack into a backrest, or to support a tarp for shelter from the weather. Trekking poles—a pair of modified ski poles—are popular but usually come with metal tips. On rocky Arizona trails, metal tips are noisy and tend to slip. Look for trekking poles with replaceable rubber tips, which are quiet and grip rocky surfaces.

Sleeping Bag

Your sleeping bag is one of the most important items in your pack. With a good one you'll most likely have a comfortable sleep; a poor bag will guarantee a miserable experience. The length of the manufacturer's warranty is a good indicator of quality. The occasional user may be happy with a backpacker-style mummy bag insulated with a synthetic fill. Synthetic fills have the advantages of lower initial cost and of retaining some of their insulating ability when soaking wet. High quality down fill, though more expensive, is still unsurpassed in insulating capability for its weight. Since it is more durable, down is actually less costly than synthetics over the lifetime of the bag. People who do longer backpack trips usually prefer down bags. Down is also more water resistant than commonly thought, as anyone who has tried to wash a down bag by hand can tell you. Sleeping bags are rated by temperature and sometimes by recommended seasons. A three-season bag is adequate for most backpackers. If you sleep cold, consider a warmer bag.

Sleeping Pad

Since lightweight sleeping bags don't provide much insulation or padding underneath, you'll need a sleeping pad. The best type currently available is the self-inflating foam-filled air mattress. These are less prone to punctures than a traditional air mattress, are much warmer, and are very comfortable. Closed-cell foam pads are a cheaper alternative. They insulate very well but are not especially comfortable.

Shelter

Most hikers depend on a tent for shelter. Sound construction and high quality is important. A three-season, two-man dome or free-standing tent is the most versatile. Larger tents are more awkward to carry and require more spacious campsites. Nearly all tents use a separate waterproof fly, which provides rain protection and allows moisture to escape from within the tent. The tent canopy should have plenty of windows and doors for ventilation, each covered with fine "no-see-um" netting to keep bugs out. Small children can share a tent with parents, but as they get older, kids like having their own tent.

Some experienced hikers avoid the weight and expense of a tent by carrying a nylon tarp with a separate groundsheet. A tarp provides good weather protection if set up properly, and is versatile enough to use as a sunshade or windbreak during lunch stops. Using a tarp effectively does take some practice. Also, a tarp provides no protection from mosquitoes and other insects. Another ultra-lightweight shelter is a waterproof, breathable bivouac sack. Some bivy sacks have bug netting and poles that transform them into tiny one-man tents, but a bivy sack can still be a miserable place during a long storm.

First Aid Kit

A small first aid kit will do for day hikes, but you'll definitely need a more complete kit for backpacking. Make sure that you get one intended specifically for wilderness sports. You'll want to include a few repair items, such as spare bulbs and batteries for your flashlight, stove and pack parts, and a sewing kit. At least one member of your party should have current first aid training. Check with your local outdoor retailer or online to pick up one of several excellent books on wilderness medical information.

Personal Locator Beacon

Personal locator beacons (PLBs) are the hiker's equivalent of the emergency locator beacons carried by ships and aircraft. When activated, a PLB determines your location with GPS (the Globe Positioning System) and transmits a coded signal that contains the owner's name and contact information to the search-and-rescue satellites cooperatively maintained by the United States and Russia. The satellite relays the PLB signal to the search-and-rescue coordination center. The center attempts to contact the owner, and, if no contact is made, initiates a search. Because the PLB locates you within a few feet, rescuers can respond directly to your position.

If you frequently hike in remote areas, and especially if you hike solo, a PLB is a wise investment. PLBs weigh just a few ounces, so won't add significantly to a backpack's weight. Anyone can twist an ankle, no matter how experienced, and a twisted ankle far from a water source can quickly develop into a life-threatening emergency.

PLBs must be registered with the national authority in your country every two years—the National Oceanic and Atmospheric Administration (NOAA) is the authority in the United States. Instructions on how to register come with your PLB. PLBs are designed to transmit for at least 24 hours after being activated and have a shelf life of five years. After five years, or upon being activated, PLBs must be returned to the manufacturer for battery replacement.

Always test your PLB before each wilderness trip. And never activate a PLB except in a life-threatening emergency. There are severe penalties for false use of PLBs, or any other distress signal.

Accessories

A camera is probably the most common "extra" item carried on day hikes. You can use small nylon ditty bags or plastic bags to protect cameras and other fragile items from rain and dust. Even the most waterproof packs can leak through seams and zippers, and dust and sand seems to get into everything.

Equipment Sources

Consider supporting local outdoor shops, especially stores staffed by people who use the gear and are willing to share their knowledge with you. Mail order is an alternative if you can't find a good local shop.

Trip Planning

Maps are essential for trip planning and should be obtained in advance. Guidebooks allow you to learn about an area more quickly than maps alone. Once you are comfortable with an area and have done many of the hikes in the guidebooks, you will be able to plan your own hikes, using maps and information from other hikers to help you.

When planning a backpacking trip, think about alternatives to traditional campsites. Dry camping, or camping with just the water you carry, is a valuable skill with many advantages. Dry camping eliminates the danger of inadvertently contaminating wilderness streams and lakes. You can avoid heavily used campsites and their camp-robbing animal attendants, which include skunks, mice, gray jays, and insects. Dry camping also lets you choose from many beautiful, uncrowded campsites. The technique is simple: Use a collapsible water container to pick up water at the last reliable source of the day, then use minimal water for camp chores. If possible, plan your route so that you pass at least one reliable water source each day of the trip.

Note that certain areas may be closed to overnight camping. Such closures may be temporary or permanent. Closures are mentioned in the hike descriptions; check with the listed agency for the latest information.

Backcountry Navigation

Maps

Several different types of maps are available for wilderness navigation. Topographic maps are the most useful because they show the elevation and shape of the land through the use of contour lines. All of the Mazatzal and Superstition Mountains are covered by the quadrangle series published by the US Geological Survey (USGS). Each hike description in this book lists the USGS topographic maps that cover the hike. The USGS maps are produced from aerial photos to high standards of accuracy. At a scale of 1:24,000 (2.6 inches to the mile) and printed in sheets that cover about 7 by 9 miles, these are usually the most detailed maps available. The catch is that the USGS does not update maps all that often, so man-made features such as trails and roads may be out of date. USGS maps are sold at some outdoor shops and bookstores and are also available by mail order from the USGS at store.usgs.gov; (888) ASK-USGS.

The Tonto National Forest publishes wilderness maps of the Mazatzal and Superstition Wildernesses at a scale of 1 inch to 1 mile. These two maps show the trail system and are more up to date than USGS maps but at a smaller scale with less topographic detail. They are adequate for trail hiking and excellent for trip planning. Cross-country hikers will want to supplement the wilderness maps with the USGS maps. The USDA Forest Service also publishes a map of the entire Tonto National Forest, which shows the forest road system at a scale of 1:126,720 (0.5 inch to the mile). It also shows the official road numbers as shown on road signs. This map is useful for finding trailheads but doesn't have enough detail for hiking.

Several privately produced maps of varying accuracy are available from time to time. I suggest using these to supplement the government maps.

Another option is digital, computer-based maps. Mapping programs such as TopoFusion (topofusion.com) and ExpertGPS (expertgps.com) work with GPS and a large variety of maps, as well as with aerial and satellite imagery, and are invaluable for trip planning. Google Earth is another valuable resource, especially in desert areas where you can often pick out the trails on the satellite photos.

If you use digital maps for trip planning, always print a copy of the maps you'll need on your trip and carry them in a plastic bag with a zip closure

Map reading is a skill that requires practice, but it pays off in increased safety in the backcountry. The best way to learn is to get a map of an area that you already know. Go to a place with an overview of the terrain and spend some time relating what you see to the map symbols. Before entering the backcountry, study the relevant maps to become familiar with the general lay of the land. On the ground, you may find trail signs have been vandalized or are inaccurate. It is wise to stay aware of your location at all times and use the trail signs as confirmation. While hiking, refer to the map often and locate yourself in reference to visible landmarks. If you do this consistently, without relying on trail signs, you will never become lost.

Compass

Always carry a reliable, liquid-filled compass so that you can determine directions in dense forest or bad weather. Because backcountry navigation in the generally open terrain of central Arizona consists primarily of map reading, your compass will probably languish in your pack for years before you use it. When you finally do need it, you will need it badly, which is not a good time to find out that the needle has fallen off.

Global Positioning System

The satellite navigation system maintained by the US Department of Defense makes it possible to find your location nearly anywhere on Earth. The Global Positioning System (GPS) consists of 24 active satellites orbiting 12,000 miles above the Earth, transmitting navigation signals to low-cost, portable receivers. A GPS receiver's display shows your position within 33 feet (10 meters) or better. Weather conditions do not affect the accuracy of GPS, but the receiver must have a clear view of the sky. This means that dense forest, narrow canyons, or poor satellite geometry can prevent an accurate fix.

When buying a receiver for hiking, make sure it uses the Universal Transverse Mercator (UTM) coordinate system, as well as latitude and longitude. UTM is found on USGS topographic maps and all digital maps and is easier to use than the latitude and longitude system. Any map accurate enough for wilderness navigation will have at least one coordinate system. All digital mapping products work with GPS. You can upload and download routes and position fixes from your computer to your GPS unit, saving a lot of time over entering information on the GPS keypad.

A GPS unit is no substitute for a good map and a reliable compass. Remember that a GPS unit is useless if the batteries die: Take spares!

And a cell phone is no substitute for a dedicated trail GPS unit. The GPS in a cell phone is designed to locate the phone during a 911 emergency call and is not as sensitive as a dedicated GPS receiver. Also, most cell phones have a short battery life, and the batteries are proprietary and can't be replaced in the field. Trail GPS receivers have much longer battery lives and use commonly available AA or AAA batteries, which are field-replaceable.

And never depend on a cell phone for trail maps. Again, the battery life is short, and you may need a cell signal to download maps.

Walking

Walking in wild country is not just a matter of "picking 'em up and putting 'em down." Most novice hikers try to go too fast, then find themselves out of breath and having to stop frequently. The group should move at a speed that allows easy conversation among all members. Long hikes, especially uphill sections, should be paced so that rest breaks are needed only about once an hour. That's not to say that you shouldn't stop at scenic viewpoints or other points of interest, but if you find yourself taking many breaks, you're probably going too fast. Keep rest stops short so that you don't become chilled. It's harder to get going after a long break.

As you walk, pay attention to the stretch of ground immediately in front of you. Hazards such as spiny plants, overhanging sharp branches, and sunbathing rattlesnakes are easy to miss if you only have eyes for the scenery. On the other hand, daydreaming is an important part of hiking. There are always sections of trail that aren't interesting. The experienced hiker can let her mind wander far away but still pay attention to the trail underfoot and the route ahead. Or she can focus on aspects of the environment such as birdsong or identifying trees from a distance by their general shape. Either technique lets the miles pass almost unnoticed.

Hikes taken with young children should have extremely modest goals. A day hike of a few hundred yards may be far enough. Children find all sorts of interesting things in a small area that their parents would not otherwise notice. Introduce your children to short day hikes at an early age, gradually lengthening the distance as they grow older and their stamina and interests increase. The first overnight hikes can be kept short, as such trips should be for any novice hiker, child or adult. Once a child is old enough to carry a pack, keep the load light. If you progressively introduce your children to backpacking, by the time they are energetic teenagers they'll be addicted to hiking. Then, maybe, you can persuade them to carry some of your load!

Trail Courtesy

Never cut switchbacks on trails. Shortcutting actually takes more physical effort than staying on the trail. It also increases erosion and trail maintenance costs.

Give horses and other pack animals the right-of-way by stepping off the trail on the downhill side. Talk in a normal tone of voice and don't make sudden movements or loud noises, which can spook an animal.

Mountain bikes are not allowed on trails in any designated wilderness, which includes the Mazatzal, Four Peaks, and Superstition Wildernesses. You may encounter bikes outside these areas. Although hikers have the right-of-way over bikes, I prefer to step off the trail to let riders past, feeling that feet cause less damage than tires. On the other hand, mountain bikers should respect the desire of others for a quiet backcountry experience and refrain from excessive noise or speed near hikers.

Smokers should stop at a bare spot or rock ledge, then make certain that all smoking materials are out and stowed to pack out before continuing. Please remember that cigarette butts are not biodegradable—they should be carried out with the rest of your garbage. Never smoke or light any kind of fire on windy days or when fire danger is high, because wildfires can start easily and spread explosively under these conditions.

Dogs are allowed in the national forests, but must be kept under control. A leash is a good idea. If your dog barks or runs up to other people, it should be left at home. Barking dogs disturb other hikers, and their presence places unnecessary stress on wildlife.

Cutting live trees or plants of any kind, blazing or carving initials on trees or rocks, picking wildflowers, and building rock campfire rings are destructive activities. We all need to consider the next hiker and leave the environment as we would like to find it ourselves. Visit the Leave No Trace Center for Outdoor Ethics website (lnt.org) for more information; the site includes resources on how to walk lightly on the land.

Never disturb ruins, historic sites, or artifacts. All such sites are protected by the National Historic Preservation Act and the Archeological Resources Preservation Act. These laws are intended to preserve our historic and prehistoric heritage. Archaeologists study artifacts in their original settings because the context reveals more information than the artifact alone. Once a site is disturbed, another piece of the puzzle is gone forever.

Camping

Start looking for a campsite at least a couple of hours before dark. Campsites become harder to find as the group size increases: a good reason to avoid groups larger than five or six people. The best camps are on reasonably level sites with dry, sandy soil, bare rock, or forest duff. Avoid fragile, easily damaged sites such as grassy meadows and stream banks. Select a site that's screened from trails, meadows, and other campsites. As a rule of thumb, camp out of sight and sound of others, and respect their desire for wilderness solitude. Land managers sometimes close specific areas to camping to allow them to recover from heavy use. Please respect these closures.

During hot weather, look for shade, especially from the morning sun. If camping in forest, check overhead for "widow-makers"—large dead branches that may break off and crash down. Ponderosa pines and cottonwood trees are notorious for producing widow-makers. If bad weather threatens, look for a campsite sheltered from wind and blowing rain, preferably with natural drainage and an absorbent surface such as forest duff or sand. Heavy forest provides protection from rain at the beginning of a storm, but trees drip for hours after the rain stops. Never dig drainage ditches or excavate dirt to level a campsite; these obsolete practices cause erosion and severe damage. A slight slope will keep groundwater from pooling under your tent. Modern sleeping pads make it possible to camp on gravel—or even rock slabs—in comfort.

Campfires

Don't build campfires, except in an emergency. Too much of the backcountry is scarred by campfire rings and heaps of trash and aluminum cans that campers have tried, futilely, to burn. Campfires are prohibited in some areas, and are likely to be outlawed elsewhere. Campfires are also prohibited in the Tonto National Forest during periods of high fire danger.

If you must build a campfire, use an existing fire ring, if possible. Otherwise, dig a shallow pit in a sandy or gravelly area clear of organic ground litter. Use the dirt from the hole to make a berm around the fire pit. Do not use rocks to construct a fire ring—they become permanently blackened. Before leaving camp, put your fire out thoroughly by mixing the coals with water or dirt. Make absolutely certain the embers are cold by putting your hand in the ashes and feeling around for heat. If you doubt the need to make sure your fire is out, consider the 60,000 acres burned in the southern Mazatzal Mountains in 1996. That fire started in a careless camper's abandoned campfire, as did the half-million-acre Wallow Fire, the second largest wildfire in American history., which burned the eastern Mogollon Rim country in Arizona and New Mexico during June 2011.

Trash

If you carried it in, you can also carry it out. Food scraps such as banana peels and orange peels take months or years to decompose—carry them out, too. Lightweight food that has been carefully repacked to eliminate excess packaging produces little trash, even if you carry enough food for a week or more in the backcountry. Avoid burying food or trash. After you leave, animals will smell it, dig it up, and scatter it all over the place. Don't feed wild creatures; they will become dependent on human food, which is not good for them and can lead to their starvation during the winter. Also, animals that become used to human food become more aggressive in seeking out those sources, which leads to unpleasant human/wildlife encounters and the possible destruction of your expensive equipment.

Sanitation

We all need to be experts in wilderness sanitation. Naturally occurring diseases such as giardiasis are aggravated by poor human practices. If possible use the facilities that are often available at trailheads and campgrounds. In the backcountry, select a site at least 200 yards from streams, lakes, springs, and dry washes. Avoid barren, sandy soil, if possible. Next, dig a small "cat-hole" about 6 inches down into the organic layer of the soil. (Some people carry a small plastic trowel for this purpose.) When finished, refill the hole, making the site as natural as possible. Land managers now recommend that all toilet paper be carried out. Use double zipper bags, adding a small amount of baking soda to absorb odor.

Weather

During the summer, heat can be a hazard, especially at the lower elevations. In hot weather, each hiker will need up to two gallons of water every day to avoid serious heat injury. To avoid dehydration, drink more water than required to quench your thirst. Sport drinks that replace electrolytes are also useful.

Protection both from the heat and the sun is important; a lightweight sun hat is essential. During hot weather, plan hikes at higher elevations, or hike early in the day to avoid the afternoon heat.

Thunderstorms may occur during the summer. Towering cumulus clouds appear first and warn of the heavy rain, hail, high winds, and lightning that are likely to follow.

In thunderstorm season, plan a hike that avoids high ridges and peaks during the afternoon. If a thunderstorm does occur, get off exposed ridges and stay away from lone trees. If lightning begins to strike in your immediate area, crouch on a sleeping pad or other insulating object with your feet together, keeping your contact with the ground to a minimum. This reduces your exposure to the ground currents caused by a lightning bolt, which spread several hundred feet from the point of the actual strike.

Avoid continuous exposure to chilling weather. Cool winds, especially with rain, are the most dangerous because the heat loss is insidious. Once your body temperature has cooled beyond a critical point, hypothermia sets in, which is a life-threatening condition. You can prevent hypothermia by wearing enough layers of clothing to avoid chilling, and by eating and drinking regularly so that your body continues to produce heat.

Snow may fall at any time of year on the higher mountains. Be prepared for it by bringing more layers of warm clothing than you think you will need. During the winter season, use synthetic garments made of polypropylene or polyester fibers, because these fibers retain their insulating ability when wet better than any natural fiber, including wool.

Insects and Their Kin

Insects can be a hazard at times. Mosquitoes are occasionally found at all elevations in the spring and summer after wet winters. The common, larger, brown scorpion is found nearly everywhere in the region, but its sting has about the same potency as a bee sting. In the lower desert areas you may encounter the smaller, but much more dangerous, straw-colored bark scorpion. Scorpions lurk under rocks and bark and are mainly active at night in warmer weather. You can reduce the risk of a sting to nearly zero by never placing your hands or feet where you can't see. Always kick rocks and sticks before picking them up.

Black widow spiders, identifiable by the red, hourglass-shaped mark on the underside of mature females, can inflict a dangerous bite. The brown recluse spider inflicts a bite that may cause extensive tissue damage at the site but is not generally life threatening. These bites seem minor at first, but may become very painful after several hours. There is no specific field treatment; young children should be transported to a hospital as soon as possible. The dangerous-looking centipede can produce a painful bite, and also irritate skin with its sharp, clawed feet, but it is not life threatening.

Kissing bugs, also known as conenose bugs or assassin bugs, are obnoxious insects that live in rodent nests and feed on mammal blood at night, leaving large, itchy welts on the victim. They're not a problem during the cooler months, but during the warmer half of the year they give desert backpackers one more reason to sleep in a fully closed net tent.

Ticks occur rarely in the desert. If ticks are discovered, though, do a careful full body search every day. It's important to remove embedded ticks before they have a chance to transmit disease, which takes a day or more.

Other insects, such as bees and wasps also may give nonthreatening but painful stings. But the Africanized bee can cause serious problems. Identical in appearance to the common honeybee, these bees are very aggressive in defending their hive. Never approach any beehive or swarm, wild or domestic. Be wary about peering into rock crevices or holes in dead trees. If attacked, drop your pack and run. Get into water or heavy brush. Protect your eyes and don't swat at the bees. If shelter, such as a building or vehicle is available, use it.

People who have a known allergic reaction to specific insect stings are at special risk. Since an allergic reaction can develop rapidly and be life threatening, hikers with known allergies should check with their doctors to see if desensitization treatment and/or emergency sting kits are recommended.

Snakes

Rattlesnakes are common at all elevations in the Superstition and Mazatzal Mountains. Rattlers can easily be avoided because they usually warn off intruders by rattling well before a hiker is within striking range. Never handle or tease any snake. Since rattlesnakes can strike no farther than approximately half their body length, avoid placing your hands and feet in areas that you cannot see, and walk several feet away from rock overhangs and shady ledges. Bites usually occur on the feet or ankles, so ankle-high hiking boots and loose fitting long pants will prevent most injuries. Snakes prefer surfaces at about 80°F. This means they like the shade of bushes or rock overhangs in hot weather, and in cool weather they prefer open, sunny ground. Don't confuse commonly found but nonvenomous bull snakes with rattlesnakes—bull snakes don't have rattles on their tails.

Wildlife

Wild animals normally leave hikers alone unless they are molested or provoked. Don't feed any wild animal, as it may get used to handouts rapidly, and then will vigorously defend its new food source. Around camp, problems with rodents can be avoided by hanging your food from rocks or trees. Even the toughest pack can be wrecked by a determined mouse or squirrel that has all night to work. Heavily used campsites host the worst critter problems.

Plants

Spiny plants are a hazard, especially at lower elevations. Always watch where you place your hands and feet. Spines can be removed with a pair of tweezers, a good item to have in your first aid kit.

Stinging nettle is harder to deal with because the irritating hairs are so fine. Apply a strip of adhesive tape over the affected area, then remove it to pull out the nettle hairs.

Never eat any plant unless you positively know what you are doing.

Poison ivy may be found in the lower canyons; it is easily recognized by its shiny leaves, which grow in groups of three. If you accidentally make contact with poison ivy, wash the affected area with soap and water as soon as possible. Plain water is better than nothing. Calamine lotion may help relieve the itching. Remember that dogs and clothing that have come into contact with the plants can spread the volatile oil that causes the skin reaction.

Rescue

Anyone entering remote country should be self-sufficient and prepared to take care of emergencies such as equipment failure and minor medical problems. Very rarely, circumstances may create a life-threatening situation that requires an emergency evacuation or a search-and-rescue effort. Carry and know how to use a signal mirror. Mirror flashes are visible for 50 miles or more in good weather. Always leave word of your hiking plans with a reliable individual. For backpack trips, you should provide a written itinerary and a map. The responsible person should be advised to contact the appropriate authority if you are overdue. In your instructions, allow extra time for routine delays. The appropriate county sheriff is responsible for search and rescue. The USDA Forest Service cooperates with the sheriff's department in each county and may also be contacted in the event of an emergency.

Cell Phones

Never depend on a cell phone in a backcountry emergency. The cellular system is designed for populated areas and major highways and probably won't work in remote areas, especially canyons and deep valleys. Of course, if you have a cell signal in an emergency, use your phone to call 911. But after you have communicated the vital information to the dispatcher, promise to call back if your situation changes, and turn off your phone to save the battery. Even if you can alert authorities to your problem, you will have a better chance of surviving until rescuers arrive if you are self-sufficient.

Trail Finder

Easy Day Hikes

1 Jacob's Crosscut Trail
3 Massacre Grounds
32 Pigeon Spring Loop
35 Marion Spring

Very Easy Day Hikes for Parents with Small Children

1 Jacob's Crosscut Trail
3 Massacre Grounds

Long Day Hikes

2 Siphon Draw
4 Garden Valley Loop
5 Second Water Trail
6 Lower La Barge Box
19 Randolph Canyon
25 Needle Canyon
28 Ballantine Trail
34 Four Peaks Trail
36 Squaw Flat
40 South Fork of Deer Creek
41 Y Bar Basin
42 Mazatzal Peak
44 North Peak
46 White Rock Spring
47 East Verde Confluence
48 Red Creek
51 Mountain Spring Loop

Summer Hikes

31 Browns Peak
32 Pigeon Spring Loop
38 Mazatzal Divide Trail
41 Y Bar Basin

First Night in the Wilderness

6 Lower La Barge Box
17 Reavis Creek
22 Dutchmans Loop
41 Y Bar Basin

Hikes For Photographers

1 Jacob's Crosscut Trail
3 Massacre Grounds
6 Lower La Barge Box
10 Lower Rogers Canyon
18 Angel Basin
20 Coffee Flat Mountain Loop
23 Barks Canyon
24 Cave Trail
38 Mazatzal Divide Trail
41 Y Bar Basin
43 Rock Creek
49 Verde River Trail

Hikes with Lots of Side Trips and Exploring

4 Garden Valley Loop
7 Marsh Valley Loop
8 Peters Mesa
9 Tortilla Pass–Red Tanks Divide
10 Lower Rogers Canyon
12 Upper Fish Creek
15 Fireline Loop
21 Bluff Spring Loop
22 Dutchmans Loop
29 Alder Creek Loop
38 Mazatzal Divide Trail
41 Y Bar Basin
43 Rock Creek
49 Verde River Trail
50 Wet Bottom Mesa
51 Mountain Spring Loop
52 The Park
53 Club Cabin

Hikes for Peak Baggers

2 Siphon Draw
14 Pinyon Mountain
27 Superstition Mountain
31 Browns Peak
38 Mazatzal Divide Trail

Map Legend

═══(17)═══	Interstate Highway	🛥	Boat Launch
═══(60)═══	US Highway	⏝	Bridge
═══(88)═══	State Highway	▪	Building/Point of Interest
═══[213]═══	County/Forest Road	▲	Campground
───────	Local Road	∩	Cave
══════	Unpaved/Jeep Road	!	Gate
▬▬▬▬▬▬	Featured Trail	🅿	Parking
----------	Trail	⏝	Pass
··················	Off-trail Route	▲	Peak/Summit
–··–··–···	State Line	⌸	Picnic Area
───────	River or Creek	×	Point Elevation
–·–·–·–	Intermittent Stream	🚻	Restroom
▬	Body of Water	◄	Scenic View/Viewpoint
▬	National Forest/Park/Monument	ơ	Spring
▭	State and Local Park	○	Town
		❶	Trailhead
		≋	Waterfall

Superstition Mountains

The Superstition Mountains are a small but rugged range lying east of Apache Junction, south of the Salt River, and trending west to east. Some Precambrian granite is exposed, especially in the eastern sections, but most of the Superstitions are a complex of interleaved lava flows, ash layers, and other volcanic deposits. Though the geology is difficult to decipher, the result is a spectacular and convoluted terrain of canyons, mesas, bluffs, and peaks. The potential for exploration is much greater than the size of the range would suggest. The western third of the range consists of high ridges, mesas, and deep canyons, ranging from 2,000 to 5,000 feet. Saguaro cactus and other Sonoran Desert plants grow on the lower slopes, while the higher country is desert grassland with an occasional pinyon pine or juniper tree. Eastward, the terrain becomes higher and somewhat gentler, though still complex. The eastern third of the range is dominated by deep canyons and high ridges and culminates in 6,247-foot Mound Mountain, the highest point in the Superstitions. Chaparral (an association of scrub oak, mountain mahogany, and manzanita brush) covers the highest slopes, and a few pockets of tall ponderosa pine hang on in the coolest, most protected locations.

Access

The western Superstitions are easily reached from several trailheads. East Broadway Trailhead, Lost Dutchman State Park, Weeks Trailhead, First Water Trailhead, and Canyon Lake are accessible from Apache Junction and AZ 88 with ordinary vehicles. Other trailheads for the central and eastern Superstitions reached from AZ 88 require a high-clearance or four-wheel-drive vehicle; these include Tortilla, Reavis, and Upper Horrell Trailheads. The Tule Trailhead can usually be reached with ordinary cars. On the east side of the range, the Miles Ranch Trailhead requires a high-clearance vehicle. The Woodbury Trailhead, along the southern border of the Superstition Wilderness, can normally be reached by cars, while the nearby Rogers Trough Trailhead may require a high-clearance vehicle. Peralta Trailhead on the southwest side is reachable by car.

Camping

Lost Dutchman State Park provides camping near Apache Junction. Other public campgrounds include the Tonto National Forest campgrounds along AZ 88—Acacia, Boulder, and Tortilla Campgrounds at Canyon Lake, and Burnt Coral Campground on upper Apache Lake. Windy Hill is a large campground off AZ 88 on the southern shore of Roosevelt Lake. Oak Flat and Devils Canyon are small campgrounds along US 60 between Globe and Superior. Dispersed camping away from developed sites is generally allowed in the Tonto National Forest, except where posted otherwise.

Please respect all such closures. Also be aware that private land inholdings may be found within the national forest. Please respect posted private property wherever you encounter it.

Services

Full services are located in Apache Junction and Mesa, west of the Superstition Mountains on US 60, and in Globe-Miami, east of the Superstitions along US 60. There are limited services at Canyon, Apache, and Roosevelt Lakes on AZ 88, north of the Superstition Wilderness. Other limited services are available at Florence Junction and Superior, on US 60 south of the range. Outdoor specialty shops are located in Tempe, Scottsdale, and Phoenix.

Permits and Restrictions

In the Superstition Wilderness, group size is limited to fifteen people, and the stay limit is fourteen days. Permits are not required, though this may change in the future. Check with the trail contact listed with each hike for current information.

1 Jacob's Crosscut Trail

This hike wanders along the base of the Superstitions' western escarpment using Jacob's Crosscut and Siphon Draw Trails and offers some amazing views. The hike lies outside the Superstition Wilderness and is never far from houses that have been built right up to the Tonto National Forest boundary, but it is still a very pleasant walk through some gorgeous desert landscapes. You can do this as an out-and-back hike or walk point to point by leaving a vehicle at the Siphon Draw Trailhead.

Start: Unsigned Broadway Trailhead
Distance: 8.4 miles out and back; 4.2 miles point to point with a car shuttle
Hiking time: About 4 hours (2 hours point to point)
Difficulty: Easy
Best seasons: Oct–Apr
Trail surface: Dirt
Land status: Tonto National Forest
Nearest town: Apache Junction
Other users: Horses, mountain bikes
Water availability: None

Canine compatibility: Leashed dogs permitted
Fees and permits: Entrance fee at Lost Dutchman State Park at the northern trailhead
Schedule: Year-round, 24 hours per day
Maps: USGS Goldfield AZ; USFS Superstition Wilderness map
Trail contact: Mesa Ranger District, Tonto National Forest, 5140 E. Ingram St., Mesa, AZ 85205; (480) 610-3300; www.fs.usda.gov/tonto

Finding the trailhead: From US 60 (Superstition Freeway) in Apache Junction, exit at AZ 88 (Idaho Road). Turn left onto Idaho Road, go 1.9 miles, then turn right onto Old West Highway. Continue 0.6 mile, then turn left onto Broadway Avenue and drive 3.5 miles east to the unsigned Broadway Trailhead. Parking is limited to 10 cars. GPS: N33 24.47' / W111 28.58'
   To reach the Siphon Draw Trailhead (the end of the point-to-point option) from Apache Junction, drive about 5 miles east on AZ 88, then turn right into Lost Dutchman State Park and follow the signs to the Siphon Draw Trailhead. The park charges an entrance fee. GPS: N33 27.21' / W111 28.80'

The Hike

Follow Jacob's Crosscut Trail up the broad desert slope toward the imposing cliffs of the western escarpment of the Superstition Mountains. This type of slope is known as a "bajada." It's composed of outwash debris—boulders, gravel, and sand—eroded from the steep mountains above and transported by flash floods out onto the plains. As the mountains erode, the debris piles up at their feet, forming a sloping, skirtlike base.

   At the Gold Camp Trail junction, bear left to remain on Jacob's Crosscut Trail. As the trail nears the base of the cliffs, it turns north at an unsigned junction with an informal trail to Monument Canyon. Monument Canyon is an interesting side hike.

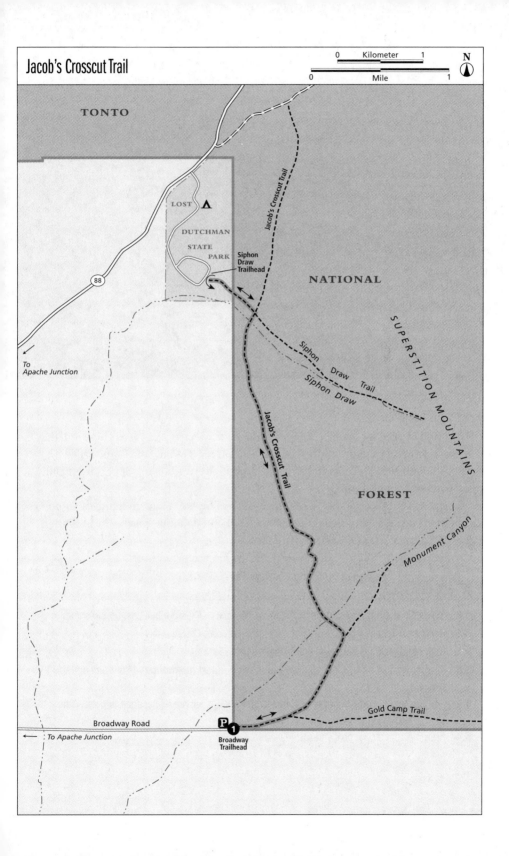

Sunrise on the Superstition crest from Jacob's Crosscut Trail

Continuing north, Jacob's Crosscut Trail stays more or less level, high on the bahada, as it swings in and out of ravines. On a clear day, the Salt River valley and greater Phoenix area are laid out before you on the west, while the Superstition cliffs loom over your right shoulder.

At about 3.8 miles, the trail passes the mouth of Siphon Draw, then meets Siphon Draw Trail. Turn left onto the Siphon Draw Trail and continue northwest to Siphon Draw Trailhead at Lost Dutchman State Park.

Unless you left a shuttle vehicle here, return the way you came.

Miles and Directions

0.0 Start from the Broadway Trailhead, following the Jacob's Crosscut Trail east up the slope.

0.4 Reach the Gold Camp Trail junction; turn left on Jacob's Crosscut Trail.

1.1 At the unsigned junction, stay left on Jacob's Crosscut Trail.

3.8 Reach the Siphon Draw Trail; turn left and hike northwest (downslope) on the Siphon Draw Trail.

4.2 Arrive at the Siphon Draw Trailhead. This is trail's end if you are hiking point to point. Otherwise, return as you came.

8.4 Arrive back at the Jacob's Crosscut Trailhead.

2 Siphon Draw

This rugged hike to the crest of Superstition Mountain features 100-mile views. As close as it is to the cities of the Valley of the Sun, the crest still has a wild, remote feel, especially as you contemplates the deep canyons, mesas, and peaks spread out to the east.

Start: Siphon Draw Trailhead
Distance: 4.6 miles out and back
Hiking time: About 3–4 hours
Difficulty: Strenuous due to elevation change and steep, unmaintained trail
Best seasons: Oct–Apr
Trail surface: Dirt trail
Land status: Tonto National Forest
Nearest town: Apache Junction
Other users: Mountain bikes up to the wilderness boundary; horses to the base of Siphon Draw

Water availability: None
Canine compatibility: Leashed dogs permitted
Fees and permits: Entrance fee at Lost Dutchman State Park. Maximum group size is 15 and the stock limit is 15.
Schedule: Year-round, 24 hours per day
Maps: USGS Goldfield AZ; USFS Superstition Wilderness map
Trail contact: Mesa Ranger District, Tonto National Forest, 5140 E. Ingram St., Mesa, AZ 85205; (480) 610-3300; www.fs.usda.gov/tonto

Finding the trailhead: From Apache Junction, drive about 5 miles east on AZ 88, then turn right into Lost Dutchman State Park and follow the signs to the Siphon Draw Trailhead. GPS: N33 27.21' / W111 28.80'

The Hike

Siphon Draw is the major canyon southeast of the state park. It's marked by a distinctive rock formation south of the draw near the crest, appropriately named the Flatiron. The trail wanders southeast across the desert foothills, at first climbing gradually toward the mouth of the canyon. You'll pass Discovery Trail just after leaving the trailhead, and Prospector and Jacob's Crosscut Trails a bit farther on. After passing the wilderness boundary, the grade begins to steepen and the impressive canyon walls and towering rock formations begin to close in. You'll also see fine examples of the stately saguaro cactus, the symbol of the Sonoran Desert, which grows up to 50 feet tall.

When the trail meets upper Siphon Draw, it becomes much steeper. Persist and you'll reach the saddle at the head of Siphon Draw on the crest of the western Superstitions, a high ridge commonly referred to as "Superstition Mountain." This 5,000-foot ridge separates the urban world to the west from the wild and broken country to the east. The crest is high desert grassland, where scattered juniper trees start to appear. You can hike cross-country north or south along the crest from the head of Siphon Draw.

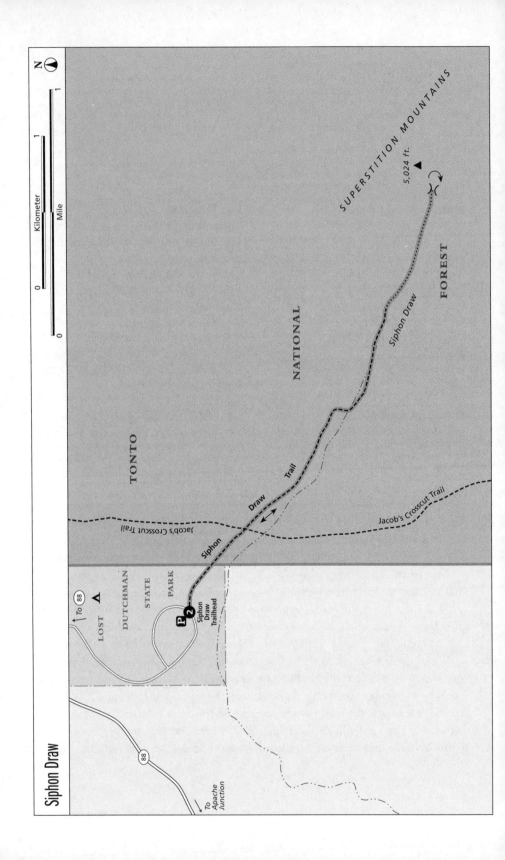

Siphon Draw

Saguaro cactus frames a view of Four Peaks from the Siphon Draw Trail.

Saguaro cacti are found in the Sonoran Desert in Arizona and northern Mexico, and only in areas where freezing temperatures are rare. The plant is supported by woody ribs just under the skin, which form cactus skeletons after the plant dies. Soft, succulent flesh fills the interior of the plant; this treasure trove of water is protected by the tough, waxy skin and an array of sharp spines. As they grow, saguaros usually develop several branching arms, which may help the plant maintain its balance. Large saguaros weigh several tons and get no support at all from their roots. The roots are shallow and spread out just below the surface to collect as much moisture as possible from the occasional rains. The volume of the cactus changes with the amount of moisture it has stored—you can see the depth of the accordion pleats in its skin change from year to year. In the spring of wet years, the cactus produces a large, showy, off-white flower at the tips of its stems.

Miles and Directions

0.0   Begin at the Siphon Draw Trailhead, hiking southeast and upslope on Siphon Draw Trail.

0.5   Cross Jacob's Crosscut Trail and continue southeast on Siphon Draw Trail.

0.8   Pass the wilderness boundary.

1.4   The trail enters upper Siphon Draw and becomes much steeper.

2.3   Reach the saddle at the head of Siphon Draw on Superstition Mountain. This is the turn-around; return the way you came.

4.6   Arrive back at the trailhead.

3 Massacre Grounds

Hike across the spectacular northwest Superstition foothills to the famous location where Spanish miners were supposedly ambushed. This is a good introduction to hiking in the Superstition Mountains.

Start: Jacob's Crosscut Trailhead
Distance: 4.8 miles out and back
Hiking time: About 3 hours
Difficulty: Moderate due to route finding on unofficial trails and old roads
Best seasons: Oct–Apr
Trail surface: Roads, old roads, and dirt trail
Land status: Tonto National Forest, Superstition Wilderness
Nearest town: Apache Junction
Other users: Horses, mountain bikes outside the wilderness area

Water availability: None
Canine compatibility: Leashed dogs permitted
Fees and permits: None
Schedule: Year-round, 24 hours per day
Maps: USGS Goldfield AZ; USFS Superstition Wilderness map
Trail contact: Mesa Ranger District, Tonto National Forest, 5140 E. Ingram St., Mesa, AZ 85205; (480) 610-3300; www.fs.usda.gov/tonto

Finding the trailhead: From Apache Junction, drive 5.7 miles east on AZ 88, then turn right onto First Water Road (FR 78). After 0.7 mile, park at the Jacob's Crosscut Trailhead (named Weekes Trailhead on some maps). GPS: N33 28.30' / W111 28.17'

The Hike

From the trailhead, follow First Water Road northeast to the old Massacre Grounds road, now closed. (There is no parking along First Water Road beyond the Jacob's Crosscut Trailhead.) Follow the old, closed road southeast toward the imposing cliffs of the northwest Superstitions. After you pass the old Massacre Grounds trailhead, the road becomes an informal trail that continues southeast toward the foot of the cliffs. The trail passes to the west of a rocky bluff, then splits below a hill crowned with a rock pinnacle. Take the left fork, which skirts below the hill and then climbs over a low saddle into a ravine. Follow the trail up this ravine and onto a broad slope. The trail turns sharply south and continues to the upper end of the slope, just below the base of the cliffs. This is the supposed site of the Massacre Grounds.

According to legend, Indians ambushed a group of Spanish miners in this area in 1848 as the miners were returning to Mexico with pack animals laden with gold ore. Unfortunately, at least as far as the legend goes, gold has never been found in the Superstition Mountains. Regardless of its past, this area of the Superstition foothills is special, and is especially delightful in spring after a wet winter, when the desert wildflowers carpet the hills. The dark, brooding cliffs of Superstition Mountain complete the scene.

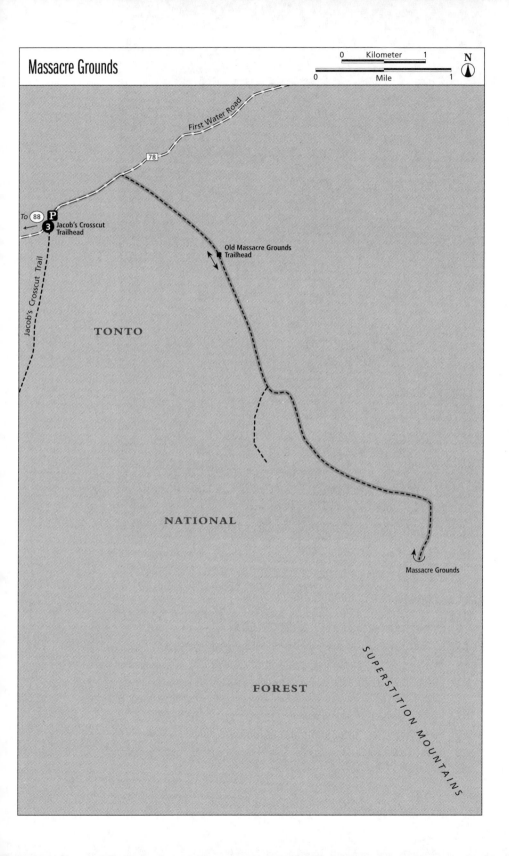

Massacre Grounds

Massacre Grounds where legend has it that a party of Spanish miners were attacked by Apaches.

Miles and Directions

0.0 Start at the Jacob's Crosscut Trailhead, walking along First Water Road.

0.3 Leave First Water Road and follow an old, closed road southwest.

0.8 Pass the old Massacre Grounds trailhead, where route becomes an informal trail.

1.3 The trail skirts a hill on the west, reaches the base of a hill crowned with a pinnacle, then splits. Go left on the trail that skirts the hill to the left and climbs through a saddle.

1.7 The trail heads southeast up a ravine.

2.2 The trail reaches a broad slope and turns south.

2.4 Reach the Massacre Grounds. This is the turnaround point; retrace your steps.

4.8 Arrive back at the trailhead.

4 Garden Valley Loop

This easily accessible day hike follows good trails through the foothills of the western Superstitions; a good introductory walk for beginning hikers and those new to the area.

Start: First Water Trailhead
Distance: 8.6-mile loop with a short cherry stem
Hiking time: About 5 hours
Difficulty: Moderate due to distance and elevation change
Best seasons: Oct–Apr
Trail surface: Dirt
Land status: Tonto National Forest, Superstition Wilderness
Nearest town: Apache Junction
Other users: Horses

Water availability: Seasonal along First Water Creek
Canine compatibility: Leashed dogs permitted
Fees and permits: None
Schedule: Year-round, 24 hours per day
Maps: USGS Goldfield AZ; USFS Superstition Wilderness map
Trail contact: Mesa Ranger District, Tonto National Forest, 5140 E. Ingram St., Mesa, AZ 85205; (480) 610-3300; www.fs.usda.gov/tonto

Finding the trailhead: From Apache Junction, drive 5.5 miles east on AZ 88, then turn right onto First Water Road (FR 78). Continue 2.6 miles to the end of the road, at the First Water Trailhead and parking area. GPS: N33 28.80' / W111 26.58'

The Hike

Start off on Dutchmans Trail, which heads southeast and soon enters a shallow canyon. This section of the trail is a very easy and popular hike—don't expect solitude. But most people walk a short distance up the trail, then turn back.

Almost immediately, you'll pass Second Water Trail, which is the return route. Keep going on Dutchmans Trail, and you'll soon get a hint of the wilder side of the Superstitions. The trail wanders through low rock formations and past stands of cholla cactus, then climbs gently over Parker Pass, the broad divide between the First Water Canyon and Boulder Canyon drainages.

Now you'll head more easterly and the trail will gradually drop into Boulder Basin. This open valley is named for the huge quantity of boulders brought down by West Boulder Canyon, which drains the area to the south. Just before the trail crosses the main wash, turn left onto Black Mesa Trail.

This trail heads northwest and climbs onto Black Mesa at 4.9 miles, passing west of Yellow Peak. Black Mesa's dark and stony surface is the result of an ancient lava flow. After the short but steep initial climb, the trail ascends a moderate grade toward a shallow saddle, which is the high point of the hike. Beyond the saddle, Black Mesa Trail descends a shallow canyon, then comes out onto the open flat of Garden Valley.

You'll meet Second Water Trail at a T intersection; turn left and head southwest.

The trail descends off the rim of Black Mesa. Where two tributaries of First Water Creek meet, Second Water Trail turns sharply right and heads west. At the junction with Dutchmans Trail, turn right to return to First Water Trailhead.

Cholla cactus, like many desert plants, is one you don't want to mess with. There are many varieties, but one of the best known is teddybear cholla, named for its cuddly appearance. This yellow-gold plant commonly is 2 to 4 feet high, and its stems are covered with a dense "fur" of sharp needles. Each needle is covered with tiny barbs. The stems are jointed, and as the plant grows the tips of the stems break off and fall to the ground. When an animal or hiker brushes one of these fuzzy

Seasonal pools along the First Water Trail

balls, it sticks to skin or clothing and hitches a ride to another place, where, if conditions are favorable, a new cactus may germinate.

Miles and Directions

0.0 From the First Water Trailhead, start on Dutchmans Trail.

0.3 Pass the Second Water Trail; stay right on Dutchmans Trail.

2.4 Cross over Parker Pass.

3.9 In Boulder Basin, turn left onto Black Mesa Trail.

5.6 Reach the saddle on Black Mesa Trail and the highest point of the hike.

6.8 In broad Garden Valley, turn left on Second Water Trail.

7.5 Two tributaries of First Water Creek meet; follow Second Water Trail as it turns sharply right (northwest).

8.3 Turn right onto Dutchmans Trail.

8.6 Arrive back at First Water Trailhead.

Garden Valley Loop

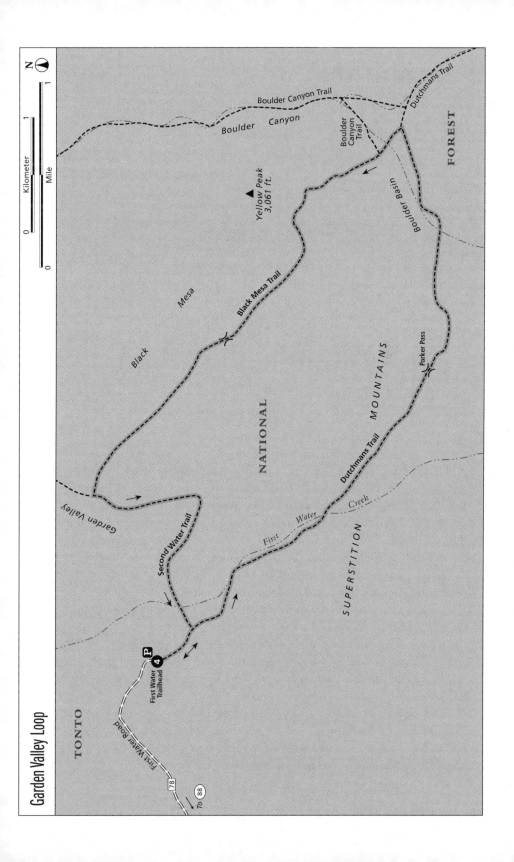

TONTO

First Water Road

78

To **88**

P
4
First Water Trailhead

Second Water Trail

Garden Valley

Black

Mesa

Black Mesa Trail

Yellow Peak
3,061 ft.

Boulder Canyon

Boulder Canyon Trail

Boulder Canyon Trail

Boulder Basin

Dutchmans Trail

FOREST

NATIONAL

First   Water   Creek

Dutchmans Trail

SUPERSTITION

MOUNTAINS

Parker Pass

N

0   1
Kilometer
0   1
Mile

5 Second Water Trail

This easily accessible hike in the western Superstition foothills crosses a volcanic mesa and descends to a remote section of rugged lower Boulder Canyon.

Start: First Water Trailhead
Distance: 7.2 miles out and back
Hiking time: About 4 hours
Difficulty: Moderate due to distance and elevation gain
Best seasons: Oct–Apr
Trail surface: Dirt
Land status: Tonto National Forest, Superstition Wilderness
Nearest town: Apache Junction
Other users: Horses

Water availability: Seasonal in Second Water Canyon
Canine compatibility: Leashed dogs permitted
Fees and permits: None
Schedule: Year-round, 24 hours per day
Maps: USGS Goldfield AZ; USFS Superstition Wilderness map
Trail contact: Mesa Ranger District, Tonto National Forest, 5140 E. Ingram St., Mesa, AZ 85205; (480) 610-3300; www.fs.usda.gov/tonto

Finding the trailhead: From Apache Junction, drive 5.5 miles east on AZ 88, then turn right on First Water Road (FR 78). Continue 2.6 miles to the end of the road at the First Water Trailhead and parking area. GPS: N33 28.80' / W111 26.58'

The Hike

Start on Dutchmans Trail, and then turn left onto Second Water Trail. The trail works its way east toward the north end of Black Mesa, the low volcanic mesa east of the trailhead area. After crossing a tributary of First Water Creek, the trail climbs north up a smaller drainage. It then turns northeast, passes a low hill on the right, then enters the broad expanse of Garden Valley. At the junction with Black Mesa Trail in Garden Valley, continue straight ahead (northeast) on Second Water Trail, heading across the valley.

The valley slopes gently down to the northeast, and shortly the trail enters a narrow canyon and starts to descend more rapidly. After an old bulldozer track branches to the left (it goes north to Cholla Tank, an old stock pond), the Second Water Trail becomes even steeper. Second Water Canyon enters from the right; Second Water Spring is a short distance up this side canyon. There is usually water in the canyon below the spring, which the trail follows to Boulder Canyon, the destination of this hike.

This rugged canyon's creek is dry most of the year, but it drains much of the western portion of the Superstition Mountains, and after heavy rains it can be an uncrossable torrent. After gentle winter rains it can be a clear, tumbling mountain stream, bordered by green grass and colorful flowers.

Camp near the Second Water Trail

The Sonoran Desert, an area encompassing the southwestern third of Arizona, Sonora state in northwest Mexico, and a bit of southeast California, is the lushest of the four North American deserts. This is due to both the influence of winter storms, which bring periods of gentle rain from December through March, and the Arizona monsoon, which brings scattered thunderstorms in late July. Of course, the amount of rainfall varies widely from year to year, and from place to place. Desert plants and animals have adapted well to these extremes. For example, wildflower seeds are capable of lying dormant within the soil for many years, until the right combination of moisture and temperature triggers them. Then the Sonoran Desert is literally carpeted with color—a display that must be seen to be believed. The plants take advantage of the unusual moisture supply to quickly complete their life cycles, and by the time summer's heat arrives, new seeds have been produced that ensure the next generation of plants.

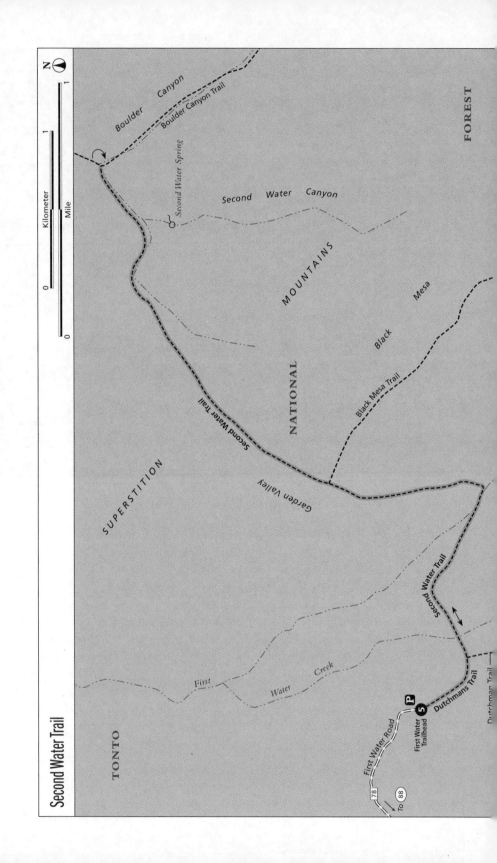

Second Water Trail

Miles and Directions

0.0 From the First Water Trailhead, start on Dutchmans Trail.

0.3 Turn left onto Second Water Trail.

1.8 At the junction with Black Mesa Trail, stay left on Second Water Trail.

3.2 Second Water Canyon comes in from the south.

3.6 Reach the turnaround point in Boulder Canyon at the junction with the Boulder Canyon Trail. Retrace your steps.

7.2 Arrive back at the trailhead.

6 Lower La Barge Box

This exceptionally scenic cross-country hike starts from one of the most accessible Superstition trailheads and takes you up a ridge with stunning views of Canyon Lake and the Four Peaks area. Descending off the ridge into La Barge Canyon gives you a feeling of deep wilderness, and the reward is a narrow canyon with towering walls and beautiful pools.

Start: Canyon Lake Marina Trailhead
Distance: 8.4 miles out and back
Hiking time: About 5 hours
Difficulty: Moderate due to elevation change and cross-country hiking
Best seasons: Oct–Apr
Trail surface: Dirt trail; cross-country on gravel and rocks
Land status: Tonto National Forest, Superstition Wilderness
Nearest town: Apache Junction

Other users: Horses
Water availability: Seasonal in La Barge Creek
Canine compatibility: Leashed dogs permitted
Fees and permits: None
Schedule: Year-round, 24 hours per day
Maps: USGS Mormon Flat Dam AZ and Goldfield AZ; USFS Superstition Wilderness map
Trail contact: Mesa Ranger District, Tonto National Forest, 5140 E. Ingram St., Mesa, AZ 85205; (480) 610-3300; www.fs.usda.gov/tonto

Finding the trailhead: From Apache Junction, drive about 14.5 miles east on AZ 88 to Canyon Lake Marina. Signed trailhead parking is on the left in the marina parking lot. GPS: N33 32.09' / W111 25.35'

The Hike

Cross the highway and start up Boulder Canyon Trail, which climbs steadily south-southeast on the ridge above La Barge Canyon. Where an unnamed spur trail branches right and descends to La Barge Canyon, stay left on Boulder Canyon Trail, which turns abruptly northeast and continues to climb via a switchback or two to the top of the main ridge. Look behind you at the expansive view of Canyon Lake and the Four Peaks region.

After climbing along the ridgecrest for a while, the trail contours around the head of a side canyon high above La Barge Canyon and soon leaves the sights and sounds of the highway and the man-made lake behind. Rounding a rock spur, the trail drops steeply into La Barge Canyon. This is a popular destination for both day hikes and overnight hikes, and there's usually water in the creek during the cool half of the year.

Follow the main trail upstream along the east bank of La Barge Creek until it crosses to the west bank. Leave the trail at this point and continue cross-country up the canyon bed. At first the going is easy up the broad wash, but as you enter Lower La Barge Box, the walls close in and travel becomes more difficult. At several places, you'll have to scramble up and around huge boulders.

The Battleship and Weavers Needle from the Boulder Canyon Trail

The hike ends where the narrows of Lower La Barge Box start, marked by a sharp left bend, followed by a sharp right bend. Here the walls seem to go straight up. Water usually trickles over polished slabs of rock, which is evidence of the powerful floods that scour the canyon bottom. Above this point the hiking becomes much rougher as the canyon bottom becomes choked with boulders and vegetation, so this is the turnaround point for this hike.

A box canyon such as Lower La Barge Box has a narrow section, bounded by tall cliffs, and generally some obstacle in the bed that makes it difficult to traverse, especially on horseback. Sometimes the obstacle is a high, dry waterfall, or, as in the case of Lower La Barge Box, the canyon floor may be choked with boulders. Obviously, a box canyon is not the place to be during a flash flood. And yes, there is an Upper La Barge Box, located miles upstream near the headwaters of the canyon below Coffee Flat Mountain.

Option: For a much shorter and easier hike, take the spur trail at 0.6 mile. This trail ends in the bed of lower La Barge Creek, not too far from Canyon Lake. The round-trip hike is 3 miles.

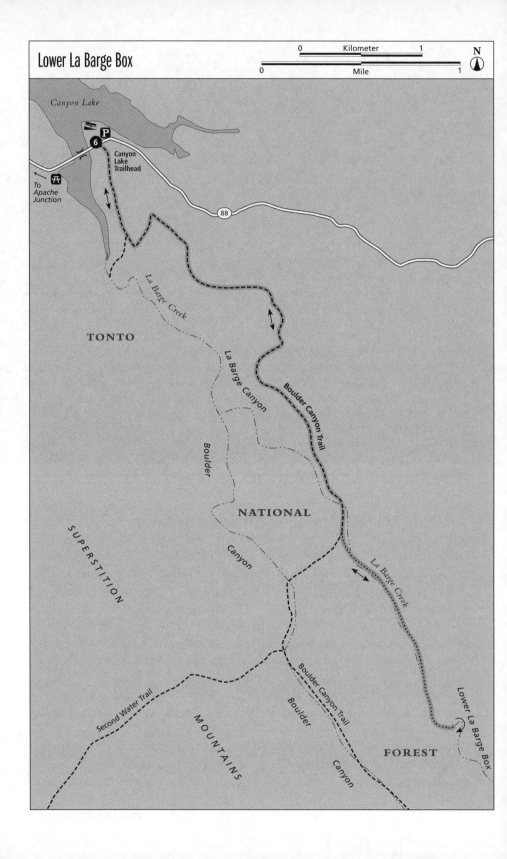

Lower La Barge Box

0 — Kilometer — 1
0 — Mile — 1

N

Canyon Lake

P 6

Canyon Lake Trailhead

To Apache Junction

88

La Barge Creek

TONTO

La Barge Canyon

Boulder

NATIONAL

Canyon

Boulder Canyon Trail

La Barge Creek

SUPERSTITION

Second Water Trail

Boulder Canyon Trail

Boulder

MOUNTAINS

Canyon

FOREST

Lower La Barge Box

Miles and Directions

0.0 From the Canyon Lake Trailhead, hike south-southeast on Boulder Canyon Trail.

0.5 At the junction with the unnamed spur trail to lower Boulder Canyon, stay left on the main Boulder Canyon Trail as it turns briefly northeast.

0.8 Boulder Canyon Trail reaches the main ridgetop and turns southeast.

2.1 The trail crosses a rock spur and starts to descend into La Barge Canyon.

2.6 Reach La Barge Creek. Follow Boulder Canyon Trail up the east side of La Barge Creek and then across the creek.

3.0 Leave Boulder Canyon Trail on the west side of La Barge Creek, and hike cross-country to the south, up La Barge Creek.

4.2 Reach Lower La Barge Box. This is the turnaround; retrace your steps.

8.4 Arrive back at the trailhead.

7 Marsh Valley Loop

This is an enjoyable overnight backpack trip or long day hike through two rugged canyons in the northwestern Superstition Mountains, with options to extend the trip and plenty of opportunities for side hikes and exploration.

Start: Canyon Lake Marina Trailhead
Distance: 16.7-mile lollipop
Hiking time: About 9 hours or 2 days
Difficulty: Moderate due to elevation change and length
Best seasons: Oct–Apr
Trail surface: Dirt
Land status: Tonto National Forest, Superstition Wilderness
Nearest town: Apache Junction
Other users: Horses

Water availability: Seasonal in La Barge and Boulder Creeks, and at White Rock Spring
Canine compatibility: Leashed dogs permitted
Fees and permits: None
Schedule: Year-round, 24 hours per day
Maps: USGS Mormon Flat Dam AZ and Goldfield AZ; USFS Superstition Wilderness map
Trail contact: Mesa Ranger District, Tonto National Forest, 5140 E. Ingram St., Mesa, AZ 85205; (480) 610-3300; www.fs.usda.gov/tonto

Finding the trailhead: From Apache Junction, drive about 14.5 miles east on AZ 88 to Canyon Lake Marina. Signed trailhead parking is on the left in the marina parking lot. GPS: N33 32.09' / W111 25.35'

The Hike

Cross the highway and start up Boulder Canyon Trail, which climbs steadily south-southeast on the ridge above La Barge Canyon. Where an unnamed spur trail branches right and descends to La Barge Canyon, stay left on Boulder Canyon Trail, which turns abruptly northeast and continues to climb via a switchback or two to the top of the main ridge. Look behind you at the expansive view of Canyon Lake and the Four Peaks region.

After climbing along the ridgecrest for a while, the trail contours around the head of a side canyon high above La Barge Canyon and soon leaves the sights and sounds of the highway and the man-made lake behind. Rounding a rock spur, the trail drops steeply into La Barge Canyon. This is a popular destination for both day hikes and overnight hikes, and there's usually water in the creek during the cool half of the year. There are numerous campsites along the creek.

The trail follows La Barge Creek upstream before veering west, crossing the creek, and climbing over a low pass into Boulder Canyon, where there are campsites on the east side of the creek. There is seasonal water in both Boulder and La Barge Creeks. When the trail reaches Boulder Creek, turn left and follow the trail up the broad, boulder-filled wash. You'll soon pass the junction with Second Water Trail on the right; there is seasonal water in Second Water Canyon. Continue south on Boulder

Weavers Needle looms through the mist of a rare rainstorm.

Canyon Trail. Turn left on Cavalry Trail, which climbs steeply out of Boulder Canyon and over a pass into the La Barge Creek drainage. The trail turns right, goes southeast up Marsh Valley, and then ends at Dutchmans Trail at the south end of the valley. White Rock Spring, just a few yards east on Dutchmans Trail, usually has water.

Turn right on Dutchmans Trail and follow it a short distance to a low pass. Turn right on Bull Pass Trail to continue the loop. The trail drops a short distance into Needle Canyon, then crosses the wash and starts to climb steeply along the north slopes of Black Mesa. You'll reach the high point of the hike at Bull Pass, and then drop steeply to rejoin Dutchmans Trail in East Boulder Canyon. Turn right and go a short distance on Dutchmans Trail to another trail junction, where you'll turn right on Boulder Canyon Trail. Hike north down East Boulder Canyon, past the confluence of West Boulder Canyon on the left and then Needle Canyon on the right. Finally, you'll pass the junction with Cavalry Trail, completing the loop portion of the trip. Return to the Canyon Lake Trailhead via the Boulder Canyon Trail.

Considering that little or no water flows through canyons such as Boulder Canyon most of the time, you might wonder how all those boulders got there. The secret is that Boulder Canyon drains a large area of the western Superstitions. Most storms produce only small, fairly steady runoff, but occasionally a heavy rain occurs, which causes rapid runoff. The dry wash can become a raging torrent in a matter of seconds as floodwaters gather from miles away and converge on the main drainage. Boulders that fell from the canyon walls and lay in the wash for many years suddenly find themselves buoyed by the massive force of the flood. The carrying capacity of moving water goes up with the cube of the velocity, so as a flow doubles in size it becomes capable of moving much larger rocks. A huge flood in a canyon like Boulder Canyon is an unforgettable sight and sound as rocks the size of small cars are jostled about.

Option 1: When the Boulder Canyon Trail first reaches La Barge Creek, you can follow La Barge Creek cross-country upstream through Lower La Barge Box and join the Cavalry Trail in Marsh Valley. This off-trail section is about 3 miles and shortens the loop by 0.9 mile, though it probably will take more time because of the rough cross-country hiking over and around boulders and thick vegetation.

Option 2: Where the Bull Pass Trail crosses Needle Canyon, you could leave the trail and follow Needle Canyon through its lower narrows. This cross-country hike is 1.7 miles, and it shortens the loop by 0.2 mile. The hiking involves boulder-hopping down the normally dry wash.

Option 3: You can do a short but scenic side hike up an old trail to the top of Black Top Mesa. This route leaves Bull Pass and climbs south about 0.6 mile to the south edge of the mesa, the high point. You may not find much of the trail, but the hiking is easy. From the end of this little side hike you'll have a great view of Weavers Needle and the rugged country surrounding this famous landmark. Weavers Needle is probably named for Pauline Weaver, an early mountain man and fur trapper.

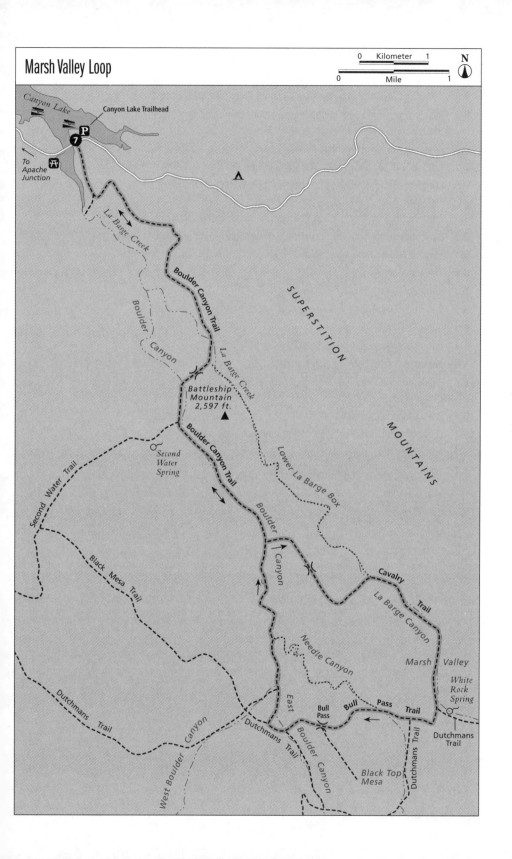

Marsh Valley Loop

0 Kilometer 1

0 Mile 1

N

Canyon Lake

Canyon Lake Trailhead

P

7

To Apache Junction

La Barge Creek

Boulder Canyon Trail

Boulder Canyon

La Barge Creek

S U P E R S T I T I O N

Battleship Mountain 2,597 ft.

Boulder Canyon Trail

Second Water Spring

Second Water Trail

Black Mesa Trail

Lower La Barge Box

Boulder Canyon

M O U N T A I N S

Cavalry Trail

La Barge Canyon

Marsh Valley

White Rock Spring

Needle Canyon

Dutchmans Trail

East Boulder Canyon

Dutchmans Trail

Bull Pass

Bull Pass Trail

Dutchmans Trail

West Boulder Canyon

Dutchmans Trail

Black Top Mesa

Miles and Directions

0.0 From the Canyon Lake Trailhead, hike south-southeast on Boulder Canyon Trail.

0.5 Pass the unnamed spur trail to lower Boulder Canyon; stay left on the main Boulder Canyon Trail as it turns briefly northeast.

0.8 Boulder Canyon Trail reaches the main ridgetop and turns southeast.

2.1 The trail crosses a rock spur and starts to descend into La Barge Canyon.

2.6 Continue up the east side of La Barge Creek, then cross the creek and go up over a low saddle.

3.3 Arrive at Boulder Creek; follow Boulder Canyon Trail left (upstream).

3.7 Pass the junction with Second Water Trail; continue south on Boulder Canyon Trail.

5.1 Turn left (east) onto Cavalry Trail.

6.4 Arrive in Marsh Valley.

7.9 Turn right (west) onto Dutchmans Trail.

8.3 Turn right (west) on Bull Pass Trail. This junction is not with Terrapin Trail.

9.3 Cross Bull Pass.

9.7 Turn right (west) onto Dutchmans Trail.

9.8 Turn right (north) onto Boulder Canyon Trail.

11.6 Close the loop at the Cavalry Trail junction; continue north (downstream) on Boulder Canyon Trail.

12.5 Pass Second Water Trail.

13.3 Leave Boulder Canyon and follow the trail over a low saddle.

13.7 Arrive back at La Barge Creek.

16.7 Arrive back at the Canyon Lake Trailhead.

8 Peters Mesa

This challenging, scenic, loop backpack trip or long day hike explores little-visited country in the north-central portion of the Superstition Wilderness.

Start: Tortilla Trailhead
Distance: 16.1 mile-loop (22.1-mile loop with the 6-mile out-and-back section if you hike FR 213)
Hiking time: About 9 hours or 2 days (12 hours or 2 days if you hike FR 213)
Difficulty: Strenuous due to distance, elevation change, and faint trails
Best seasons: Oct–Apr
Trail surface: Dirt (dirt road if you hike FR 213)
Land status: Tonto National Forest, Superstition Wilderness
Nearest town: Apache Junction
Other users: Horses

Water availability: La Barge and Charlebois Springs are usually reliable; seasonal water can be found at Upper La Barge Box, Trap Canyon Spring, Music Canyon Spring, and Kane Spring.
Canine compatibility: Leashed dogs permitted
Fees and permits: None
Schedule: Year-round, 24 hours per day
Maps: USGS Horse Mesa Dam AZ, Weavers Needle AZ; USFS Superstition Wilderness map
Trail contact: Mesa Ranger District, Tonto National Forest, 5140 E. Ingram St., Mesa, AZ 85205; (480) 610-3300; www.fs.usda.gov/tonto

Finding the trailhead: From Apache Junction, drive about 22 miles east on AZ 88 to the Tortilla Road (FR 213), on the right. Turn right onto FR 213 and continue 3 miles to the end of the road at Tortilla Trailhead. This road requires a four-wheel-drive, high-clearance vehicle—if you have a low-clearance vehicle you will need to park at the junction with AZ 88 and hike FR 213 both ways, which adds 6 miles round-trip to the hike. GPS (FR 213): N33 31.56' / W111 19.15'; GPS (Tortilla Trailhead): N33 29.57' / W111 17.73'

The Hike

Although this hike is entirely on trail, some sections are faint and difficult to follow. You should have both the USGS topo maps and the USFS Superstition Wilderness map with you, as well as skill in route finding. Start on JF Trail, which heads southeast up a gentle ridge. Turn right onto Hoolie Bacon Trail, which takes you south off the ridge and to Tortilla Creek. Follow the trail upstream around a bend, where it leaves Tortilla Creek and climbs a drainage to the southwest. This section can be difficult to find. The trail is heading for a pass on Horse Ridge, ahead.

After crossing the broad pass, the trail drops into Horse Camp Basin, which is the hilly confluence of several small drainages. Hoolie Bacon Trail, still faint, swings more to the south and drops into the Trap Canyon drainage. After crossing a tributary of Trap Canyon, the trail (incorrectly shown as Peters Trail on the USGS topo) swings farther left and heads southeast over a low pass next to the cliffs of Herman Mountain. (A branch of Peters Trail shown on the USGS topographic map heading

Trap Canyon

northwest from here does not exist.) Finally, the trail drops into La Barge Canyon and meets Red Tanks Trail.

Turn right and follow Red Tanks Trail downstream into Upper La Barge Box, a spectacular canyon formed by the towering walls of Coffee Flat Mountain and Herman Mountain. There is often seasonal water in the creek here. As Red Tanks Trail emerges from the canyon, it meets Whiskey Spring Trail. Turn right to remain on Red Tanks Trail and hike northwest down La Barge Creek past Trap Canyon. A side trail goes 0.2 mile to Trap Canyon Spring, a seasonal water source. La Barge Spring, which is more reliable, is located just before the junction with the heavily used Dutchmans Trail, on the right side of the creek.

Turn right onto Dutchmans Trail, which continues down La Barge Creek. Music Canyon Spring is another possible water source and is located 0.1 mile up a spur trail on the right (east). The next side canyon on the right is Charlebois Canyon; turn right here onto Peters Trail. Just after this trail junction, you'll pass Charlebois Spring (which is usually reliable). There are campsites along La Barge Creek.

Peters Trail starts a steep climb south, then east, out of La Barge Canyon. After reaching a ridge, the trail swings turns north and climbs up a drainage. Watch carefully for cairns—some sections of Peters Trail are faint and easy to lose. After contouring around the head of a tributary of Charlebois Canyon, the Peters Trail continues a short distance northwest, then makes an abrupt turn east and climbs over a broad saddle on the crest of Peters Mesa. (The wilderness map shows an old trail heading west from this turning point. I've found traces of this trail and an apparent continuation down Squaw Canyon to the north. It's an interesting area to explore.) If you lose

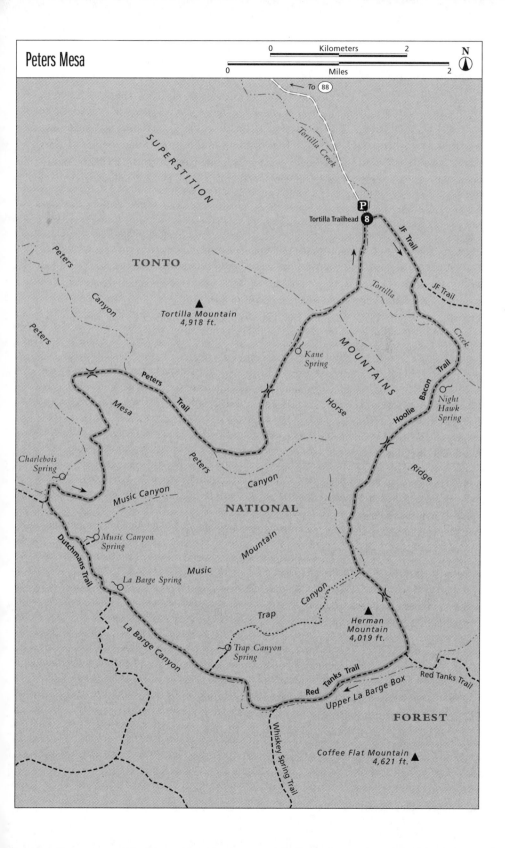

Peters Mesa

To 88

Tortilla Creek

SUPERSTITION

TONTO

P
Tortilla Trailhead 8

JF Trail

JF Trail

Tortilla

MOUNTAINS

Creek

Peters

Canyon

Peters

Tortilla Mountain
4,918 ft.

Kane
Spring

Horse

Bacon Trail

Night
Hawk
Spring

Peters

Trail

Hoolie

Mesa

Charlebois
Spring

Peters

Canyon

Ridge

Music Canyon

NATIONAL

Dutchmans Trail

Music Canyon
Spring

Mountain

La Barge Spring

Music

Trap

Canyon

Herman
Mountain
4,019 ft.

La Barge Canyon

Trap Canyon
Spring

Red Tanks Trail

Red

Upper La Barge Box

Red Tanks Trail

FOREST

Whiskey Spring Trail

Coffee Flat Mountain
4,621 ft.

the trail in this area, head east toward the pass, and you should pick up the trail as it drops into Peters Canyon.

Once in Peters Canyon, the trail follows the drainage upstream (southeast) before climbing away from Peters Canyon to the east. Follow Peters Trail over a low saddle and then east and back down to Peters Canyon. (The USGS topographic map shows a trail junction here, but the trail shown heading southeast no longer exists.) Peters Trail climbs north over a saddle between Horse Ridge and Tortilla Mountain, passes Kane Spring, then drops into a tributary of Tortilla Creek at 13.8 miles and follows the wash back to Tortilla Creek and Tortilla Trailhead.

You'll see the Arizona state tree, the paloverde, along this hike. The name means "green stick" in Spanish, which nicely describes this small desert tree. To survive long periods without water, the tree drops its leaves and depends on chlorophyll in its branches and stems to produce food. After spring rains, the tree quickly produces thousands of tiny leaves. If there's enough moisture, the tree becomes covered with a cloud of tiny yellow flowers, transforming the desert with its heady perfume.

Option 1: Where Hoolie Bacon Trail crosses Trap Canyon, it's possible to leave the trail and hike directly down Trap Canyon to the spur trail at Trap Canyon Spring, and on down to Red Tanks Trail. It's about 1.8 miles to Trap Canyon Spring, and another 0.2 mile to the Whiskey Spring Trail. This is a shortcut in distance only—the cross-country hike will take more time than the longer route on the trail. Be prepared to lower packs at several spots in this imposing and rough canyon. You might want to bring a 30-foot-length of ¼-inch nylon rope for this purpose.

Miles and Directions

0.0 From the Tortilla Trailhead, start on the JF Trail, which heads east.

0.8 Turn right on Hoolie Bacon Trail.

1.3 Reach Tortilla Creek.

1.8 Leave Tortilla Creek and follow Hoolie Bacon Trail southwest.

2.8 Cross the pass on Horse Ridge.

5.0 Turn right on Red Tanks Trail.

6.4 Pass Whiskey Spring Trail; turn right to remain on Red Tanks Trail.

8.4 Turn right onto Dutchmans Trail.

9.6 Turn right onto Peters Trail.

9.7 Pass Charlebois Spring.

11.6 At Peters Mesa, the trail turns sharply right (east).

12.1 Peters Trail drops into Peters Canyon.

13.1 The trail climbs over a low saddle above Peters Canyon.

13.8 The trail turns north, away from upper Peters Canyon.

14.2 Peters Trail crosses the saddle between Tortilla Mountain and Horse Ridge.

15.5 Reach Tortilla Creek.

16.1 Arrive back at Tortilla Trailhead.

9 Tortilla Pass–Red Tanks Divide

This fine backpacking loop explores some remote and little-visited canyons in the central Superstition Wilderness. The first section is along the scenic JF Trail, which follows a high ridge with sweeping views of the surrounding canyons and mountains.

Start: Tortilla Trailhead
Distance: 21.1-mile loop (27.1-mile loop with the 6-mile out-and-back cherry stem if you hike FR 213)
Hiking time: About 2 or 3 days
Difficulty: Strenuous due to distance and elevation change
Best seasons: Oct–Apr
Trail surface: Dirt (dirt road if you hike FR 213)
Land status: Tonto National Forest, Superstition Wilderness
Nearest town: Apache Junction
Other users: Horses
Water availability: La Barge Spring is normally reliable. You may find water seasonally at

Mullin Spring, Dripping Spring, and Night Hawk Spring, and in Fraser Canyon, Randolph Canyon, and Upper La Barge Box. In dry years, you may have to carry extra water for camp along the first part of this loop.

Canine compatibility: Leashed dogs permitted
Fees and permits: None
Schedule: Year-round, 24 hours per day
Maps: USGS Horse Mesa Dam AZ, Weavers Needle AZ, Iron Mountain AZ; USFS Superstition Wilderness map; Tonto National Forest map
Trail contact: Mesa Ranger District, Tonto National Forest, 5140 E. Ingram St., Mesa, AZ 85205; (480) 610-3300; www.fs.usda.gov/tonto

Finding the trailhead: From Apache Junction, drive about 22 miles east on AZ 88 to the Tortilla Road (FR 213), on the right. Turn right onto FR 213 and continue 3 miles to the end of the road and Tortilla Trailhead. This road requires a four-wheel-drive, high-clearance vehicle—if you have a low-clearance vehicle, you will need to park at the junction with AZ 88 and hike FR 213 both ways, which adds 6 miles round-trip to the hike. GPS (FR 213): N33 31.56' / W111 19.15'; GPS (Tortilla Trailhead): N33 29.57' / W111 17.73'

You can also start this loop from the Woodbury Trailhead. From Apache Junction, drive 19 miles east on US 60, then turn left on Queen Creek Road. Continue 2.4 miles on this paved road, then turn right on FR 537, which is maintained dirt. Go 3.3 miles, then turn left on FR 172 (Hewlitt Canyon Road). This road is maintained, but you must cross Queen Creek at the start. If either Queen Creek or Hewlitt Canyon is flooding, the approach will be impassable. Continue 8.8 miles to a locked gate, then turn right and go 0.1 mile to the Woodbury Trailhead.

Hike 0.5 mile north on JF Trail, then turn left on Coffee Flat Trail to start the loop at its southeast corner. GPS (Woodbury Trailhead): N33 24.56' / W111 12.37'

The Hike

Start by hiking southeast on JF Trail, which climbs gradually onto the unnamed ridge between Tortilla Creek and Lost Dutch Canyon. You'll pass the Hoolie Bacon Trail on the right—this will be your return trail. As JF Trail continues to work up the ridge,

Along the JF Trail

the terrain gradually becomes high desert grassland and gives you expanding views of the central part of the Superstitions. Eventually, you cross the highest point of the trail and the trip.

The trail then drops slightly, crosses through a saddle, and swings into the head of Tortilla Creek drainage. A side trail goes right about 0.5 mile to Mullin Spring. The main trail continues east to Tortilla Pass, where Rogers Canyon Trail branches left. Turn right to stay on the JF Trail, which drops steeply south down a canyon. The trail finally drops into Randolph Canyon and follows the drainage upstream to Woodbury Trail.

Turn right on Woodbury Trail and cross a broad saddle into Fraser Canyon. The trail passes JF Ranch and becomes Coffee Flat Trail, which continues southwest down the canyon. There is seasonal water in the creekbed. When Fraser Canyon ends at Randolph Canyon, you are at the low point of the loop.

Turn right on Red Tanks Trail, and follow Randolph Canyon north, upstream. Watch for Red Tanks Canyon on the left; a short distance upstream, Red Tanks Trail leaves Randolph Canyon on the left, climbs over a spur, and drops into Red Tanks Canyon. You may see traces of an old trail up Randolph Canyon—don't take this trail by mistake.

At first, the trail follows Red Tanks Canyon, which drains the imposing cliffs of Coffee Flat Mountain, towering above you to the west. Soon the route veers left (west), up an unnamed side canyon, and climbs over Red Tanks Divide. It's easy to lose the trail here, so you should have the Weavers Needle topo with you. (The trail

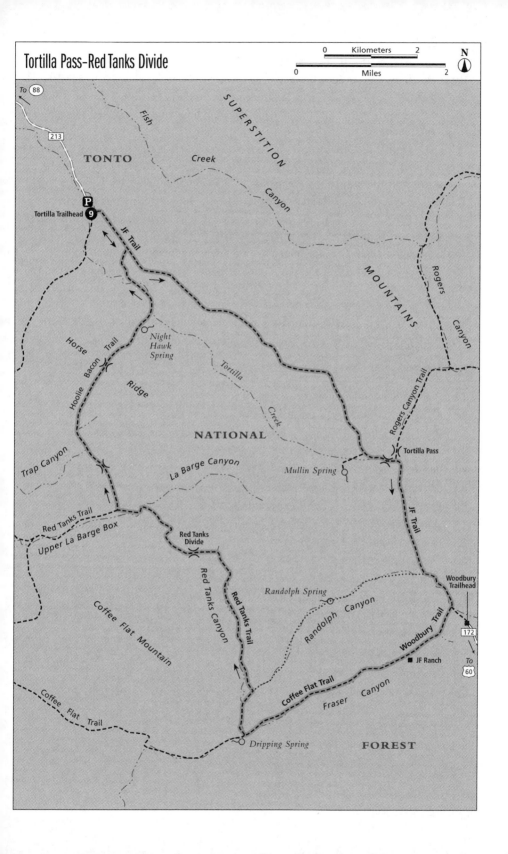

Tortilla Pass-Red Tanks Divide

0 Kilometers 2
0 Miles 2

N

To 88

213

Fish

Creek

Canyon

SUPERSTITION

TONTO

P 9
Tortilla Trailhead

JF Trail

MOUNTAINS

Rogers

Canyon

Horse

Bacon

Trail

Hoolie

Ridge

Night
Hawk
Spring

Tortilla

Creek

Rogers Canyon Trail

NATIONAL

Trap Canyon

La Barge Canyon

Mullin Spring

Tortilla Pass

Red Tanks Trail

Upper La Barge Box

Red Tanks
Divide

JF Trail

Coffee Flat Mountain

Red Tanks Canyon

Red Tanks Trail

Randolph Spring

Randolph Canyon

Woodbury
Trailhead

Woodbury Trail

172

JF Ranch

To
60

Coffee Flat Trail

Coffee Flat Trail

Fraser Canyon

Dripping Spring

FOREST

is shown incorrectly on the USGS Weavers Needle topo; it crosses the divide about 0.2 mile north of the location shown on the map. North of the pass, the trail follows a drainage down to La Barge Creek and meets Hoolie Bacon Trail just east of Upper La Barge Box. Turn right on Hoolie Bacon Trail, which can be difficult to follow through the next section.

Hoolie Bacon Trail climbs north up a slope on the east side of Herman Mountain, crosses a broad pass, then drops slightly into Trap Canyon. Heading more north-westerly, the trail follows Trap Canyon for a short distance, then turns north and heads through Horse Camp Basin. Turning northeast, Hoolie Bacon Trail climbs over Horse Ridge, then drops to Tortilla Creek. Turn left and follow the trail down Tortilla Creek. Watch for the point where the trail leaves the drainage on the right, and follow it north, up the slope, to JF Trail. Turn left on JF Trail to return to Tortilla Trailhead. **Option:** When you reach Randolph Canyon at the bottom of the descent from Tortilla Pass, turn right and hike 3.1 miles cross-country down Randolph Canyon to Red Tanks Canyon. The going is easy, though you won't see much trace of the trail shown on the Weavers Needle topo. Although Randolph Canyon is a 1.6-mile short-cut, your hiking time will be about the same. There's seasonal water in the canyon.

Miles and Directions

0.0   From the Tortilla Trailhead, head southeast on JF Trail.

0.8   At the junction with Hoolie Bacon Trail, stay left on JF Trail.

5.4   Pass the spur trail that leads 0.4 mile to Mullin Spring, a seasonal water source.

5.9   At the junction with Rogers Canyon Trail, stay right on JF Trail.

7.5   Reach Randolph Canyon.

8.1   Turn right on Woodbury Trail and follow it southwest into Fraser Canyon.

9.1   Pass JF Ranch; the trail becomes Coffee Flat Trail.

11.7   At the junction, turn right into Randolph Canyon on the Red Tanks Trail.

12.1   Pass the mouth of Red Tanks Canyon.

12.3   Turn left on Red Tanks Trail.

14.6   Cross Red Tanks Divide.

16.1   Turn right on Hoolie Bacon Trail.

18.3   Cross the pass on Horse Ridge.

19.3   Drop to Tortilla Creek.

20.4   Turn left on JF Trail.

21.1   Arrive back at Tortilla Trailhead.

10 Lower Rogers Canyon

This backpack trip or long day hike in the central Superstition Mountains points out the great contrast between ridge hiking and canyon hiking, and travels into rugged, wild, and little-visited canyons.

Start: Tortilla Trailhead
Distance: 15.8-mile loop (21-mile loop with the 6-mile out-and-back cherry stem if you hike FR 213)
Hiking time: About 10 hours or 2 days
Difficulty: Strenuous due to length, elevation change, and cross-country hiking
Best seasons: Oct–Apr
Trail surface: Dirt trails; cross-country along Fish Creek; dirt road if you hike FR 213
Land status: Tonto National Forest, Superstition Wilderness
Nearest town: Apache Junction

Other users: Horses
Water availability: Seasonal at Mullins Spring, along Rogers Canyon, and in Fish Creek
Canine compatibility: Leashed dogs permitted
Fees and permits: None
Schedule: Year-round, 24 hours per day
Maps: USGS Horse Mesa Dam AZ, Weavers Needle AZ, Iron Mountain AZ; USFS Superstition Wilderness map, Tonto National Forest map
Trail contact: Mesa Ranger District, Tonto National Forest, 5140 E. Ingram St., Mesa, AZ 85205; (480) 610-3300; www.fs.usda.gov/tonto

Finding the trailhead: From Apache Junction, drive about 22 miles east on AZ 88 to the Tortilla Road (FR 213), on the right. Turn right onto FR 213 and continue 3 miles to the end of the road and Tortilla Trailhead. This road requires a four-wheel-drive, high-clearance vehicle—if you have a low-clearance vehicle, you will need to park at the AZ 88 junction and hike FR 213 both ways, which adds 6 miles round-trip to the hike. GPS (FR 213): N33 31.56' / W111 19.15'; GPS (Tortilla Trailhead): N33 29.57' / W111 17.73'

The Hike

Start on JF Trail, heading southeast from the trailhead. As the trail climbs onto the ridge, note Lost Dutch Canyon to the northeast. You'll return through this canyon. Continue to climb steadily along the ridge, passing the high point of the trip just before descending into the head of the Tortilla Creek drainage. A side trail goes 0.5 mile to Mullin Spring.

At Tortilla Pass, turn left onto Rogers Canyon Trail. You'll descend, steeply at first, to the north, into an unnamed tributary of Rogers Canyon. After the descent moderates, the trail and canyon curve east and meet Rogers Canyon at Angel Basin. Angel Spring is a short distance up Rogers Canyon, below a cliff dwelling. Please do not disturb the fragile cliff dwelling.

To continue, hike down Rogers Canyon on Frog Tanks Trail. This trail gets less use than JF and Rogers Canyon Trails, and crosses the bottom frequently as it follows the easiest route down this remote, scenic canyon, with its towering walls and odd volcanic formations. There are usually pools of water in the streambed along the way.

Rock formations on the approach to Rogers Canyon

Rogers Canyon ends at Fish Creek, and Frog Tanks Trail climbs out on the right side of Fish Creek, just below Rogers Canyon. Look for a natural window in the rock formations high to the east of the confluence.

To continue the hike, follow Fish Creek cross-country downstream. Like lower Rogers Canyon, upper Fish Creek is deeply cut into very rough terrain. There's no trace of a trail along Fish Creek, though you can boulder hop down the bed without too much difficulty. You may find seasonal water at several points. Fish Creek heads generally east, and there are side canyons, such as Little Goat Canyon, Goat Canyon, and several unnamed canyons, that you can explore as options.

When Fish Creek turns to the north at the mouth of Lost Dutch Canyon, turn left and hike cross-country up the easy slopes to the southwest. This will take you onto the ridge between Lost Dutch Canyon and Tortilla Creek, where you meet JF Trail. Turn right and hike less than a mile to the Tortilla Trailhead.

Miles and Directions

0.0 Start at the Tortilla Trailhead on the JF Trail.

0.8 Pass the Hoolie Bacon Trail.

5.8 At Tortilla Pass and the junction with the Rogers Canyon Trail, turn left onto the Rogers Canyon Trail.

7.4 Reach Angel Basin and the Frog Tanks Trail junction. Turn left onto Frog Tanks Trail.

9.0 Turn left, down Fish Creek.

14.1 Turn left, up Lost Dutch Canyon.

15.1 Rejoin the JF Trail; turn right.

15.8 Arrive back at Tortilla Trailhead.

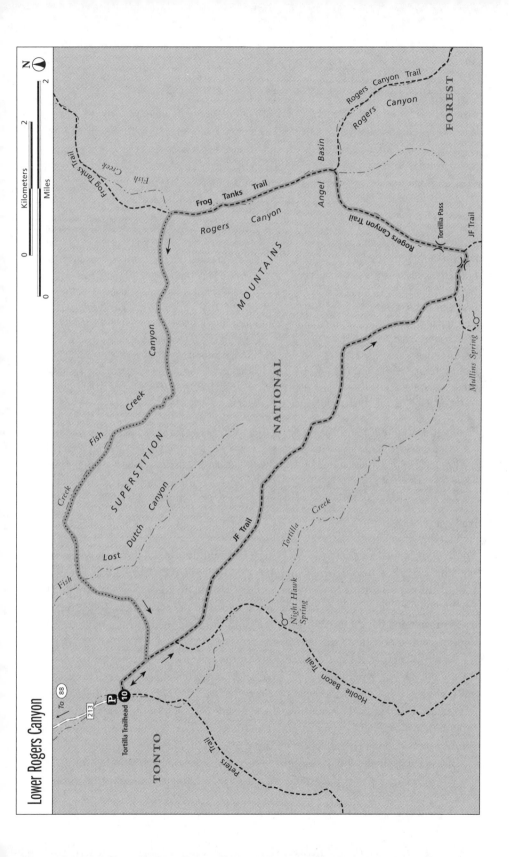

Lower Rogers Canyon

N

Kilometers
0   2

Miles
0   2

FOREST

Rogers Canyon Trail

Rogers Canyon

Frog Tanks Trail

Fish Creek

Angel Basin

Rogers Canyon

M O U N T A I N S

Rogers Canyon Trail

Tortilla Pass

JF Trail

N A T I O N A L

Mullins Spring

Fish Creek

S U P E R S T I T I O N

Creek Canyon

Dutch Canyon

JF Trail

Tortilla Creek

Lost

Fish Creek

Night Hawk Spring

To 88

213

P   10

Tortilla Trailhead

Hoolie Bacon Trail

T O N T O

Peters Trail

11 Reavis Ranch

This popular hike follows the north end of the Reavis Ranch Trail to the historic Reavis Ranch, a former cattle ranch that operated from the 1870s until the late 1960s. One reason this hike is popular is the old Reavis apple orchard, which still produces delicious fruit in the late summer. You'll also hike part of the Arizona National Scenic Trail, an 800-mile trail that crosses Arizona from Utah to Mexico.

Start: Reavis Trailhead
Distance: 18.2 miles out and back
Hiking time: About 10 hours or 2 days
Difficulty: Strenuous due to distance and elevation change
Best seasons: Oct–Apr
Trail surface: Old road
Land status: Tonto National Forest, Superstition Wilderness
Nearest town: Apache Junction
Other users: Horses
Water availability: Seasonal at Plow Saddle

Spring and in Reavis Creek south of the ranch site
Canine compatibility: Leashed dogs permitted
Fees and permits: None
Schedule: Year-round, 24 hours per day
Maps: USGS Pinyon Mountain AZ and Iron Mountain AZ; USFS Superstition Wilderness map; Tonto National Forest map
Trail contact: Mesa Ranger District, Tonto National Forest, 5140 E. Ingram St., Mesa, AZ 85205; (480) 610-3300; www.fs.usda.gov/tonto

Finding the trailhead: From Apache Junction, drive 20 miles east on AZ 88 to the end of the pavement. Continue for 7.4 miles on the gravel road (AZ 88) to the Reavis Ranch Road (FR 212), and turn right. Drive 3 miles on FR 212 to the Reavis Trailhead at the end of the road. GPS: N33 33.38' / W111 13.55'

The Hike

The Reavis Ranch was the only working ranch within the Superstition Wilderness after the wilderness was designated in 1964, and vehicle access to the ranch was via a long and winding road from AZ 88. After the USDA Forest Service bought the ranch, the ranch site and road corridor were added to the wilderness. Today, the old road is maintained as a foot and horse trail, and the route makes a fine hike though the east-central portion of the Superstition Mountains.

Reavis Ranch Trail climbs steadily, at first heading east as it works its way along the complex ridge system north of Lewis and Pranty Creek. After several miles the trail swings south, around the head of the creek, and climbs toward Castle Dome, a prominent rounded peak. Note how the vegetation changes from low desert scrub to high desert grassland as you ascend. The old road skirts the peak on the east and climbs over an unnamed saddle, which is the highest elevation of the hike.

Beyond the saddle you'll descend slightly and hike through Windy Pass, at the head of Fish Creek Canyon. Turning more to the east, the trail passes through broad

Cooking dinner at a backpacker's camp near the Reavis Ranch Trail

Plow Saddle, then climbs over a ridge. It crosses another broad saddle at the head of Willow Creek; here Frog Tanks Trail forks right. Reavis Ranch Trail now turns south along the west side of Reavis Creek. Reavis Creek is graced with numerous Arizona sycamores, and there are scattered ponderosa pines mixed with pinyon pines and juniper trees.

You'll meet Reavis Gap Trail (Arizona Trail) joining from the left. The trail passes the old Reavis apple orchard, then emerges into a meadow next to Reavis Creek.

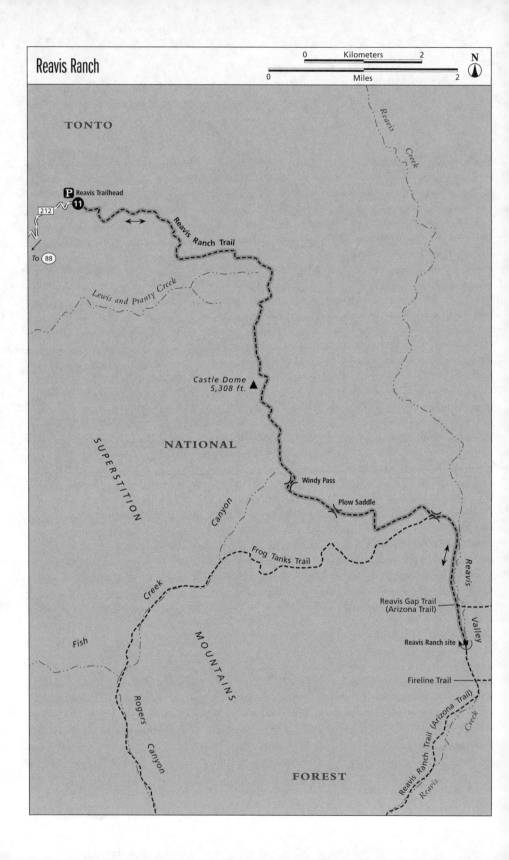

This was the site of the old ranch house. You can usually find flowing water in the creek upstream from the ranch site. There are numerous campsites nearby.

When the ranch was sold to the USDA Forest Service in the 1960s, the historic ranch house was still intact and usable as an emergency shelter. Unfortunately, years of weather and vandalism took their toll, and the building was finally burned to the ground by careless campers. Although the ruins of the house were cleaned up and removed, you may find artifacts from the old ranching days—please leave everything as you find it.

Miles and Directions

0.0 From the Reavis Trailhead, start on Reavis Ranch Trail.

5.1 Pass the first saddle.

5.6 Reach Windy Pass.

6.2 Reach Plow Saddle.

7.5 At the junction with Frog Tanks Trail, stay left on Reavis Ranch Trail.

8.7 At the junction with Reavis Gap Trail, stay right on Reavis Ranch Trail.

9.1 Reach the Reavis Ranch site; this is the turnaround point.

18.2 Arrive back at the trailhead.

12　Upper Fish Creek

This rugged but scenic backpack trip leads past the popular, historic Reavis Ranch site and through remote canyons in the upper Fish Creek drainage.

Start: Reavis Trailhead
Distance: 30.5-mile lollipop
Hiking time: About 3 days
Difficulty: Strenuous due to distance, elevation gain, and cross-country hiking
Best seasons: Oct–Apr
Trail surface: Old roads, dirt trails
Land status: Tonto National Forest, Superstition Wilderness
Nearest town: Apache Junction
Other users: Horses
Water availability: Seasonal in Reavis Creek

south of the ranch site, in Fish Creek, and at Frog Spring and Plow Saddle Spring
Canine compatibility: Leashed dogs permitted
Fees and permits: None
Schedule: Year-round, 24 hours per day
Maps: USGS Pinyon Mountain AZ and Iron Mountain AZ; USFS Superstition Wilderness map; Tonto National Forest map
Trail contact: Mesa Ranger District, Tonto National Forest, 5140 E. Ingram St., Mesa, AZ 85205; (480) 610-3300; www.fs.usda.gov/tonto

Finding the trailhead: From Apache Junction, drive 20 miles east on AZ 88 to the end of the pavement. Continue for 7.4 miles on the gravel road (AZ 88) to the Reavis Ranch Road (FR 212), and turn right. Drive 3 miles on FR 212 to the Reavis Trailhead at the end of the road. GPS: N33 33.38' / W111 13.55'

The Hike

Reavis Ranch Trail climbs steadily, at first heading east as it works its way along the complex ridge system north of Lewis and Pranty Creek. After several miles the trail swings south, around the head of the creek, and climbs toward Castle Dome, a prominent rounded peak. Note how the vegetation changes from low desert scrub to high desert grassland as you ascend. The old road skirts the peak on the east and climbs over an unnamed saddle, which is the highest elevation of the hike.

Beyond the saddle you'll descend slightly and hike through Windy Pass, at the head of Fish Creek Canyon. Turning more to the east, the trail passes through broad Plow Saddle, then climbs over a ridge. About a mile east of Plow Saddle, Frog Tanks Trail turns sharply right into the Fish Creek drainage—this is the return route; continue on the Reavis Ranch Trail. Next you'll pass the junction with Reavis Gap Trail (Arizona Trail), and then reach the site of the old ranch. There is usually flowing water in the creek south of the ranch. Continue south on the Reavis Ranch Trail, past the junction with Fireline Trail, to Reavis Saddle at the head of Reavis Creek. From

A dry spring at the start of the Frog Tanks Trail. ▶
Never depend on any single water source.

the saddle, follow Reavis Ranch Trail as it drops down Grave Canyon into Rogers Canyon.

Turn right in Rogers Canyon, leaving Reavis Ranch Trail (Arizona Trail), and follow Rogers Canyon Trail down its namesake canyon. This section of the canyon is very rugged and scenic—watch for a huge boulder jammed in a crack high up on the southwest wall. There is usually water in a few pools along the creekbed. As the canyon swings a bit west, watch for a cliff dwelling in a cave on the north wall. This well-preserved ruin is a popular destination, but please don't climb on the walls or otherwise disturb the fragile remains. There is seasonal water in the creekbed below the ruin. There are plenty of campsites just downstream at Angel Basin.

At Angel Basin, turn right and hike down Rogers Canyon on Frog Tanks Trail. This trail gets less use than JF and Rogers Canyon Trails, and crosses the bottom frequently as it follows the easiest route down this remote, scenic canyon, with its towering walls and odd volcanic formations. There are usually pools of water in the streambed along the way.

Rogers Canyon ends at Fish Creek. Look for a natural window in the rock formations high to the east of the confluence. It's a good idea to pick up water from one of the pools in Rogers Canyon, as it's a long, dry hike after the trail climbs out of the bed at Fish Creek. There are small campsites here.

Follow Frog Tanks Trail north out of Fish Creek. The trail leaves the bed of Fish Creek on the right just below the end of Rogers Canyon; there are seasonal water pockets in the bed of the canyon. Follow the steep, rough trail to Frog Spring, which is marked by an old water trough almost completely buried by flood debris. The spring itself is a couple hundred yards up the ravine from the trail, but it's much easier to pick up water before leaving Fish Creek.

After passing the old trough, the trail plunges steeply back to Fish Creek. The trail follows Fish Creek until just past Paradise Canyon, then climbs the slopes east of Fish Creek and contours to Plow Saddle Spring. The portion of the trail from Fish Creek to the Reavis Ranch Trail is a former jeep trail, and is easier going than the sections in Rogers Canyon and Fish Creek. Though the trough at Plow Saddle Spring is no longer maintained, you may find seasonal water in the ravine bed above and below the trail crossing. Beyond the spring, the trail climbs gradually to Reavis Ranch Trail in an unnamed saddle, completing the loop. Turn left on Reavis Ranch Trail and hike northwest to return to the trailhead.

Pre-Columbian ruins are common throughout the Superstition Mountains. They take the form both of cliff dwellings, such as the ruin at Angel Basin, and pit houses. One mysterious structure is thought to be an astronomical observatory. The major occupation of the Superstition area lasted until about 700 years ago.

Option: Instead of following the Reavis Ranch, Rogers Canyon, and Frog Tanks Trails down Rogers Canyon, you can leave the Reavis Ranch Trail near Reavis Saddle at the head of Reavis Creek, southeast of White Mountain, for a rugged but rewarding cross-country route across high ridges. You'll need the USGS topographic

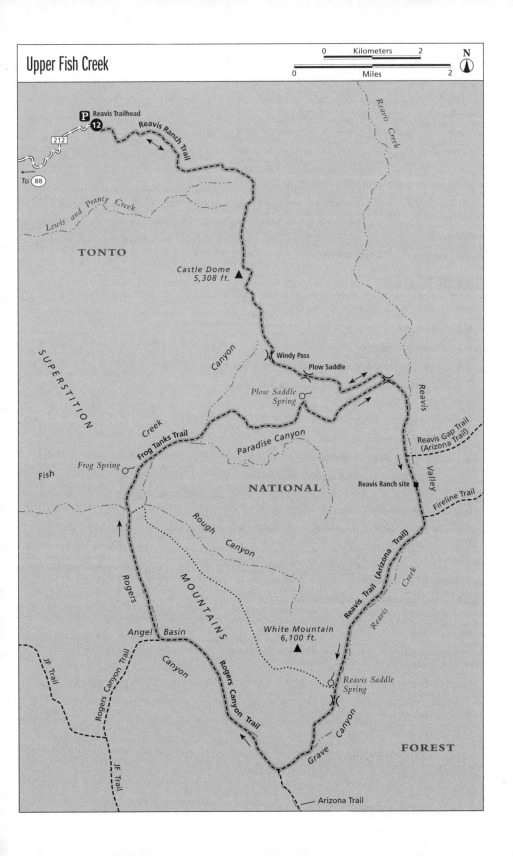

Upper Fish Creek

0   Kilometers   2

0   Miles   2

N

Reavis Creek

Reavis Trailhead

P 12

212

To 88

Reavis Ranch Trail

Lewis and Pranty Creek

TONTO

Castle Dome
5,308 ft.

Canyon

Windy Pass

Plow Saddle

Plow Saddle
Spring

Reavis

Creek

Frog Tanks Trail

Paradise Canyon

Reavis Gap Trail
(Arizona Trail)

Fish

Frog Spring

NATIONAL

Reavis Ranch site

Valley

Fireline Trail

SUPERSTITION

Rough

Canyon

Rogers

MOUNTAINS

White Mountain
6,100 ft.

Reavis Trail (Arizona Trail)

Reavis Creek

JF Trail

Angel Basin

Rogers Canyon Trail

Canyon

Rogers Canyon Trail

Reavis Saddle
Spring

Grave Canyon

FOREST

JF Trail

Arizona Trail

maps, the USFS wilderness map, and skill in cross-country hiking and route finding to follow this route. Work your way through the chaparral brush toward the ridge south of the summit of White Mountain. It becomes less brushy as you climb onto the ridge. You can easily hike to the summit of White Mountain as a side trip, which is only 0.1 mile north. Turn southwest along the ridge to the major ridge running northwest to the confluence of Rogers Canyon and Fish Creek. The views along this open, grassy ridge are spectacular. The ridge gradually descends as you follow it above the depths of well-named Rough Canyon. At the end of the ridge, drop west directly to the end of Rogers Canyon, working your way around small cliffs. This route is 3.7 miles shorter than the route along the trails, but the cross-country hiking will be slow enough that you won't save much time, if any. You'll also have an additional 800 feet of elevation gain because of the climb over White Mountain.

Miles and Directions

0.0 Start at the Reavis Trailhead on Reavis Ranch Trail.

5.6 Reach Windy Pass.

6.1 Reach Plow Saddle.

7.5 At the Frog Tanks Trail junction, stay left on Reavis Ranch Trail.

8.7 At Reavis Gap Trail, stay right on Reavis Ranch Trail.

9.1 Reach the Reavis Ranch site.

9.5 At the junction with the Fireline Trail, stay right on Reavis Ranch Trail.

12.3 Reach Reavis Saddle.

13.7 Turn right on Rogers Canyon Trail.

16.3 At Angel Basin, turn right on Frog Tanks Trail.

18.0 Reach Fish Creek; leave the canyon bottom and climb north on Frog Tanks Trail.

18.6 Pass Frog Spring.

19.9 The trail leaves Fish Creek and climbs the slope to the northeast.

21.5 Pass Plow Saddle Spring.

23.1 Close the loop at the junction with Reavis Ranch Trail. Turn left of Reavis Ranch Trail and retrace your steps.

30.5 Arrive back at the Reavis Trailhead.

13 Lower Pine Creek

This rugged cross-country backpack trip or long day hike takes you into remote canyon country in the northeastern Superstition Wilderness. You'll also hike a section of the 800-mile Arizona Trail along scenic Two Bar Ridge.

Start: Pine Creek Bridge at AZ 88
Distance: 15.1-mile lollipop
Hiking time: About 11 hours or 2 days
Difficulty: Strenuous due to cross-country travel and elevation change
Best seasons: Oct–Apr
Trail surface: Boulder hopping along canyon bottom, dirt trails
Land status: Tonto National Forest, Superstition Wilderness
Nearest town: Apache Junction
Other users: Horses on the Arizona Trail

Water availability: Seasonal in lower and upper Pine Creek
Canine compatibility: Leashed dogs permitted
Fees and permits: None
Schedule: Year-round, 24 hours per day
Maps: USGS Pinyon Mountain AZ and Two Bar Ridge AZ; USFS Superstition Wilderness map; Tonto National Forest Map
Trail contact: Tonto Basin Ranger District, Tonto National Forest, 28079 N. AZ 188, Roosevelt, AZ 85545; (928) 467-3200; www.fs.usda.gov/tonto

Finding the trailhead: From Apache Junction, drive 20 miles east on AZ 88 to the end of the pavement. Continue for another 12.7 miles on the gravel road (AZ 88) to the bridge across Pine Creek and park along the road. GPS: N33 35.90' / W111 12.17'

The Hike

You should have both the USGS topos and the wilderness map, as well as skill in cross-country route finding, before attempting this hike. The Arizona Trail (Two Bar Ridge Trail) is not shown on the USGS quad.

Begin by hiking cross-country up Pine Creek above the bridge. There is seasonal water along this low Sonoran Desert creek as you pass through groves of stately saguaro cactus. Pinecones washed down from the pinyon and ponderosa pine stands at the head of this long drainage hint at the variety of plantlife to be found in the eastern Superstition Mountains. Where the Pinyon Mountain USGS topo shows the crossing of a nonexistent trail from Yellowjacket Spring, take note of the slope to the east. This is the return route.

No serious obstacles present themselves on the hike up lower Pine Creek, but the canyon gradually steepens as it turns more to the east. You should pick up water for camp or plan on camping along Pine Creek, as there is no water on the return along Two Bar Ridge.

At 4.6 miles, turn east (left) up an unnamed side canyon that heads east toward Two Bar Mountain. Climb up this canyon, which becomes narrow and brushy in spots, until you intercept the Arizona Trail (Two Bar Ridge Trail) at about the 4,000-foot level.

Four Peaks from Pine Creek

Turn left on the Two Bar Ridge/Arizona Trail and climb steeply to the north onto Two Bar Ridge, then head north along the ridge. There are some great views of the Pine Creek drainage on the west and the Campaign Creek drainage on the east. Now in high desert grassland, cross a minor summit along the ridge that is the high point of the hike. The trail continues north, eventually swinging west to the head of Two Bar Canyon, and then meeting Tule Canyon Trail. Stay on Arizona Trail as it follows the ridge above Tule Canyon.

When Arizona Trail starts to turn northeast to skirt Pinyon Mountain, leave the trail and head cross-country northwest along the slopes of Pinyon Mountain for about 0.2 mile, then turn west and descend the ridge just south of the 4,083-foot elevation point on the USGS topo. There are a few steep, rocky sections, but overall the descent is straightforward. You'll leave the high desert grassland behind and descend back into the saguaro cactus forest. The last 1.5 miles is a pleasant walk along desert ridges to Pine Creek. Once back at the creek, turn right and hike downstream to AZ 88 and your vehicle.

If you've done many hikes in the western Superstitions, you might have noticed that the rocks in the northeastern portion of the range are different. Granite rocks dominate in the Pine and Campaign Creek drainages. Most of the rock in the Superstition Mountains is volcanic and flowed or was blasted out of volcanic vents onto the landscape. Granitic rocks, in contrast, form deep underground, when molten rock invades a weakness in the earth's crust. The molten mass cools slowly so that rock crystals grow to large sizes. As the mountains of central Arizona were uplifted and eroded, the deeply buried granitic rocks were exposed. Today, you can readily see the large crystals that make up the rock.

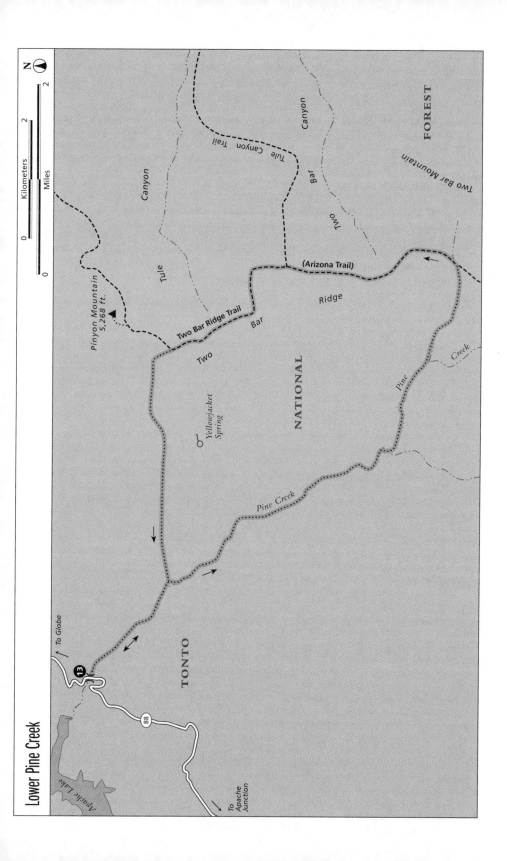

Lower Pine Creek

Option: At the point where you leave the Two Bar Ridge Trail to descend to Pine Creek, you can easily make a side trip to climb Pinyon Mountain for an excellent view of the eastern Superstitions. Stay on the Two Bar Ridge Trail for about 0.5 mile, until it turns east and starts to contour, then continue north, cross-country, another 0.2 mile to the rounded summit. This side hike would add 1.4 miles and 750 feet of climbing to the hike.

Miles and Directions

0.0 Start at the Pine Creek Bridge, hiking cross-country (south) up Pine Creek.

1.5 Pass the Yellowjacket Spring drainage; this is the return route.

4.6 Turn left up unnamed side canyon north of Klondyke Spring.

7.0 At Arizona Trail (Two Bar Ridge Trail), turn left.

8.9 At the Tule Canyon Trail junction, stay left on Arizona Trail.

10.9 Leave Arizona Trail and descend a ridge north of Yellowjacket Spring to Pine Creek.

12.9 At Pine Creek, turn right and head downstream.

15.1 Arrive back at the Pine Creek Bridge.

14 Pinyon Mountain

This nice hike along Two Bar Ridge and over Pinyon Mountain, one of the highest peaks in the northeastern Superstition Mountains, also features a short but scenic portion of the Arizona Trail.

Start: Tule Trailhead
Distance: 11.5-mile loop
Hiking time: About 8 hours
Difficulty: Strenuous due to elevation gain and cross-country hiking
Best seasons: Oct–Apr
Trail surface: Dirt trails, dirt roads, cross-country terrain
Land status: Tonto National Forest, Superstition Wilderness
Nearest town: Globe
Other users: Horses

Water availability: None
Canine compatibility: Leashed dogs permitted
Fees and permits: None
Schedule: Year-round, 24 hours per day
Maps: USGS Pinyon Mountain AZ and Two Bar Ridge AZ; USFS Superstition Wilderness map; Tonto National Forest map
Trail contact: Tonto Basin Ranger District, Tonto National Forest, 28079 N. AZ 188, Roosevelt, AZ 85545; (928) 467-3200; www .fs.usda.gov/tonto

Finding the trailhead: From Apache Junction, drive 20 miles east on AZ 88 to the end of the pavement. Continue for another 20 miles on the gravel road (AZ 88) to Roosevelt Dam, then turn right to remain on AZ 88, which is now paved. Continue 8.6 miles, then turn right on FR 449, the Campaign Creek Road, which is maintained dirt. Go 1.9 miles, turn right at a fork to remain on FR 449, and continue 0.6 mile to the Tule Trailhead. GPS: N33 35.61' / W111 4.60'
  You can also reach FR 449 from Globe by driving about 20 miles west on AZ 88, which is paved.

The Hike

This hike is a good introduction to this less-traveled portion of the Superstition Wilderness. You'll encounter a wide variety of terrain, from Sonoran Desert to pinyon–juniper forest. Start on Tule Trail, which wanders southwest from the trailhead, working its way through the foothills toward Tule Canyon. A few short switchbacks lead down to Tule Canyon. After crossing Tule Canyon, the trail turns more to the west for a distance and climbs onto a ridge south of Tule Canyon. Then the trail abruptly turns south and climbs steeply to the top of a ridge north of Two Bar Canyon. Follow the trail west along the ridge.

Tule Trail ends on the top of Two Bar Ridge. Turn right and follow the Arizona Trail (Two Bar Ridge Trail) north toward the rounded bulk of Pinyon Mountain.

Notice that you left the saguaro cactus of the Sonoran Desert behind as you climbed. The grassy top of Two Bar Ridge has scattered pinyon pines and juniper trees. The trail wanders north, then west, then north again as it follows the twists and turns of the ridge. Finally, the route climbs partway up Pinyon Mountain, contouring around the southeast slopes of the peak before descending northeast to end at FR 83.

Coyotes have increased their range, and it's a rare desert backpacker who hasn't been awakened by their twilight serenades.

Turn right and follow the forest road as it drops off the ridge, then turns north into a drainage system. After leaving the drainage, it climbs over a low pass to the east. As you emerge from the mountains onto the gently sloping desert plain, the road turns north. Leave the road at this point and hike cross-country directly to Tule Trailhead and your vehicle.

Junipers and pinyon pines commonly occur together in the mountains of central Arizona and combine to create a pygmy forest 10–20 feet high. The several species of junipers are slow growing, drought-resistant trees, and they appear first as you gain elevation. Pinyon pines need a little more water, and gradually mix with the junipers as you climb. These shaggy pines are taller than the junipers and have short needles. The pinecones produce a tasty nut that has long been a staple food for Native Americans. Occasionally, pinyon pines grow up to 40 feet tall and often provide a soft bed of needles and an inviting patch of shade around their bases. They also produce a lot of sticky sap, which runs down the trunk and drips from the branches.

Option: You can easily climb Pinyon Mountain from this route for some great views. Leave the trail where it starts to contour below the summit, and hike cross-country about 0.2 mile north to the rounded summit. This option adds 0.4 mile and less than 300 feet of climbing to the hike.

Pinyon Mountain

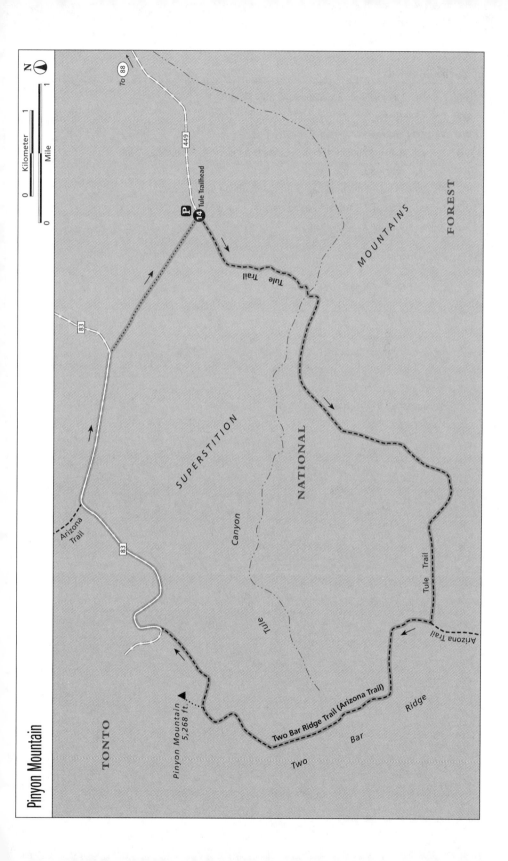

Miles and Directions

0.0 From the Tule Trailhead, hike southwest on Tule Trail.

1.2 Cross Tule Canyon.

4.4 Turn right on Arizona Trail (Two Bar Ridge Trail).

7.0 The trail skirts the southeast slopes below the summit of Pinyon Mountain.

7.7 Turn right on FR 83.

9.2 Arizona Trail leaves the road and heads north; follow the road east.

10.3 Leave the road (FR 83) and hike cross-country southeast.

11.5 Arrive back at the Tule Trailhead.

15 Fireline Loop

This is a most enjoyable hike through the high country in the eastern Superstitions. You'll have a chance to climb the highest peak in the range, visit the site of historic Reavis Ranch, and hike along beautiful Campaign Creek.

Start: Campaign Trailhead
Distance: 14.8-mile loop
Hiking time: About 10 hours or 2 days
Difficulty: Strenuous due to length, elevation change, and faint trails
Best seasons: Oct–Apr
Trail surface: Dirt
Land status: Tonto National Forest, Superstition Wilderness
Nearest town: Globe
Other users: Horses
Water availability: Campaign Creek near the trailhead, Walnut Spring, seasonal in Pine Creek and Reavis Creek, Whiskey Spring, Black Jack Spring, Brushy Spring, seasonal in upper Campaign Creek
Canine compatibility: Leashed dogs permitted
Fees and permits: None
Schedule: Year-round, 24 hours per day
Maps: USGS Pinyon Mountain AZ, Two Bar Mountain AZ, Haunted Canyon AZ, and Iron Mountain AZ; USFS Superstition Wilderness map; Tonto National Forest map
Trail contact: Tonto Basin Ranger District, Tonto National Forest, 28079 N. AZ 188, Roosevelt, AZ 85545; (928) 467-3200; www .fs.usda.gov/tonto

Finding the trailhead: From Apache Junction, drive 20 miles east on AZ 88 to the end of the pavement. Continue for another 20 miles on the gravel road (AZ 88) to Roosevelt Dam, then turn right to remain on AZ 88, which is now paved. Continue 8.6 miles, then turn right on FR 449 (Campaign Creek Road), which is maintained dirt. Go 1.9 miles, then turn left at a fork onto FR 449A. Continue 5.2 miles to the end of the road at the Reavis Mountain School. FR 449A follows Campaign Creek and crosses it numerous times. This route requires a high-clearance vehicle and may be washed out and impassable after major storms. The trailhead is on private land—please park in the signed trailhead parking area. There is no camping at the trailhead. GPS: N33 31.89' / W111 4.76'

You can also reach FR 449 from Globe by driving about 20 miles west on AZ 88, which is paved.

The Hike

After leaving the Campaign Trailhead on Campaign Trail, hike through the Reavis Mountain School (there are several buildings and tent camps—please respect private property and stay on the trail) and continue southwest along Campaign Creek. This section of the creek has a permanent flow of water from several nearby springs. Just beyond a side canyon that comes in from the right, turn right on Reavis Gap Trail.

The Reavis Gap Trail is not shown on the USGS topos, and sections can be difficult to follow. First climb over a low ridge, then head west up an unnamed canyon system, climbing steadily. After you cross the normally dry wash, the grade steepens as

Backpacker descending to Reavis Creek on the Fireline Trail

the trail heads for Reavis Gap, a saddle on Two Bar Ridge. Just after passing through Reavis Gap, the Two Bar Ridge Trail (Arizona Trail) branches right. (Walnut Spring is about 0.5 mile north on Two Bar Ridge Trail.) Stay on the Reavis Gap Trail (now part of the Arizona Trail) as it passes through another saddle, then swings south and drops into Pine Creek. There is seasonal water in Pine Creek, and good camping.

After crossing Pine Creek, follow the trail southwest and climb gradually toward another saddle. The trail then drops gradually west down a tributary of Reavis Creek and ends at the Reavis Ranch Trail (the route of the Arizona Trail southward), on the west side of Reavis Creek. Turn left, and hike a short distance upstream to the historic ranch site. There is usually water in the creek south of the ranch site.

Continue the hike by heading south on Reavis Ranch Trail. You may also find water along this section of Reavis Creek. Turn left (east) on the Fireline Trail, which intersects before you reach the first major drainage entering on the left.

Parts of Fireline Trail follow an old bulldozer track made by the USDA Forest Service while fighting a forest fire in 1966. Wildfires are common in this remote country and difficult to fight. In the early days of the Superstition Wilderness, it was thought that all wildfires should be aggressively suppressed, and bulldozers were used to build access roads and construct fire lines, leaving prominent scars. The forest service now recognizes that lightning-caused fires are part of the natural forest life cycle and are necessary to keeping the wilderness wild. Now, fires with natural causes are allowed to burn uncontrolled, except for monitoring and containment efforts to keep the blaze from threatening developed areas outside the wilderness. Another fire burned the area in the 1980s, but because low-impact firefighting techniques were used, there was much less impact to the landscape.

You'll mostly be in mixed chaparral and pinyon-juniper forest along the first part of Fireline Trail. After passing Whiskey Spring, the trail turns to the northeast and climbs up a drainage to the divide between Reavis Creek and Pine Creek, at 8 miles. From this point, the route heads southeast and descends gradually into the head of the Pine Creek drainage. There are pockets of tall ponderosa pines growing in favored locations—hence the name of the creek. The old bulldozer trail suddenly turns east and drops steeply into the bed of Pine Creek, then follows the drainage for a short distance before climbing out to the east and crossing the divide between Pine and Campaign Creeks. The trail then plunges steeply into Campaign Creek, passing Black Jack Spring (shown on the USFS wilderness map but not on the USGS topo) just before ending at Campaign Trail in Campaign Creek.

Turn left, and follow Campaign Trail down Campaign Creek. After the rugged country you've just crossed, it's a joy to wander down the scenic canyon bottom. There's seasonal water in the creekbed. Finally, the trail climbs over a low saddle to avoid a narrow, rough section of the canyon bottom, then the trail meets Reavis Gap Trail, closing the loop. Stay right to return to the Campaign Trailhead.

The high country of the eastern Superstitions is frequently burned by wildfires. You might wonder how any pine trees manage to grow here. Ponderosa pines are actually well adapted to fire. The thick, platelike bark of mature trees insulates the living cambium from the heat of a fire. As long as the fire is not so hot that it jumps into the crowns of the trees, most ponderosa pines survive wildfires. Frequent fires keep underbrush and deadwood from accumulating, and lower the average intensity of fires.

Option 1: At Reavis Gap, turn right onto Two Bar Ridge Trail (Arizona Trail) and hike 1.2 miles north, past Walnut Spring, to the point where the trail starts to drop into a tributary of Pine Creek. This point is a fine overlook of lower Pine Creek and

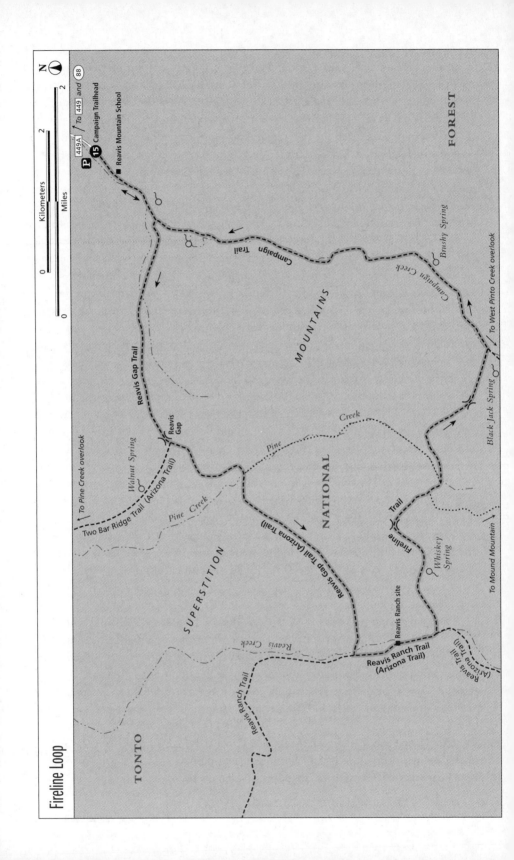

Fireline Loop

Two Bar Ridge. This option adds 2.4 miles and 200 feet of elevation change to the hike.

Option 2: Where Reavis Gap Trail (Arizona Trail) crosses Pine Creek, turn left and hike cross-country up Pine Creek to Fireline Trail. Sections of upper Pine Creek are rough and slow-going because of large boulders and dense brush. It's 1.8 miles to the Fireline Trail, and you'll climb about 620 feet. This option shortens the loop by 5.6 miles but is much more difficult than staying on the formal trails.

Option 3: When Fireline Trail starts down into Pine Creek, leave the trail to the right (south) and hike cross-country along the pinyon-juniper-covered ridge. Though the upper part of this ridge is brushy, with some route finding you can find a reasonably brush-free route to the top of Mound Mountain. At 6,266 feet, this round summit is the highest point in the Superstition Mountains and has an appropriately commanding view of the range. This option adds 2.6 miles and 800 feet of elevation change to the trip.

Option 4: At the junction of Fireline Trail and Campaign Trail, turn right and hike up Campaign Trail to the saddle at the head of Campaign Creek. You'll get good views of upper Pinto Creek and the rugged country around Iron Mountain and Pinto Peak in the southeast corner of the Superstition Mountains. This hike adds 3.2 miles to the trip and 690 feet of elevation gain.

Miles and Directions

0.0 From the Campaign Trailhead, hike southwest on Campaign Trail.

0.8 Turn right on Reavis Gap Trail.

3.0 Reach Reavis Gap and the Two Bar Ridge Trail (Arizona Trail) junction. Stay left on Reavis Gap Trail (Arizona Trail).

3.9 Cross Pine Creek.

6.0 Turn left on Reavis Ranch Trail (Arizona Trail).

6.5 Reach the Reavis Ranch site.

6.8 Turn left on Fireline Trail.

8.0 Cross the saddle marking the Reavis Creek–Pine Creek divide.

10.1 Turn left on Campaign Trail and follow it northeast down Campaign Creek.

13.9 Close the loop and stay right at the Reavis Gap Trail, retracing your steps to the trailhead.

14.8 Arrive back at the Campaign Trailhead.

16 West Pinto Creek

This rugged hike leads through the southeast portion of the Superstition Wilderness—probably the most remote and least-visited region.

Start: Miles Trailhead
Distance: 17.3-mile lollipop
Hiking time: About 10 hours or 2 days
Difficulty: Strenuous due to length, elevation change, and faint trails
Best seasons: Oct–Apr
Trail surface: Dirt trails, dirt roads, cross-country terrain
Land status: Tonto National Forest, Superstition Wilderness
Nearest town: Globe
Other users: Horses; mountain bikes and vehicles on FR 650

Water availability: Seasonal in West Pinto Creek, at Iron Mountain and Rogers Springs, and in Rock Creek
Canine compatibility: Leashed dogs permitted
Fees and permits: None
Schedule: Year-round, 24 hours per day
Maps: USGS Iron Mountain AZ and Haunted Canyon AZ; USFS Superstition Wilderness map; Tonto National Forest map
Trail contact: Globe Ranger District, Tonto National Forest, 7680 S. Six Shooter Canyon Rd., Globe, AZ 85501; (928) 402-6200; www.fs.usda.gov/tonto

Finding the trailhead: From Apache Junction, go about 31 miles east on US 60, through the town of Superior. Continue another 15 miles, then turn left onto the paved Pinto Valley Road (this turnoff is about 4 miles east of Top of the World). Go 3.2 miles, then turn left onto a maintained dirt road, just before the mine gatehouse. The next few miles are on private land in an active mining area. Stay on the main road, which is marked with Public Access Road signs. There are many side roads, and the public access road is subject to change. Because this area is confusing, the following mileages are from US 60. At 5.8 miles, turn left at the FR 287 sign. You'll leave the private land at 7.1 miles. At 7.3 miles, turn right. At 7.4 miles, turn left onto FR 287A. Park at the Miles Trailhead, 13.3 miles from the highway. FR 287A is rocky in places, and a high-clearance vehicle is recommended. GPS: N33 26.27' / W111 4.02'

The Hike

Follow the West Pinto Trail westward through pinyon pine, juniper, and Arizona cypress forest. The trail first skirts private land, then descends to West Pinto Creek and meets the Rock Creek Trail. This trail is used on the return. Stay right on West Pinto Trail as it continues up its namesake creek, which is usually a dry wash. Fine examples of Arizona sycamore trees grow along the drainage, which proves that water is not far below the surface, even in dry periods. Flowing water and pools can usually be found at several places along the creekbed as the trail continues upstream into a narrow section of the canyon.

The canyon opens out into Oak Flat, a broad oak-covered flat, and both Cuff Button and Campaign Trails branch to the right. At the west end of Oak Flat, Spencer Spring Trail forks left, up Spencer Spring Canyon; stay right and continue on West Pinto Trail.

Pool in lower Campaign Creek

Beyond the flat, West Pinto Trail climbs along the south side of the canyon to avoid narrow, rocky sections of the bed, and the stands of Arizona cypress start to give way to dense chaparral brush. After a while, the trail crosses the creek and contours along the north side. The upper sections of the West Pinto Trail are little traveled and may be overgrown with brush in places.

The trail descends back to the creekbed at Crockett Spring. (Crockett Spring is shown correctly on the Superstition Wilderness map but incorrectly on the Iron

Mountain USGS map.) The trail then starts a steep climb up the north side of the canyon toward Iron Mountain. Sections of very steep grade are interspersed with almost level sections along scenic ridges. You can look back at most of upper West Pinto Creek from these vantage points.

The trail continues up a ridge to the east shoulder of Iron Mountain, then turns abruptly south and descends a short distance to Iron Mountain Spring. The old USGS topo maps show numerous trails in the Iron Mountain area that have disappeared; refer to the USFS wilderness map for more current trail information.

After passing Iron Mountain Spring, the trail again climbs steeply, this time to a saddle on the south shoulder of Iron Mountain, just below a prominent cliff. The route then descends the west slopes of the mountain, passing Rogers Spring, which is in an old corral. West Pinto Trail ends shortly below the corral, when it meets the Reavis Ranch Trail (Arizona Trail). Turn left here and walk to the Rogers Trough Trailhead.

From the trailhead, hike south on FR 172A (the only road leaving the trailhead), then turn left on FR 650, a four-wheel-drive road. This road is the route of the Arizona Trail and is marked occasionally with Arizona Trail symbols. A short, steep climb on FR 650 takes you over a saddle and into a drainage, which the road follows southeast to gain the top of the ridge leading to Montana Mountain. From here eastward, the road stays near the ridgecrest and offers fines views of the southeast Superstitions and the sprawling deserts far to the south.

Just before the road swings around the north side of Montana Mountain, the Reavis Trail/Arizona Trail leaves the road to the right. Stay on FR 650. Where Sawtooth Ridge joins the west shoulder of Montana Mountain, the Spencer Spring Trail drops off the ridge to the left, into its namesake canyon. This junction is marked only by a cairn. Continue east along FR 650 to another junction marked by a cairn; turn left here onto the little-used Rock Creek Trail. Watch carefully for these cairns, as FR 650 and these two trails are not shown correctly on the USGS topo or the USFS wilderness map.

Rock Creek Trail descends steeply through stands of Arizona cypress and soon reaches the bed of upper Rock Creek. The southern portion of this trail is faint and overgrown in places, but the route stays in or very near Rock Creek after the initial descent. After the Arizona sycamores make their appearance along the bed, you'll find several seasonal pools of water, and there are possible campsites.

The trail emerges onto a broad flat and meets Bull Basin Trail, which merges from the right. The trail is much better down the lower mile of Rock Creek and ends at the junction with West Pinto Trail. Turn right here to retrace your steps to the Miles Trailhead.

Option 1: At Oak Flat, take Cuff Button Trail to Iron Trough Spring. This side hike adds 1.9 miles and 710 feet of elevation gain to the trip.

Option 2: At Oak Flat, turn right on Campaign Trail and climb to the pass at the head of Campaign Creek. This vantage point gives good views of the heads of Pinto

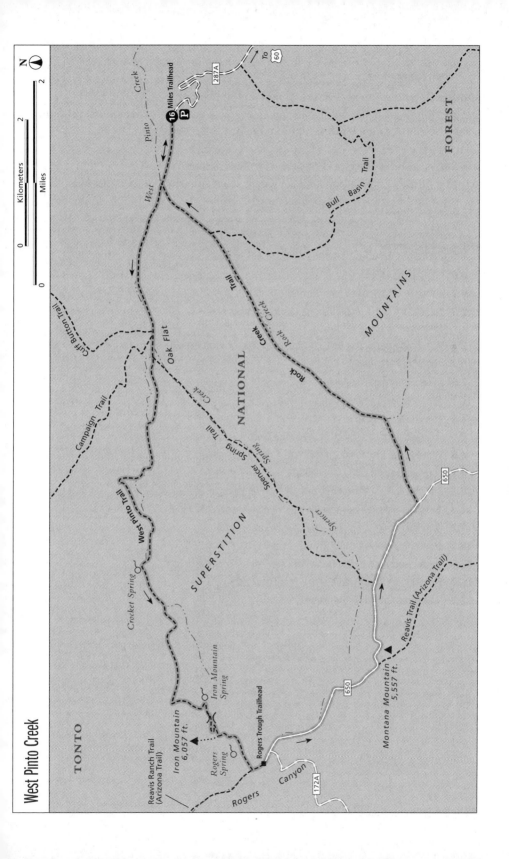

West Pinto Creek

and Campaign Creeks, two of the major drainages of the eastern Superstition Mountains. This option adds 5 miles and 1,610 feet of elevation change to the hike.

Option 3: You can climb Iron Mountain, a prominent summit in the eastern Superstition Mountains, by leaving West Pinto Trail west of the pass. Work your way up the southwest slopes of the mountain to join the east ridge above the cliffs. This side hike adds 0.7 mile and 600 feet of elevation gain to the hike.

Option 4: You can leave FR 650 at the Spencer Spring Trail and use this trail as your return route. It's 3.5 miles to Oak Flat, where you'll turn right on the West Pinto Trail to return to the Miles Trailhead. This shortcut makes the hike 2.8 miles shorter, for a total loop distance of 12.1 miles, but the elevation gain is the same.

Miles and Directions

0.0   Start at the Miles Trailhead, and hike west on West Pinto Trail.

0.7   At the Rock Creek Trail junction at the mouth of Rock Creek, stay right on West Pinto Trail.

2.3   Reach Oak Flat. Cuff Button and Campaign Trails branch off on the right; stay left on West Pinto Trail.

2.5   At the Spencer Spring Trail junction, keep right on West Pinto Trail.

5.3   Pass Crockett Spring.

7.3   Pass Iron Mountain Spring.

7.7   Pass the south ridge of Iron Mountain.

8.1   Pass Rogers Spring.

8.5   Turn left on Reavis Ranch Trail (Arizona Trail).

8.6   Arrive at the Rogers Trough Trailhead. Continue south on FR 172A (Arizona Trail).

9.1   Turn left onto FR 650 (Arizona Trail).

10.3   The Reavis Trail/Arizona Trail branches off on the right; stay left on FR 650.

11.3   Pass the unsigned Spencer Spring Trail on left; stay right on FR 650.

12.2   Turn left onto the unsigned Rock Creek Trail.

13.2   Reach Rock Creek; continue downstream.

15.9   At the junction with Bull Basin Trail, stay left on Rock Creek Trail.

16.6   Turn right on West Pinto Trail and retrace your step.

17.3   Arrive back at the Miles Trailhead.

17 Reavis Creek

This hike takes you on a scenic trip around Iron and Mound Mountains through the highest portion of the Superstition Mountains, at the eastern end of the wilderness. Part of the hike follows the Arizona Trail.

Start: Rogers Trough Trailhead
Distance: 20.1-mile loop
Hiking time: About 12 hours or 2 days
Difficulty: Strenuous due to distance and elevation change
Best seasons: Oct–Apr
Trail surface: Dirt
Land status: Tonto National Forest, Superstition Wilderness
Nearest town: Apache Junction
Other users: Horses
Water availability: Seasonal at Rogers Spring, Iron Mountain Spring, Crockett Spring, and in

Reavis Creek, Campaign Creek, and West Fork Pinto Creek
Canine compatibility: Leashed dogs permitted
Fees and permits: None
Schedule: Year-round, 24 hours per day
Maps: USGS Iron Mountain AZ and Haunted Canyon AZ; USFS Superstition Wilderness map; Tonto National Forest map
Trail contact: Mesa Ranger District, Tonto National Forest, 5140 E. Ingram St., Mesa, AZ 85205; (480) 610-3300; www.fs.usda.gov/tonto

Finding the trailhead: From Apache Junction, go about 18 miles east on US 60, then turn left on the Queen Creek Road. Follow this paved road for 1.9 miles, then turn right on FR 357, a maintained dirt road. Continue 3.1 miles to the junction with FR 172, then turn left. Go 12.5 miles on FR 172, a maintained dirt road, then turn right onto FR 172A. After 3.6 miles, turn left at the junction with FR 650, and continue 0.4 mile to the Rogers Trough Trailhead. The last section of FR 172A is rough and may require a high-clearance vehicle. GPS: N33 25.35' / W111 10.41'

The Hike

Start by following Reavis Ranch Trail (Arizona Trail) down Rogers Canyon, heading northwest from the trailhead. At the junction with West Pinto Trail, stay left on Reavis Ranch Trail. At the mouth of Grave Canyon and the junction with Rogers Canyon Trail, turn right and follow Reavis Ranch Trail (Arizona Trail) up this side canyon. The trail climbs steeply to Reavis Saddle, on the ridge northwest of Iron Mountain. Continue along the trail as it descends gently to the northeast along the headwaters of Reavis Creek. Chaparral and pinyon–juniper forest are the dominant vegetation, but some nice groves of ponderosa pines also grow along the valley floor.

Turn right on Fireline Trail before you reach the site of Reavis Ranch. (There's usually water in the creek just above the ranch site, and small campsites.) Fireline Trail climbs past Whiskey Spring, then over the saddle between Reavis and Pine Creeks. It drops into Pine Creek, then climbs over another saddle on the divide between Pine and Campaign Creeks. A steep descent takes you past Black Jack Spring (shown on

Ponderosa pines along Reavis Creek

the USFS wilderness map but not the USGS topo) and into the Campaign Creek drainage.

Continue by turning right on Campaign Trail and hiking up Campaign Creek to the pass at its head. From the pass, the trail drops southeast, down a ridge system into the Pinto Creek drainage and meets the West Fork Pinto Creek at Oak Flat. Turn right onto West Pinto Trail and hike west. After passing the junction with Spring Creek Trail, West Pinto Trail climbs along the slopes south of the creek for about

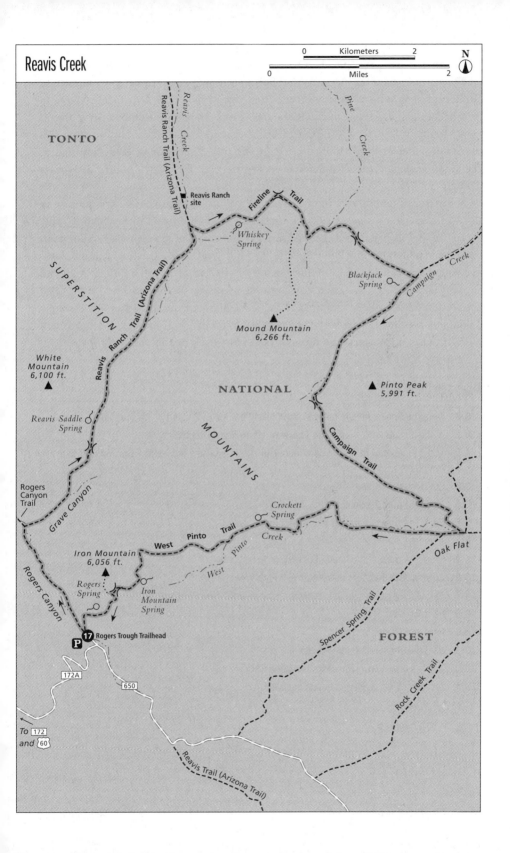

a mile, then crosses the creekbed to the north side. The trail descends back to the creekbed at Crockett Spring. (Crockett Spring is shown correctly on the Superstition Wilderness map but incorrectly on the Iron Mountain USGS map.) After staying in or near the creek for less than a mile, the trail leaves the bed and climbs a ridge toward Iron Mountain. It descends south to Iron Mountain Spring, then climbs over a pass on the shoulder of Iron Mountain. Finally, the trail descends past Rogers Spring to the junction with Reavis Ranch Trail (Arizona Trail). Turn left to return to Rogers Trough Trailhead.

Chaparral is common at intermediate elevations in Arizona. It's a community of shrubs rather than a single plant. Common members are manzanita, which is easily recognized by its brittle, red-barked branches and small, oval, green leaves; mountain mahogany, which has smaller, ridged leaves; and scrub oak, which is a tough, low-growing evergreen oak. Really thick stands of chaparral can reach 10 feet high and are very difficult to force your way through. Most stands are lower and have open lanes, often made by deer and other animals, that allow to you to find a route through. Though a pain for hiking, chaparral is valuable cover for a number of animals and birds. It burns furiously after a drought but grows back rapidly from its roots, which can survive a fire's heat.

Miles and Directions

0.0 From the Rogers Trough Trailhead, start hiking on Reavis Ranch Trail (Arizona Trail).

0.1 At the junction with West Pinto Trail, stay left on Reavis Ranch Trail (Arizona Trail).

1.5 At the junction with Rogers Canyon Trail, turn right and stay on Reavis Ranch Trail (Arizona Trail).

2.8 Cross Reavis Saddle.

5.7 Turn right onto Fireline Trail.

6.9 Cross the saddle between Reavis and Pine Creeks.

9.2 Turn right onto Campaign Trail.

11.2 Cross the pass at the head of Campaign Creek.

13.8 Arrive at Oak Flat. Turn right onto West Pinto Trail.

14.0 At the junction with Spring Creek Trail, stay right on West Pinto Trail.

16.8 Pass Crockett Spring.

18.8 Pass Iron Mountain Spring.

19.1 Pass the shoulder of Iron Mountain.

20.0 Turn left onto Reavis Ranch Trail (Arizona Trail).

20.1 Arrive back at the Rogers Trough Trailhead.

18 Angel Basin

This hike leads through one of the most scenic canyons in the Superstition Mountains and to a well-preserved pre-Columbian ruin. It can be done as a long day hike or an overnight backpack.

Start: Woodbury Trailhead
Distance: 12.7-mile lollipop
Hiking time: About 8 hours or 2 days
Difficulty: Strenuous due to length and elevation change
Best seasons: Oct–Apr
Trail surface: Dirt trails and dirt roads
Land status: Tonto National Forest, Superstition Wilderness
Nearest town: Apache Junction
Other users: Horses; vehicles and mountain bikes on FR 172A

Water availability: Seasonal along Rogers Canyon
Canine compatibility: Leashed dogs permitted
Fees and permits: None
Schedule: Year-round, 24 hours per day
Maps: USGS Iron Mountain AZ; USFS Superstition Wilderness map; Tonto National Forest map
Trail contact: Mesa Ranger District, Tonto National Forest, 5140 E. Ingram St., Mesa, AZ 85205; (480) 610-3300; www.fs.usda.gov/tonto

Finding the trailhead: From Apache Junction, go about 18 miles east on US 60, then turn left on the Queen Creek Road. Follow this paved road for 1.9 miles, then turn right onto FR 357, a maintained dirt road. Continue 3.1 miles to the junction with FR 172, then turn left. Go 12.5 miles on FR 172, a maintained dirt road, to FR 172B and turn left. Continue 1.5 miles on FR 172B to a locked gate, then turn right and park at the Woodbury Trailhead. This road is passable for ordinary vehicles except after a major storm. GPS: N33 24.56' / W111 12.37'

The Hike

Begin by hiking north on the JF Trail, then turn right at 0.5 mile on the Woodbury Trail, an old mining road. (The JF Trail is the return route.) Follow the Woodbury Trail 1.2 miles as it climbs steeply east to meet FR 172A, the Rogers Trough Road. Follow the road to Rogers Trough Trailhead at 3.7 miles.

The hike then takes you down Rogers Canyon on the Reavis Ranch Trail. Stay left at 5 miles, where the Reavis Ranch Trail veers right up Grave Canyon, and follow the Rogers Canyon Trail northwest, down Rogers Canyon. This section of the canyon is very rugged and scenic—watch for a huge boulder jammed in a crack high up on the southwest wall. There is usually water in a few pools along the creekbed. As the canyon swings a bit west, watch for a cliff dwelling in a cave on the north wall. This well-preserved ruin is a popular destination, but please don't climb on the walls or otherwise disturb the fragile remains. There is seasonal water in the creekbed below the ruin. There are plenty of campsites just downstream at Angel Basin.

Rogers Canyon near Angel Basin

From Angel Basin, follow the Rogers Canyon Trail as it leaves Rogers Canyon at 7.4 miles (the Frog Tanks Trail continues down the canyon). The route heads west, and then south, up a tributary canyon. A steady climb leads to Tortilla Pass at 9 miles, and the junction with the JF Trail. Turn left here and start a steep descent down a tributary of Randolph Canyon. At the bottom of this long descent (at 11.4 miles), cross the Woodbury Trail. From this junction, continue south to the trailhead.

Option: If you have two vehicles, you can leave one at Woodbury Trailhead and start the hike from Rogers Trough Trailhead. From Woodbury Trailhead, drive 1.5 miles, then turn left on FR 172A. After 3.6 miles, turn left at the junction with FR 650, and continue 0.4 mile to the Rogers Trough Trailhead. The last section of FR 172A is rough and may require a high-clearance vehicle. GPS: N33 25.35' / W111 10.41' This avoids the 2.9-mile climb on Woodbury Trail and Rogers Trough Road at the start of the hike.

Miles and Directions

0.0 From the Woodbury Trailhead, start on JF Trail.

0.3 Turn right onto Woodbury Trail.

1.8 Turn left onto FR 172A.

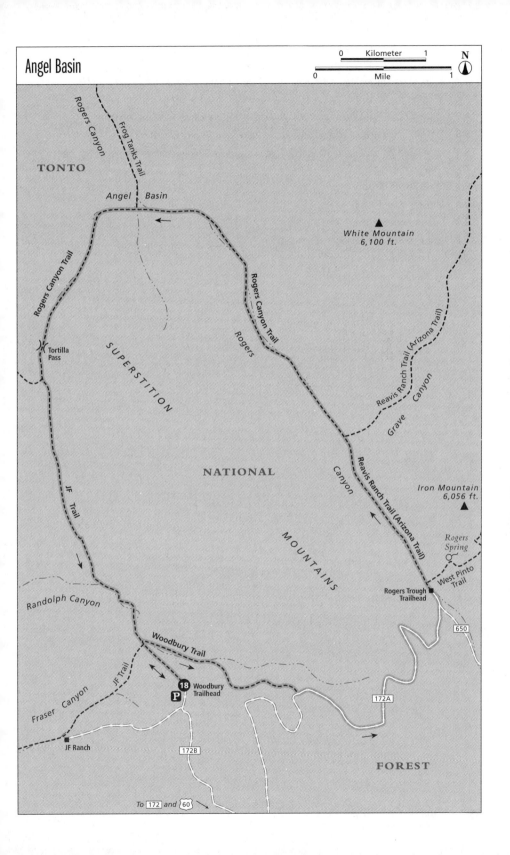

Angel Basin

0 Kilometer 1
0 Mile 1

N

TONTO

Rogers Canyon

Frog Tanks Trail

Angel Basin

White Mountain
6,100 ft.

Rogers Canyon Trail

S U P E R S T I T I O N

Rogers Canyon Trail

Rogers

Reavis Ranch Trail (Arizona Trail)

Grave Canyon

Tortilla Pass

Canyon

NATIONAL

Reavis Ranch Trail (Arizona Trail)

Iron Mountain
6,056 ft.

JF Trail

M O U N T A I N S

Rogers Spring

West Pinto Trail

Rogers Trough Trailhead

Randolph Canyon

650

Woodbury Trail

JF Trail

172A

18 Woodbury Trailhead
P

Fraser Canyon

JF Ranch

172B

FOREST

To 172 and 60

4.4 At the junction with FR 650, stay left on FR 172A.

4.6 Arrive at the Rogers Trough Trailhead. Leave the trailhead on Reavis Ranch Trail (Arizona Trail).

4.7 At the junction with West Pinto Trail, stay left on Reavis Ranch Trail (Arizona Trail).

5.9 Turn left onto Rogers Canyon Trail and continue down Rogers Canyon.

8.4 Arrive at Angel Basin and the junction with Frog Tanks Trail; turn left to remain on Rogers Canyon Trail.

9.8 Cross Tortilla Pass.

10.1 Turn left onto JF Trail.

12.4 Cross Woodbury Trail.

12.7 Arrive back at the Woodbury Trailhead.

19 Randolph Canyon

This trail and cross-country hike takes you through scenic Randolph and Fraser Canyons in the south-central Superstitions. Seasonal pools and a waterfall are among the attractions of this area.

Start: Woodbury Trailhead
Distance: 9-mile lollipop
Hiking time: About 6 hours
Difficulty: Moderate due to length and cross-country hiking
Best seasons: Oct–Apr
Trail surface: Dirt trails, gravel and rocks along dry washes
Land status: Tonto National Forest, Superstition Wilderness
Nearest town: Apache Junction
Other users: Horses

Water availability: Randolph Canyon, Dripping Spring
Canine compatibility: Leashed dogs permitted
Fees and permits: None
Schedule: Year-round, 24 hours per day
Maps: USGS Weavers Needle AZ and Iron Mountain AZ; USFS Superstition Wilderness map, Tonto National Forest map
Trail contact: Mesa Ranger District, Tonto National Forest, 5140 E. Ingram St., Mesa, AZ 85205; (480) 610-3300; www.fs.usda.gov/tonto

Finding the trailhead: From Apache Junction, go about 18 miles east on US 60, then turn left on the Queen Creek Road. Follow this paved road for 1.9 miles, then turn right on FR 357, a maintained dirt road. Continue 3.1 miles on FR 357 to the junction with FR 172, then turn left. Go 12.5 miles on FR 172, a maintained dirt road, then go left on FR 172B. Continue for 1.5 miles on FR 172B to a locked gate, then turn right and go 0.1 mile to the Woodbury Trailhead. This road is passable to ordinary vehicles except after a major storm. GPS: N33 24.56' / W111 12.37'

The Hike

Hike north on the JF Trail, past the junction with the Woodbury Trail at 0.5 mile, which is the return. The JF Trail follows Randolph Canyon downstream to the northwest, then leaves the canyon to climb north. Turn left at this point, and follow Randolph Canyon downstream to the west.

The going is easy down the wash, and at first the canyon is broad and open. It narrows somewhat as it swings to the southwest. You should find seasonal water in the bed, near where the Superstition Wilderness map shows Randolph Spring.

Downstream, Red Tanks Trail drops over a low ridge into Randolph Canyon. Turn left and follow Red Tanks Trail downstream. Just below this junction, Red Tanks Canyon comes in from the right, and a short hike up this canyon features a seasonal waterfall.

Continue on Red Tanks Trail to Fraser Canyon, which joins from the left. At this junction, Dripping Spring normally has water. Turn left onto Coffee Flat Trail and follow it up Fraser Canyon. You'll pass through a narrow section, then the canyon opens up.

Backpackers in Randolph Canyon

After passing JF Ranch, a historic ranch that is still active, you meet JF Trail, completing the loop. At the junction with Woodbury Trail, turn right on JF Trail to return to the Woodbury Trailhead.

Along Randolph and Fraser Canyons, you'll see tamarisk, a tall, slender shrub with leaves that resemble the common juniper's. Also known as salt cedar, tamarisk is a native of the Middle Eastern deserts but was imported into California as an ornamental plant and to control erosion. It soon got out of control and has since spread

Randolph Canyon

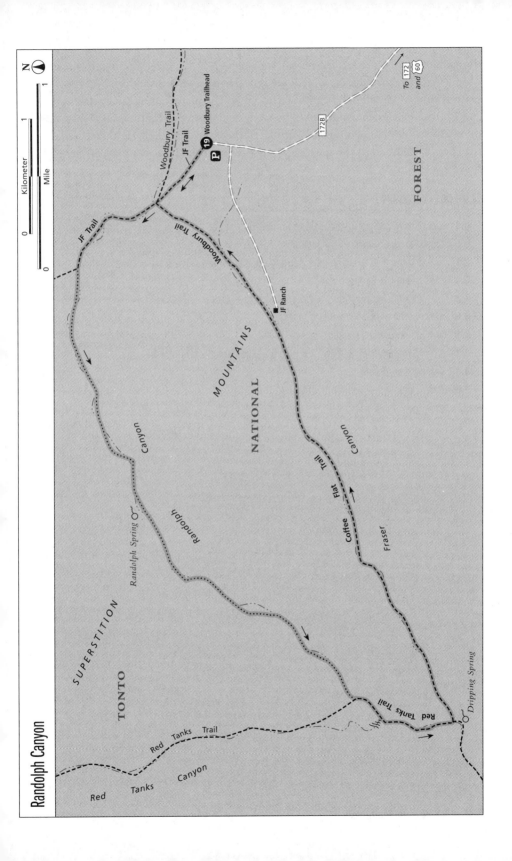

throughout the Colorado River basin, of which both the Superstition and Mazatzal Mountains are a part. Tamarisk seeds are spread by the wind, and it can take root any place with enough underground water to support it, including normally dry washes and isolated springs. It competes aggressively with native streamside vegetation and often grows so thickly it's difficult to hike through. In the fall, the feathery branches turn bright gold, and in the spring and early summer the plant is a mass of tiny pink flowers.

Miles and Directions

0.0 From the Woodbury Trailhead, start on JF Trail.

0.5 Cross Woodbury Trail.

1.1 Turn left and hike cross-country down Randolph Canyon.

2.6 Pass Randolph Spring.

4.3 Turn left on Red Tanks Trail.

4.6 Arrive at the mouth of Red Tanks Canyon.

5.1 Turn left on Coffee Flat Trail.

7.7 Pass JF Ranch; the trail becomes Woodbury Trail. Continue northeast.

8.6 Turn right on JF Trail.

9.0 Arrive back at the Woodbury Trailhead.

20 Coffee Flat Mountain Loop

This very scenic loop begins from an easily accessible trailhead and passes through classic Sonoran desert wilderness as it loops around Coffee Flat Mountain.

Start: Peralta Trailhead
Distance: 18.5-mile lollipop
Hiking time: About 11 hours or 2 days
Difficulty: Strenuous due to distance, elevation change, and faint trails
Best seasons: Oct–Apr
Trail surface: Dirt
Land status: Tonto National Forest, Superstition Wilderness
Nearest town: Apache Junction
Other users: Horses
Water availability: Seasonal at Dripping Spring, lower Red Tanks Canyon, Upper La Barge Box, Whiskey Spring
Canine compatibility: Leashed dogs permitted
Fees and permits: None
Schedule: Year-round, 24 hours per day
Maps: USGS Weavers Needle AZ; USFS Superstition Wilderness map; Tonto National Forest map
Trail contact: Mesa Ranger District, Tonto National Forest, 5140 E. Ingram St., Mesa, AZ 85205; (480) 610-3300; www.fs.usda.gov/tonto

Finding the trailhead: From Apache Junction, drive about 8.5 miles east on US 60, then turn left onto Peralta Road (FR 77), which is maintained dirt. Continue 8 miles to the end of the road at Peralta Trailhead. GPS: N33 23.83' / W111 20.89'

The Hike

Start on the Dutchmans Trail, and stay right at the junction with Bluff Spring Trail. Continue on Dutchmans Trail, hiking east over a low pass. The broad, well-traveled trail continues east along the saguaro cactus–studded foothills at the north edge of Barkley Basin and heads for the base of Miners Needle, a collection of stone towers visible ahead.

Just before the trail starts to switchback up the canyon southeast of Miners Needle, turn right on Coffee Flat Trail (Dutchmans Trail is the return route). This trail heads southeast, then climbs over a low pass into Coffee Flat. It follows the Whitlow Canyon drainage for a short distance downstream to the south, then veers east and climbs across low hills and drops into a tributary of Randolph Canyon at Reeds Water, the site of an old windmill (not a reliable water source). The trail continues south for a short distance, then turns east up Randolph Canyon. When Fraser Canyon enters from the north, turn left on Red Tanks Trail and follow it up Fraser Canyon. There is usually water at Dripping Spring at this junction, and there are a few small campsites.

Watch for Red Tanks Canyon, which enters Fraser Canyon on the left. There is seasonal water and a small waterfall here. Follow Red Tanks Trail a short distance past Red Tanks Canyon, where it veers left, climbs out of Fraser Canyon, crosses a low ridge, then drops into Red Tanks Canyon itself. The trail then heads north up the canyon and climbs west over Red Tanks Divide. (The trail is shown incorrectly

"Fickle of Finger of Fate," pinnacles near the Dutchmans and Coffee Flat Trail junction in Barkley Basin

on the USGS Weavers Needle topo. It crosses the divide about 0.2 mile north of the location shown on the topo. GPS: N33 25.73' / W111 16.23') This section of the trail is faint in places. At the pass you have great views of imposing Coffee Flat Mountain to the southwest.

The trail continues northwest and north, down the slopes into La Barge Canyon. Pass the junction with the Hoolie Bacon Trail, and then turn more to the west as the

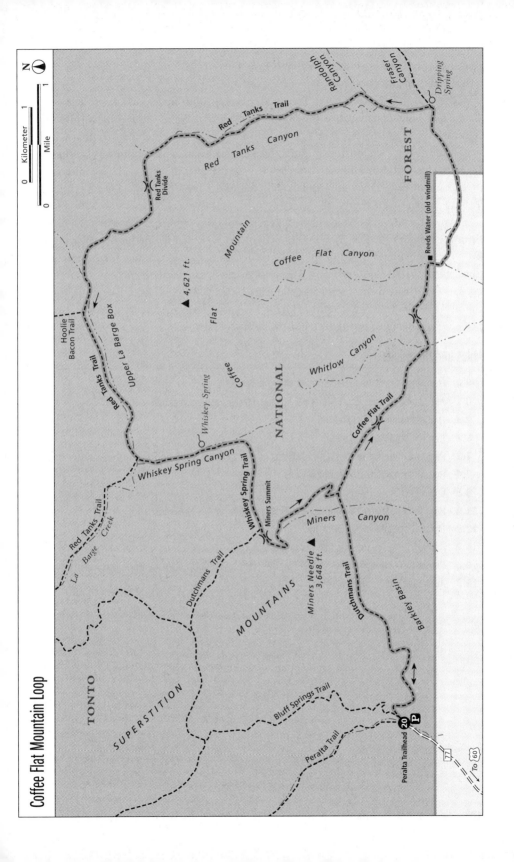

Coffee Flat Mountain Loop

TONTO

SUPERSTITION

MOUNTAINS

NATIONAL

FOREST

N

0   Kilometer   1

0   Mile   1

Red Tanks Trail

Red   Tanks   Canyon

Randolph Canyon

Fraser Canyon

Dripping Spring

Red Tanks Divide

Mountain

Coffee   Flat   Canyon

Reeds Water (old windmill)

Flat

4,621 ft.

Whitlow   Canyon

Hoolie Bacon Trail

Upper La Barge Box

Red Tanks Trail

Coffee

Whiskey Spring

Whiskey Spring Canyon

Whiskey Spring Trail

Coffee Flat Trail

La Barge Creek

Red Tanks Trail

Dutchmans Trail

Miners Summit

Miners   Canyon

Miners Needle
3,648 ft.

Dutchmans Trail

Barkley Basin

Bluff Springs Trail

Peralta Trail

Peralta Trailhead

20

P

77

To 60

Red Tanks Trail enters Upper La Barge Box. There is seasonal water where the trail crosses the bed and good campsites downstream.

Turn left on Whiskey Spring Trail, which heads south up a tributary of La Barge Canyon. Whiskey Spring is in the bed below the trail. After passing the spring, the trail turns west and climbs over a pass, then drops to meet Dutchmans Trail at Miners Summit. Turn left on this popular, heavily used trail, and continue past Miners Needle. The trail drops down a couple of switchbacks southeast of the needle, then meets Coffee Flat Trail at 15.1 miles, completing the loop. Stay right on Dutchmans Trail to return to the trailhead.

Two of the common volcanic rock types found throughout the western Superstitions are tuff and rhyolite. Tuff is a soft, yellowish rock that formed from ash spewed from ancient volcanoes. Rhyolite is a somewhat harder, gray rock that forms from ash flows. Both rhyolite and tuff cooled from the molten state very quickly, so the mineral crystals that formed the rock had little time to grow. In contrast, the granitic rocks found in the eastern Superstitions formed deep underground, where cooling took place very slowing, allowing time for the crystals to grow.

Miles and Directions

0.0 From the Peralta Trailhead, start on the Dutchmans Trail.

0.1 At the junction with Bluff Springs Trail, stay right on Dutchmans Trail.

2.5 Turn right onto Coffee Flat Trail.

6.7 Turn left onto Red Tanks Trail.

7.2 Pass the entrance to Red Tanks Canyon.

7.4 Red Tanks Trail leaves Randolph Canyon.

9.8 Cross Red Tanks Divide.

11.4 Pass the junction with Hoolie Bacon Trail; stay left on Red Tanks Trail.

12.9 Turn left onto Whiskey Spring Trail.

14.2 Turn left onto Dutchmans Trail at Miners Summit.

16.0 Return to the junction with Coffee Flat Trail, closing the loop. Stay right on Dutchmans Trail.

18.5 Arrive back at Peralta Trailhead.

21 Bluff Spring Loop

This enjoyable and scenic hike on good trails leads through varied country in the southwest Superstitions.

Start: Peralta Trailhead
Distance: 8.5-mile loop
Hiking time: About 5 hours
Difficulty: Easy
Best seasons: Oct–Apr
Trail surface: Dirt
Land status: Tonto National Forest, Superstition Wilderness
Nearest town: Apache Junction
Other users: Horses
Water availability: Seasonal at Crystal Spring and Bluff Spring

Canine compatibility: Leashed dogs permitted
Fees and permits: None
Schedule: Year-round, 24 hours per day
Maps: USGS Weavers Needle AZ; USFS Superstition Wilderness map; Tonto National Forest map
Trail contact: Mesa Ranger District, Tonto National Forest, 5140 E. Ingram St., Mesa, AZ 85205; (480) 610-3300; www.fs.usda.gov/tonto

Finding the trailhead: From Apache Junction, drive about 8.5 miles east on US 60, then turn left onto Peralta Road (FR 77), which is maintained dirt. Continue 8 miles to the end of the road at Peralta Trailhead. GPS: N33 23.83' / W111 20.89'

The Hike

Start off by hiking Dutchmans Trail northeast, passing Bluff Springs Trail on the left (Bluff Springs is the return route). Dutchmans Trail climbs over a low ridge and then continues east along the foothills, passing the base of turreted Miners Needle. Stay left at the junction with Coffee Flat Trail; the trail turns northwest. Switchback up to Miners Summit and meets Whiskey Spring Trail. Stay left on Dutchmans Trail as it descends a broad drainage toward the imposing cliffs of Bluff Spring Mountain.

At the base of the mountain, turn left onto Bluff Springs Trail at 3.8 miles. Crystal Spring is located at this trail junction. Bluff Springs Trail heads west and climbs gradually up Bluff Spring Canyon to a pass, then turns south and descends a tributary of Barks Canyon. Stay left at the Terrapin Trail junction and remain on the Bluff Springs Trail, continuing across Barks Canyon. This is an especially scenic area of cliffs and pinnacles, and the canyon often has flowing water during the cool season. The trail climbs south out of the canyon, swings around a ridge, then descends into Peralta Canyon. Turn right on Dutchmans Trail to return to Peralta Trailhead.

You can see several old mines and prospect holes along the cliffs of Bluff Spring Mountain. Because of the stories of a lost gold mine, the Superstition Mountains have long been the target of prospectors. Up until about 1970, the Bluff Spring Mountain and Weavers Needle areas were fiercely contested by competing prospectors, in spite

Weavers Needle from the Bluff Springs Trail

of the fact that most of the Superstition Mountains are composed of relatively young volcanic rocks that are not known for gold-bearing deposits. The forest service finally put an end to the destructive prospecting by withdrawing the area from mineral location.

Miles and Directions

0.0   From the Peralta Trailhead, start on Dutchmans Trail.

0.1   Pass the junction with Bluff Springs Trail; stay right on Dutchmans Trail.

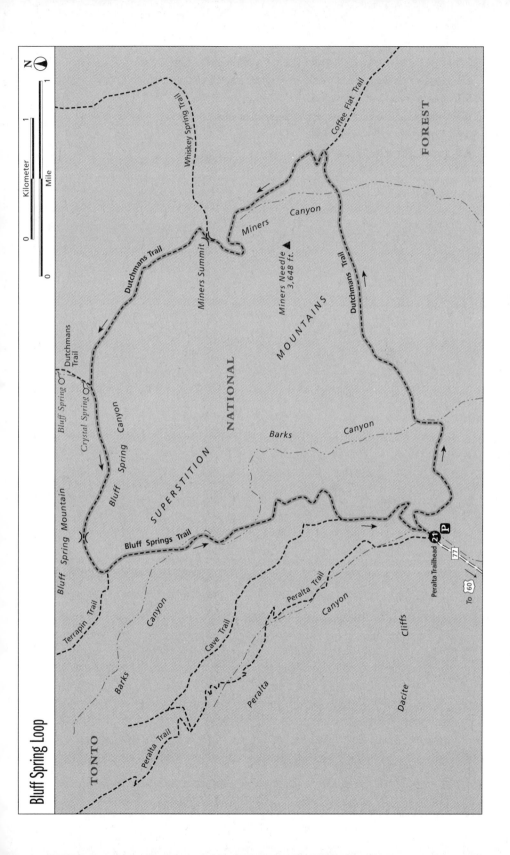

Bluff Spring Loop

TONTO

FOREST

SUPERSTITION

MOUNTAINS

NATIONAL

Whiskey Spring Trail

Coffee Flat Trail

Dutchmans Trail

Miners Summit

Miners · Canyon

Miners Needle
3,648 ft.

Dutchmans Trail

Bluff Spring ○
Crystal Spring ○

Dutchmans Trail

Bluff Spring Canyon

Barks · Canyon

Bluff Spring Mountain

Bluff Springs Trail

Terrapin Trail

Barks · Canyon

Cave Trail

Peralta Trail

Peralta · Canyon

Dacite · Cliffs

Peralta Trail

Peralta Trailhead
21
P
77
To 60

N

0   Kilometer   1
0   Mile   1

2.5 Pass the intersection with Coffee Flat Trail; stay left on Dutchmans Trail.

3.9 Pass Miners Summit and Whiskey Spring Trail; stay left on Dutchmans Trail.

5.1 Turn left onto Bluff Springs Trail.

6.2 Pass the junction with Terrapin Trail; keep left on Bluff Springs Trail.

8.4 Turn right onto Dutchmans Trail.

8.5 Arrive back at the Peralta Trailhead.

22 Dutchmans Loop

This popular loop through the western Superstitions covers a lot of interesting country, and it follows well-graded, easy trails throughout. The hike is a good overnight trip for newcomers to backpacking. It also makes a long day hike.

Start: Peralta Trailhead
Distance: 17.9-mile loop
Hiking time: About 10 hours or 2 days
Difficulty: Moderate if done as an overnight backpacking trip; strenuous as a day hike due to length and elevation change
Best seasons: Oct–Apr
Trail surface: Dirt
Land status: Tonto National Forest, Superstition Wilderness
Nearest town: Apache Junction
Other users: Horses

Water availability: Seasonal at Crystal Spring, Bluff Spring, La Barge Spring, Charlebois Spring, White Rock Spring
Canine compatibility: Leashed dogs permitted
Fees and permits: None
Schedule: Year-round, 24 hours per day
Maps: USGS Weavers Needle AZ; USFS Superstition Wilderness map; Tonto National Forest map
Trail contact: Mesa Ranger District, Tonto National Forest, 5140 E. Ingram St., Mesa, AZ 85205; (480) 610-3300; www.fs.usda.gov/tonto

Finding the trailhead: From Apache Junction, drive about 8.5 miles east on US 60, then turn left onto Peralta Road (FR 77) at a traffic light. After passing through a subdivision, the road becomes maintained dirt. Continue 8 miles to the end of the road at Peralta Trailhead. GPS: N33 23.83' / W111 20.89'

The Hike

Hike east on Dutchmans Trail from the trailhead. Pass Bluff Springs Trail; stay right on Dutchmans Trail and follow it over a low ridge. The trail passes along the north side of a broad desert plain, then passes Coffee Flat Trail. Stay left at the junction and follow Dutchmans Trail up Miners Canyon to Miners Summit via a couple of switchbacks.

Stay left on Dutchmans Trail at the Whiskey Spring Trail junction. Dutchmans Trail then descends northwest to Crystal Spring at the base of Bluff Spring Mountain, and the junction with Bluff Springs Trail. Turn right on Dutchmans Trail and follow it down into Bluff Spring Canyon. At the mouth of Bluff Spring Canyon, Red Tanks Trail comes in from the right. La Barge Spring is on the east side of La Barge Creek about 0.1 mile up Red Tanks Trail.

Stay left on Dutchmans Trail and follow it down La Barge Creek to the northwest. An unsigned spur trail leads right to Music Spring. At the junction with Peters Trail, stay left on Dutchmans Trail. (Charlebois Spring is 0.1 mile up Peters Trail.) Dutchmans Trail continues down La Barge Canyon to Marsh Valley and White Rock Spring. Stay left on Dutchmans Trail at the junction with Cavalry Trail.

The imposing cliffs of Bluff Spring Mountain above the Dutchmans Trail

Dutchmans Trail continues south and west to a low saddle and Bull Pass Trail. Stay left on Dutchmans Trail and follow it west into Needle Canyon. After following Needle Canyon for a while, turn right at the junction with Terrapin Trail and follow Dutchmans Trail up an unnamed drainage south of Black Top Mesa. The trail reaches Black Top Mesa Pass, then descends west into East Boulder Canyon to meet the Peralta Trail. This scenic basin is dominated by towering Weavers Needle to the south. You can sometimes find water in the bed of the wash.

Turn left onto Peralta Trail, which climbs west on well-graded switchbacks to the ridge south of Palomino Mountain, then heads south on the slopes above a tributary of Little Boulder Canyon. A few switchbacks take the trail over a saddle next to a rock outcrop, then the trail descends back into East Boulder Canyon, below triple-summited Weavers Needle. The route then works its way up the scenic head of East Boulder Canyon, past Pinyon Camp, which is marked by a few of its namesake pinyon pines. Water can sometimes be found in the creekbed, and there are numerous campsites. Follow Peralta Trail as it climbs to Fremont Saddle in a couple of switchbacks, then descends scenic Peralta Canyon to the Peralta Trailhead.

Yucca plants grow throughout the western Superstition Mountains. There are several varieties, but they all feature a base of slender, stiff, sharp-tipped leaves that

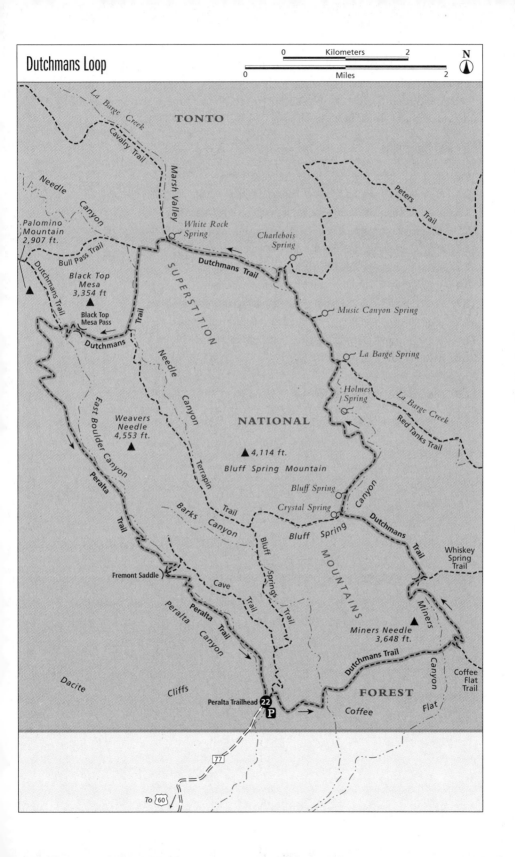

Dutchmans Loop

Kilometers
0   2

Miles
0   2

N

La Barge Creek

TONTO

Cavalry Trail

Marsh Valley

Needle Canyon

Peters Trail

Palomino
Mountain
2,907 ft.

White Rock
Spring

Charlebois
Spring

Bull Pass Trail

Dutchmans Trail

Black Top
Mesa
3,354 ft

Dutchmans Trail

SUPERSTITION

Music Canyon Spring

Black Top
Mesa Pass

Dutchmans

Needle Trail

La Barge Spring

Needle Canyon

Holmes
Spring

La Barge Creek

East Boulder Canyon

Weavers
Needle
4,553 ft.

NATIONAL

Red Tanks Trail

▲ 4,114 ft.

Bluff Spring Mountain

Peralta

Terrapin Trail

Barks Canyon

Crystal Spring

Bluff Spring

Canyon

Trail

Bluff Spring

Dutchmans Trail

Fremont Saddle

Cave Trail

Bluff Springs Trail

Whiskey
Spring
Trail

MOUNTAINS

Peralta Trail

Miners Needle
3,648 ft.

▲ Miners

Peralta Canyon

Dacite

Cliffs

Peralta Trailhead **22**
P

Dutchmans Trail

Canyon

Coffee
Flat
Trail

FOREST

Coffee   Flat

77

To **60**

point out in all directions and a tall central stalk that appears when the plant flowers. Each species of yucca has its own interdependent moth, which pollinates that species of yucca and no other. Yuccas were important to Native Americans, who ate the fruits and made baskets from the tough fibers.

Miles and Directions

0.0 From the Peralta Trailhead, start on Dutchmans Trail.

0.1 At the junction with Bluff Springs Trail, stay right on Dutchmans Trail.

2.5 At the junction with Coffee Flat Trail, stay left on Dutchmans Trail.

3.9 Pass Miners Summit and the Whiskey Spring Trail; stay left on Dutchmans Trail.

5.1 At the Bluff Springs Trail junction, turn right on Dutchmans Trail.

7.2 At the junction with Red Tanks Trail, stay left on Dutchmans Trail.

8.4 At the Peters Trail junction, stay left on Dutchmans Trail.

9.8 Reach Marsh Valley and Cavalry Trail; stay left on Dutchmans Trail.

10.2 At the junction with Bull Pass Trail, turn left on Dutchmans Trail.

11.0 At the Terrapin Trail junction, stay right on Dutchmans Trail.

11.9 Turn left onto Peralta Trail.

15.7 Cross Fremont Saddle.

17.9 Arrive back at the Peralta Trailhead.

23 Barks Canyon

This hike takes you up Peralta Canyon to the classic view of Weavers Needle from Fremont Saddle and returns via a cross-country descent into scenic Barks Canyon.

Start: Peralta Trailhead
Distance: 5.5-mile loop
Hiking time: About 4 hours
Difficulty: Moderate due to cross-country travel and elevation change
Best seasons: Oct–Apr
Trail surface: Dirt trails, cross-country terrain
Land status: Tonto National Forest, Superstition Wilderness
Nearest town: Apache Junction
Other users: Horses on Bluff Springs Trail

Water availability: Seasonal in Barks Canyon
Canine compatibility: Leashed dogs permitted
Fees and permits: None
Schedule: Year-round, 24 hours per day
Maps: USGS Weavers Needle AZ; USFS Superstition Wilderness map; Tonto National Forest map
Trail contact: Mesa Ranger District, Tonto National Forest, 5140 E. Ingram St., Mesa, AZ 85205; (480) 610-3300; www.fs.usda.gov/tonto

Finding the trailhead: From Apache Junction, drive about 8.5 miles east on US 60, then turn left onto Peralta Road (FR 77) at a traffic light. After passing through a subdivision, the road becomes maintained dirt. Continue 8 miles to the end of the road at Peralta Trailhead. GPS: N33 23.83' / W111 20.89'

The Hike

Start the loop on the well-graded but rocky Peralta Trail, which heads northwest up Peralta Canyon, climbing steadily. The trail generally stays near the bed of the canyon, occasionally crossing it. Numerous stone pinnacles, known locally as "stone ghosts," are scattered along the canyon and its rims. The pinnacles are mostly carved from rhyolite, a volcanic rock. As the mountains eroded, erosion followed cracks in the rock and carved out odd-looking fins and pinnacles. The trail steepens somewhat near the head of the canyon, and a few short switchbacks lead to Fremont Saddle at the head of Peralta Canyon. Fremont Saddle is one of many places throughout the American West named for John C. Fremont, the noted American explorer who led several government-sponsored survey trips.

The Peralta Trail continues north from the saddle, but this loop heads cross-country onto the broken plateau northeast of the saddle. You'll need the topographic map and skill in cross-country route finding to follow this route. Follow the unmarked Cave Trail east, and then northeast, onto the mesa. Turn left on the unmarked Weavers Needle Overlook Trail at a junction on the mesa. Follow the trail north toward Weavers Needle and descend off the rim of the mesa into a saddle. Leave the trail from the saddle and descend directly east. Work your way through the pinnacles and rock slabs onto a drainage heading northeast toward Barks Canyon. Follow Barks Canyon

Weavers Needle from upper Barks Canyon

downstream a short distance about 0.4 mile, then leave the bed and climb northeast over a low saddle to Terrapin Trail.

Because the Barks Canyon terrain is confused with numerous "stone ghost" pinnacles, rock formations, and drainages, just remember to head generally east-northeast after leaving the Weavers Needle Overlook Trail to intercept either Terrapin or Bluff Springs Trail. In either case, turn right.

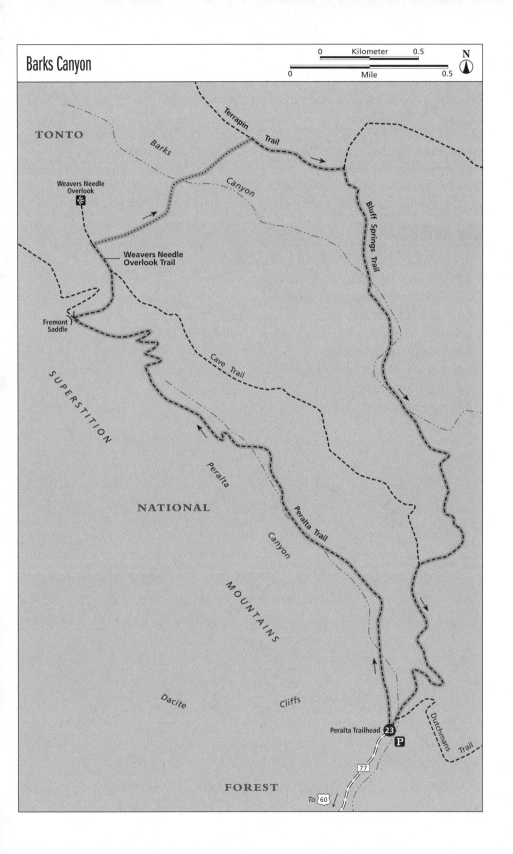

Barks Canyon

0 — Kilometer — 0.5
0 — Mile — 0.5

N

TONTO

Barks

Terrapin Trail

Canyon

Bluff Springs Trail

Weavers Needle
Overlook

Weavers Needle
Overlook Trail

Fremont
Saddle

Cave Trail

SUPERSTITION

Peralta

NATIONAL

Canyon

Peralta Trail

MOUNTAINS

Dacite   Cliffs

Peralta Trailhead **23**

P

Dutchmans

Trail

77

FOREST

To 60

This loop uses Terrapin Trail. Turn right on Terrapin and follow it down to a tributary of Barks Canyon, east of the main canyon. Turn right on Bluff Springs Trail and follow it as it descends along Barks Canyon and then climbs over a ridge to return to Peralta Trailhead.

Option: At the junction with Weavers Needle Overlook Trail, continue 0.2 mile north on this informal trail to Weavers Needle Overlook for a spectacular view of Weavers Needle. This option adds 0.4 mile to the trip. A large pinyon pine marks this spot. The area at the head of East Boulder Canyon, below you to the west, is home to a few scattered pinyon pines at the extreme lower elevation of their range.

Miles and Directions

0.0 From the Peralta Trailhead, start on the Peralta Trail.

2.0 Reach Fremont Saddle; turn right on the unmarked Cave Trail.

2.2 Turn left on Weavers Needle Overlook Trail.

2.3 Leave the trail from the saddle and descend east into Barks Canyon.

2.6 Arrive in Barks Canyon; leave the canyon and climb northeast over a low saddle.

3.0 Turn right onto Terrapin Trail.

3.3 Turn right onto Bluff Springs Trail.

5.4 Turn left onto Dutchmans Trail.

5.5 Arrive back at Peralta Trailhead.

24 Cave Trail

The Cave Trail was established by the Dons Club, which used to have an outing in the Peralta Canyon area each year that included a rugged hike in the area. The trail is no longer officially maintained or marked, but you can still follow the route, which descends the ridge east of Peralta Canyon and features views of much of the western Superstition Mountains.

Start: Peralta Trailhead
Distance: 4.7-mile loop
Hiking time: About 4 hours
Difficulty: Moderate due to cross-country hiking and elevation change
Best seasons: Oct–Apr
Trail surface: Dirt trails, cross-country terrain
Land status: Tonto National Forest, Superstition Wilderness
Nearest town: Apache Junction
Other users: None

Water availability: None
Canine compatibility: Leashed dogs permitted
Fees and permits: None
Schedule: Year-round, 24 hours per day
Maps: USGS Weavers Needle AZ; USFS Superstition Wilderness map; Tonto National Forest map
Trail contact: Mesa Ranger District, Tonto National Forest, 5140 E. Ingram St., Mesa, AZ 85205; (480) 610-3300; www.fs.usda.gov/tonto

Finding the trailhead: From Apache Junction, drive about 8.5 miles east on US 60, then turn left onto Peralta Road (FR 77) at a traffic light. After passing through a subdivision, the road becomes maintained dirt. Continue 8 miles to the end of the road at Peralta Trailhead. GPS: N33 23.83' / W111 20.89'

The Hike

Start the loop on the well-graded but rocky Peralta Trail, which heads northwest up Peralta Canyon, climbing steadily. The trail generally stays near the bed of the canyon, occasionally crossing it. The trail steepens somewhat near the head of the canyon, and a few short switchbacks lead to Fremont Saddle at the head of Peralta Canyon.

From the saddle, turn right on the unmarked Cave Trail, which heads northeast onto a small mesa. As the mesa becomes broader, turn right at the unmarked junction with Weavers Needle Overlook Trail, remaining on Cave Trail. Although not maintained, Cave Trail generally works its way southeast along the crest of the ridge northeast of Peralta Canyon. The only place the trail leaves the crest is at Geronimo Cave.

Follow Cave Trail southeast to the edge of the mesa and descend to a saddle. At this point, the route is blocked by cliffs of yellow volcanic tuff. Bear right and follow the trail on wide ledges around the west side of the yellow cliffs to Geronimo Cave.

Although Geronimo, a war chief of the Chiricahua Apache and the last Native American to surrender to the US Army, never came anywhere near the Superstition Mountains, this shallow cave in the tuff cliffs somehow acquired his name. The spot

Looking into Barks Canyon from the Cave Trail

is spectacular, looking down on Peralta Canyon and far out across the deserts to the south.

Follow Cave Trail around the base of the yellow tuff cliff to the top of a series of yellow tuff slabs. Hike northeast about 100 yards before descending the slabs to the southeast. If you descend too soon, the slabs are steeper and more difficult to negotiate. The correct descent puts you near the top of the main ridge, northeast of a small basin. The trail crosses bare rock in this area and is marked by rock cairns, many of which have been placed by confused hikers. Ignore the cairns and find your own way. And don't build any more cairns!

Work your way along the ridge above the small basin, aiming for the middle of the broad ridge ahead, southeast of the small basin. Cave Trail becomes distinct as it descends the slope southeast of this broad ridge. After a level section, the trail drops off the ridge to the south and meets Bluff Springs Trail at the bottom of the slope.

Turn right on Bluff Springs Trail. After descending into Peralta Canyon, turn right on Dutchmans Trail to return to Peralta Trailhead.

Option: At the junction with Weavers Needle Overlook Trail, continue 0.2 mile north on this informal trail to Weavers Needle Overlook for a spectacular view of Weavers Needle. This option adds 0.4 mile to the trip. A large pinyon pine marks this

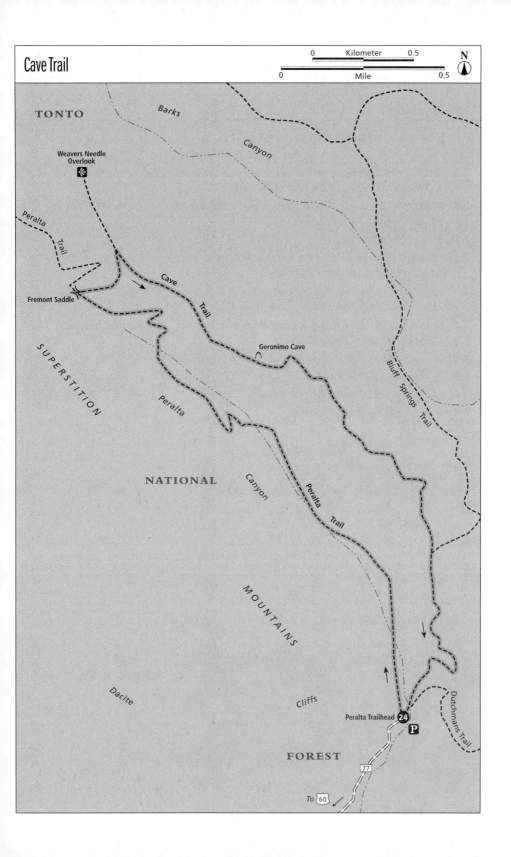

spot. The area at the head of East Boulder Canyon, below you to the west, is home to a few scattered pinyon pines at the extreme lower elevation of their range.

Miles and Directions

0.0 From Peralta Trailhead, start on the Peralta Trail.

2.0 Reach Fremont Saddle; turn right on the unmarked Cave Trail.

2.2 Reach the unmarked junction with Weavers Needle Overlook Trail. Turn right and hike southeast on Cave Trail, off the edge of the mesa.

2.5 Arrive on the first saddle. Follow Cave Trail around the right (southwest) side of the yellow tuff ridge ahead.

2.8 Arrive at Geronimo Cave.

2.9 At the end of the yellow tuff ridge, turn sharply northeast for 100 yards, then descend yellow slabs of tuff to the southeast.

3.0 Work your way along the ridge northeast of the shallow basin (GPS: N33 24.71' / W111 21.12'). This area is confused by multiple trails.

3.2 Cross the middle of the ridge southeast of the small basin and descend the slope to the southeast. The trail becomes distinct

3.5 Cross a broad ridge, then follow the trail south off the ridge.

3.8 Turn right onto Bluff Springs Trail.

4.6 Turn right onto Dutchmans Trail.

4.7 Arrive back at the Peralta Trailhead.

25 Needle Canyon

This day hike or overnight backpack takes you through the scenic and rugged country around Weavers Needle, the most famous Superstition landmark.

Start: Peralta Trailhead
Distance: 12-mile loop
Hiking time: About 8 hours or 2 days
Difficulty: Moderate due to distance and elevation change
Best seasons: Oct–Apr
Trail surface: Dirt trails
Land status: Tonto National Forest, Superstition Wilderness
Nearest town: Apache Junction
Other users: Horses on Terrapin Trail

Water availability: Seasonal in Barks Canyon, Needle Canyon, and East Boulder Canyon
Canine compatibility: Leashed dogs permitted
Fees and permits: None
Schedule: Year-round, 24 hours per day
Maps: USGS Goldfield AZ and Weavers Needle AZ; USFS Superstition Wilderness
Trail contact: Mesa Ranger District, Tonto National Forest, 5140 E. Ingram St., Mesa, AZ 85205; (480) 610-3300; www.fs.usda.gov/tonto

Finding the trailhead: From Apache Junction, drive about 8.5 miles east on US 60, then turn left onto Peralta Road (FR 77) at a traffic light. After passing through a subdivision, the road becomes maintained dirt. Continue 8 miles to the end of the road at Peralta Trailhead. GPS: N33 23.83' / W111 20.89'

The Hike

From Peralta Trailhead, start out on the Dutchmans Trail. Almost immediately, turn left onto Bluff Springs Trail and follow the well-graded trail across Barks Canyon. The trail climbs north up a tributary of Barks Canyon. Turn left onto Terrapin Trail. A gradual climb to the northwest leads over Bluff Saddle and then north into the head of Needle Canyon. The triple summits of Weavers Needle dominate the view to the northwest, and the cliffs of Bluff Spring Mountain tower above you on the west.

The Weavers Needle area is alleged to be the location of the fabulous Lost Dutchman gold mine. The "Dutchman" was actually Jacob Waltz, a German immigrant who apparently did have a gold mine somewhere, because he was seen returning to Phoenix with packsaddles full of gold ore. Unscrupulous people attempted to follow Waltz back to his mine, but he would lead them on wild goose chases through the mountains near Phoenix, and often through the Superstition Mountains. Waltz died in Phoenix in 1891, but not before whispering to a neighbor that his rich gold mine was located where the shadow of Weavers Needle fell at 4 p.m. There are a couple of major problems with this statement. First, he didn't specify a date, and over the course of a year the tip of the shadow covers dozens of square miles of extremely rugged country. And second, the Superstitions do not consist of gold-bearing rocks. The Dutchman did appear in Phoenix with rich gold ore from time to time, but his mine

Weavers Needle is the most distinctive landmark in the Superstition Mountains.

was more likely located in the Goldfield or Mazatzal Mountains. It seems likely that the Dutchman's statement was a final joke on the greedy people who had been trying to steal his mine. If so, it was wildly successful—thousands of people have scoured the Superstitions since his death and have found nothing—except, possibly, adventure.

Terrapin Trail descends gradually into the drainage of Needle Canyon, working its way generally north-northwest through complex country. It climbs a bit to reach Terrapin Pass at 3.8 miles, then descends north into Needle Canyon. Turn left on Dutchmans Trail and follow Dutchmans Trail over Black Top Mesa Pass. The trail descends to East Boulder Canyon, where there is seasonal water along the wash.

Turn left onto Peralta Trail, which climbs west on well-graded switchbacks to the ridge south of Palomino Mountain, then heads south on the slopes above a tributary of Little Boulder Canyon. A few switchbacks take the trail over a saddle next to a rock outcrop, then the trail descends back into East Boulder Canyon below triple-summited Weavers Needle. It then works its way up the scenic head of East Boulder Canyon, past Pinyon Camp, which is marked by its namesake pinyon pines. Water can sometimes be found in the creekbed. There are plenty of campsites nearby.

Follow Peralta Trail as it climbs to Fremont Saddle in a couple of switchbacks, then descends scenic Peralta Canyon to the Peralta Trailhead.

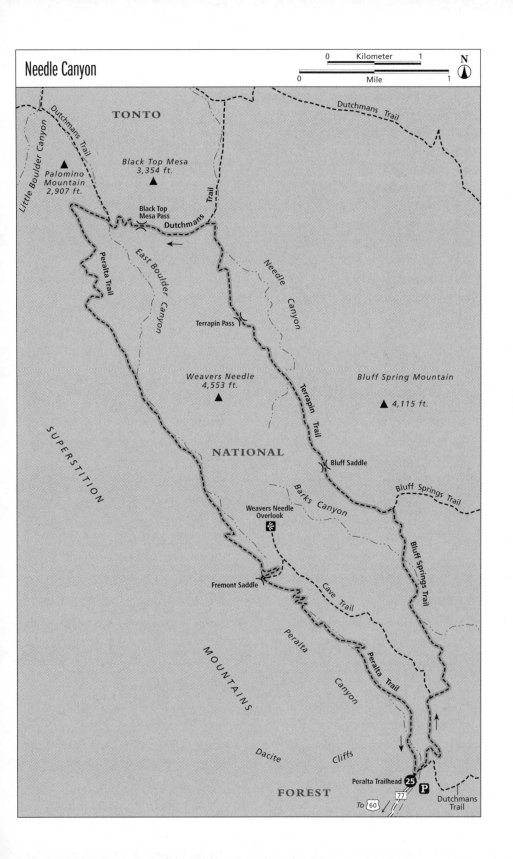

Miles and Directions

0.0 From the Peralta Trailhead, start on Dutchmans Trail.

0.1 Turn left onto Bluff Springs Trail.

2.3 Turn left onto Terrapin Trail.

2.9 Cross Bluff Saddle.

4.2 Cross Terrapin Pass.

5.1 Turn left onto Dutchmans Trail.

5.5 Cross Black Top Mesa Pass and start the descent to East Boulder Canyon.

6.0 Turn left onto Peralta Trail.

6.3 Cross the low pass south of Palomino Mountain.

7.4 Cross a saddle and start the descent into upper East Boulder Canyon.

9.9 Cross Fremont Saddle.

12.0 Arrive back at the Peralta Trailhead.

26 West Boulder Canyon

This day hike or overnight trip loops through West Boulder Canyon, a remote and little-visited portion of the western Superstition Mountains.

Start: Peralta Trailhead
Distance: 15.1-mile loop
Hiking time: About 10 hours or 2 days
Difficulty: Strenuous due to cross-country hiking, distance, and elevation change
Best seasons: Oct-Apr
Trail surface: Dirt trails, rocky washes
Land status: Tonto National Forest, Superstition Wilderness
Nearest town: Apache Junction
Other users: Horses on Gold Camp and Dutchmans Trails

Water availability: Seasonal in West Boulder Canyon, at Willow Spring, and in East Boulder Canyon
Canine compatibility: Leashed dogs permitted
Fees and permits: None
Schedule: Year-round, 24 hours per day
Maps: USGS Goldfield AZ and Weavers Needle AZ; USFS Superstition Wilderness map; Tonto National Forest map
Trail contact: Mesa Ranger District, Tonto National Forest, 5140 E. Ingram St., Mesa, AZ 85205; (480) 610-3300; www.fs.usda.gov/tonto

Finding the trailhead: From Apache Junction, drive about 8.5 miles east on US 60, then turn left onto Peralta Road (FR 77) at a traffic light. After passing through a subdivision, the road becomes maintained dirt. Continue 8 miles to the end of the road at Peralta Trailhead. GPS: N33 23.83' / W111 20.89'

The Hike

Route-finding skills and the USGS topographic maps are required for this demanding hike. All of the cross-country travel is on the first half of the loop; the return is on well-graded trails.

Start by walking down Peralta Road to Gold Camp Trailhead. Cross the parking area and hike west on Gold Camp Trail, which follows the wilderness boundary fence.

Where an old road comes in from the left, turn right, go through the wilderness boundary fence, and follow an unmarked trail northeast into a canyon. Follow this trail over a ridge and then to a saddle on the main crest above West Boulder Canyon.

From the saddle, head northwest down West Boulder Canyon. Except for occasional boulder piles and a few brushy sections, the going is not too difficult. During the cool season there will be water at several places along this long canyon, and after wet weather the entire length may be flowing. The old Goldfield USGS map shows a trail following the canyon, but little trace of this trail remains.

After Old West Boulder Canyon enters from the left, the canyon walls begin to open out. Soon you'll find yourself heading north, and then northeast, down a broad, open wash. You'll meet the well-traveled Dutchmans Trail, which crosses this wash.

A seasonal pool in upper West Boulder Canyon

Turn right on Dutchmans Trail, and follow it past the Black Mesa, Boulder Canyon, and Bull Pass trail junctions to East Boulder Canyon. Here the trail turns south and gradually ascends East Boulder Canyon past Palomino Mountain. There is seasonal water in the creek, and good campsites nearby.

Turn right onto Peralta Trail, which climbs west on well-graded switchbacks to the ridge south of Palomino Mountain, then heads south on the slopes above a tributary of Little Boulder Canyon. A few switchbacks take the trail over a saddle next to a rock outcrop, then the trail descends back into East Boulder Canyon below triple-summited Weavers Needle. The route then works its way up the scenic head of East Boulder Canyon, past Pinyon Camp, which is marked by its namesake pinyon pines. Water can sometimes be found in the creekbed. There are numerous campsites nearby.

Follow Peralta Trail as it climbs to Fremont Saddle via a couple of switchbacks, then descends scenic Peralta Canyon to the Peralta Trailhead.

Miles and Directions

0.0 From the Peralta Trailhead, start by hiking down Peralta Road to the southwest.

0.4 Reach the Gold Camp Trailhead on the right; hike west on Gold Camp Trail.

1.3 Turn right on an unmarked trail.

2.5 Cross the saddle at the head of West Boulder Canyon Hike cross-country north, down into West Boulder Canyon.

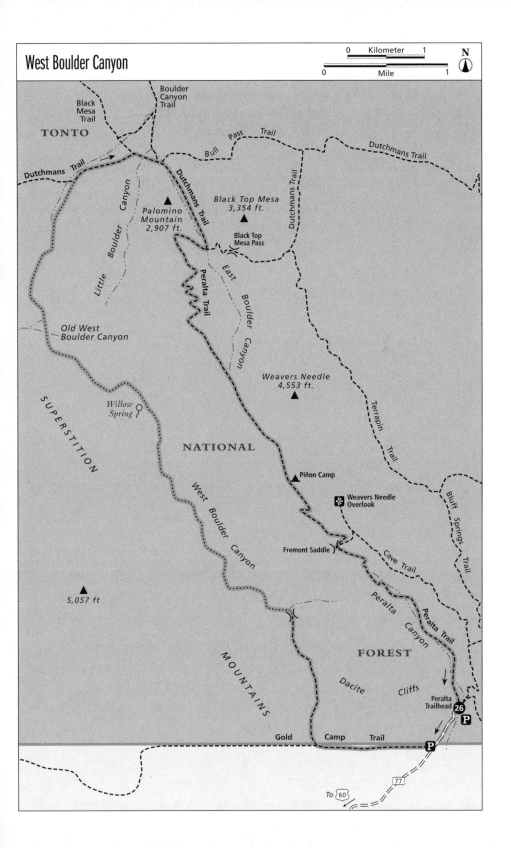

West Boulder Canyon

0   Kilometer   1

0   Mile   1

N

Black Mesa Trail

Boulder Canyon Trail

TONTO

Bull Pass Trail

Dutchmans Trail

Dutchmans Trail

Dutchmans Trail

Dutchmans Trail

Little Boulder Canyon

Palomino Mountain 2,907 ft.

Black Top Mesa 3,354 ft.

Black Top Mesa Pass

Dutchmans Trail

Peralta Trail

East Boulder Canyon

Old West Boulder Canyon

Weavers Needle 4,553 ft.

SUPERSTITION

Willow Spring

NATIONAL

Terrapin Trail

Piñon Camp

Weavers Needle Overlook

West Boulder Canyon

Bluff Springs Trail

5,057 ft

Fremont Saddle

Cave Trail

Peralta Canyon

Peralta Trail

FOREST

M O U N T A I N S

Dacite   Cliffs

Peralta Trailhead

26

P

Gold   Camp   Trail

P

77

To 60

5.0 Pass Willow Spring (seasonal).

7.5 Turn right on Dutchmans Trail.

8.1 At the junction with Black Mesa Trail, stay right on Dutchmans Trail.

8.2 At the Boulder Canyon Trail junction, stay right on Dutchmans Trail.

8.3 At the junction with Bull Pass Trail, stay right on Dutchmans Trail.

9.1 Turn right onto Peralta Trail.

13.0 Cross Fremont Saddle.

15.1 Arrive back at the Peralta Trailhead.

27 Superstition Mountain

This demanding backpack features a traverse of the famous "Superstition Mountain" ridgeline that dominates the eastern view from Mesa and Apache Junction. The cross-country ridge hike splits the view between the 100-mile expanse of greater Phoenix to the west and countless wilderness canyons, mesas, and summits to the east.

Start: Peralta Trailhead
Distance: 19.4-mile lollipop
Hiking time: About 2 days
Difficulty: Strenuous due to cross-country hiking, distance, and elevation gain
Best seasons: Oct–Apr
Trail surface: Cross-country terrain and dirt trails
Land status: Tonto National Forest, Superstition Wilderness
Nearest town: Apache Junction
Other users: Horses on Dutchmans Trail

Water availability: Seasonal in West Boulder Canyon, at Willow Spring, and in East Boulder Canyon
Canine compatibility: Leashed dogs permitted
Fees and permits: None
Schedule: Year-round, 24 hours per day
Maps: USGS Goldfield AZ and Weavers Needle AZ; USFS Superstition Wilderness map; Tonto National Forest map
Trail contact: Mesa Ranger District, Tonto National Forest, 5140 E. Ingram St., Mesa, AZ 85205; (480) 610-3300; www.fs.usda.gov/tonto

Finding the trailhead: From Apache Junction, drive about 8.5 miles east on US 60, then turn left onto Peralta Road (FR 77) at a traffic light. After passing through a subdivision, the road becomes maintained dirt. Continue 8 miles to the end of the road at Peralta Trailhead. GPS: N33 23.83' / W111 20.89'

The Hike

You'll need route-finding skills and the USGS topos for this hike. There's no water along the crest, so you'll have to carry extra water if you plan to camp up high. All of the cross-country travel is on the first half of the loop, and the return is on well-graded trails.

Start the hike by following Peralta Trail to Fremont Saddle. Leave the trail at Fremont Saddle and hike cross-country southwest, to the crest of the ridge. Work your way west through the "stone ghost" pinnacles to the saddle at the head of West Boulder Canyon.

From the saddle, follow a faint, informal trail west, and when the terrain permits, continue west up to the main crest of Superstition Mountain, aiming for Peak 4,391. Hiking becomes much easier along the crest. Follow the main crest of Superstition Mountain generally northwest, though there are many twists and turns. On a clear day, the views from the crest are tremendous. The cities of the Salt River valley lie below to the west, and much of the western and central Superstition Mountains

The southeast end of the Superstition Crest from the head of West Boulder Canyon

stretch out to the east. You can also see Four Peaks in the Mazatzal Mountains to the northeast, and to the south, the Santa Catalina Mountains near Tucson are often visible.

The ridge climbs steadily toward Peak 5,057, the highest point of the crest and the highest summit in the western Superstitions. This summit is locally called "Superstition Peak." You can pass the rocky summit on either side, but it's easiest to climb from the west side.

Continuing northward, the crest dips down to a saddle, then climbs over Peak 4,869. Beyond this peak, long sections of the ridge are nearly level and provide very enjoyable cross-country hiking. A second saddle at the head of Old West Boulder Canyon, beyond Peak 4,613, proves to be the most difficult section of the crest. To avoid the cliffs in the saddle, you'll have to descend a few hundred feet to the northeast.

After passing Peak 4,562, just northwest of the second saddle, turn sharply east and descend the ridge that lies just north of Old West Boulder Canyon. Continue down the crest of the ridge until you can descend a gentler slope into Old West Boulder Canyon, then follow this canyon to West Boulder Canyon. There is often seasonal water here.

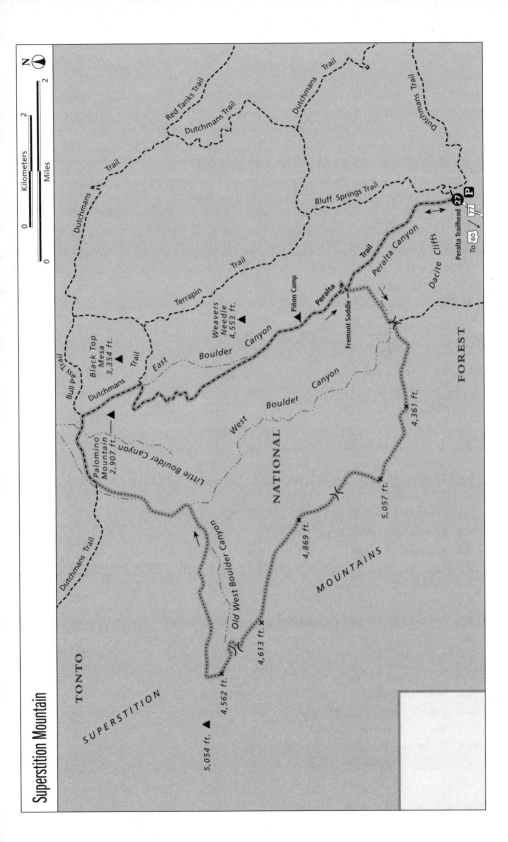

Superstition Mountain

Turn left and follow West Boulder Canyon downstream to the north. The canyon walls begin to open out, and you'll find yourself heading north, and then north-east, down a broad, open wash. You'll meet the well-traveled Dutchmans Trail, which crosses this wash. Turn right on Dutchmans Trail, and follow it past the Black Mesa, Boulder Canyon, and Bull Pass trail junctions to East Boulder Canyon. The trail turns south and gradually ascends East Boulder Canyon past Palomino Mountain. There is seasonal water in the creek, and good campsites nearby.

Turn right onto Peralta Trail, which climbs west in well-graded switchbacks to the ridge south of Palomino Mountain, then heads south on the slopes above a tributary of Little Boulder Canyon. A few switchbacks take the trail over a saddle next to a rock outcrop, then the trail descends back into East Boulder Canyon below triple-summited Weavers Needle. The route then works its way up the scenic head of East Boulder Canyon, past Pinyon Camp, which is marked by its namesake pinyon pines. Water can sometimes be found in the creekbed.

Follow Peralta Trail as it climbs to Fremont Saddle via a couple of switchbacks, closing the loop. Then descend scenic Peralta Canyon to the Peralta Trailhead.
Option: From Peak 4,562, just north of the second saddle, you can hike cross-country 0.6 mile east to Peak 5,024, the other 5,000-foot summit along the western crest. This adds 1.2 miles to the hike.

Miles and Directions

0.0 From the Peralta Trailhead, start northwest on Peralta Trail.

2.0 At Fremont Saddle, leave the trail and hike cross-country, heading southwest to the ridgecrest.

2.8 Reach the saddle at the head of West Boulder Canyon (GPS: N33 24.47' / W111 22.29'); follow an informal trail west.

3.9 Reach the crest of Superstition Mountain. (GPS: N33 24.37' / W111 23.29')

4.8 Pass west of Peak 5,057.

5.5 Reach the first saddle.

7.7 Reach the cliffs above the second saddle. Avoid these cliffs by descending east, and then climbing northwest to the saddle.

8.4 Turn east and descend the ridge.

10.0 Reach Old West Boulder Canyon. Descend the canyon to the east.

10.6 Reach West Boulder Canyon; turn left and descend the canyon.

11.9 Turn right onto Dutchmans Trail.

12.4 At the junction with Black Mesa Trail, stay right on Dutchmans Trail.

12.5 At the Boulder Canyon Trail junction, stay right on Dutchmans Trail.

12.6 At the Bull Pass Trail junction, stay right on Dutchmans Trail.

13.5 Turn right onto Peralta Trail.

17.4 Cross Fremont Saddle, closing the loop portion of the route.

19.4 Arrive back at the Peralta Trailhead.

Four Peaks Wilderness

The Mazatzal Mountains rise abruptly north of the Salt River. The deep river gorge, now filled by the Canyon and Apache Reservoirs, divides the Superstition Mountains from the Mazatzal Mountains. The two ranges are completely different in character, which is surprising considering how few air miles separate them. The Mazatzal Mountains are one of a number of ranges that trend from north-northwest to south-southeast in central Arizona. The range is bounded by Tonto Basin on the east and the Verde River on the west. Sonoran Desert foothills covered with mesquite, saguaro and cholla cactus, and other desert plants border the Verde River. The southern portion of the range culminates at Four Peaks, a group of four distinctive 7,000-foot summits easily visible from the Phoenix area on clear days.

The terrain rises more gradually on the west side of the range and falls off steeply on the east. North of Four Peaks, the crest of the range dips somewhat, rises again at the summit of Mount Ord, then falls abruptly to Slate Creek Divide, which separates the south and north halves of the range. This pass is crossed by AZ 87 (Beeline Highway), a four-lane highway connecting the city of Mesa in the desert Salt River valley to the forested high country around Payson.

The lowest slopes of the Four Peaks Wilderness are covered by the lower Sonoran Desert ecosystem, the intermediate elevations are pinyon pine and juniper woodland, and the highest areas are covered with dense chaparral. The north-facing slopes on the highest peaks are covered with a mixed ponderosa pine and Gambel oak woodland. Wildfires have repeatedly scorched the Four Peaks area. The largest of these burned the entire mountain from desert to summits in summer 1996, one of the driest fire seasons on record. Because of this, dead trees commonly fall across the trails in the Four Peaks Wilderness, and hikers should expect slow going at times. Despite all the fires, pockets of tall pines have survived, and smaller plants always grow back quickly. After a wet winter or summer rainy season, the open, burned areas are a riot of wildflowers.

Access

The Four Peaks Wilderness can be reached from the west via AZ 87, FR 143, and FR 401 to Cottonwood Camp Trailhead. FR 143 continues to the Mazatzal crest and the Cline Cabin, Mud Spring, and Lone Pine Saddle Trailheads. This is a long, rough road requiring a high-clearance vehicle. The Ballantine Trailhead is located on the east side of AZ 87 and is the easiest trailhead to reach in the southern Mazatzal Mountains. Along AZ 188, on the east side of the range, several short, primitive roads can be used to gain access to trails north of the Four Peaks Wilderness. Farther south along AZ 188, near Roosevelt Lake, the east end of FR 143, also known as the El Oso Road, climbs west onto the crest. This section of FR 143 is generally in better shape than the western portion, and ordinary cars can reach the Lone Pine Saddle Trailhead from here. Farther south along AZ 188, a four-wheel-drive, high-clearance road, FR 445, provides access to Oak Flat Trailhead. Rock Creek Trailhead can also be reached via FR 445; turn left on FR 445A after 3 miles, then right on the short spur road to the trailhead. Avoid parking in or near the wash to avoid possible flood damage to your vehicle. Even farther south along AZ 188, FR 429 provides access to the Mills Ridge Trailhead; a four-wheel-drive vehicle is recommended.

Camping

The only public campgrounds in the Four Peaks area are located on the shores of Roosevelt Lake, on the east side of the range. Indian Point Campground is reached via AZ 188, FR 60, and FR 661. Cholla Campground is off AZ 188 north of Roosevelt Dam. Dispersed camping away from developed sites is generally allowed in the Tonto National Forest, except where posted otherwise. Please respect all such closures and all posted private land.

Services

Full services are located in Mesa, southwest of the wilderness on AZ 87. Limited services can be found in Sunflower, along AZ 87 northwest of the wilderness, and in Punkin Center, on AZ 188 east of the wilderness. Outdoor specialty shops are found in Tempe, Scottsdale, and Phoenix.

Permits and Restrictions

In the Four Peaks Wilderness, group size is limited to fifteen people, and the stay limit is fourteen days. Permits are not required, though this may change in the future. Check with the trail contact listed with each hike for current information.

28 Ballantine Trail

This trail is north of the Four Peaks Wilderness and south of Slate Creek Divide, in the southern half of the Mazatzal Mountains. The hike starts amid granite boulders in classic Sonoran Desert terrain and climbs along Camp Creek and Ballantine Canyon to the chaparral and pine zones near the crest of the range.

Start: Ballantine Trailhead
Distance: 10.5 miles point to point (shuttle)
Hiking time: About 8 hours
Difficulty: Strenuous due to elevation gain and distance
Best seasons: Oct–Apr
Trail surface: Dirt
Land status: Tonto National Forest
Nearest town: Mesa
Other users: Horses
Water availability: Seasonal in Camp Creek and at Mountain Spring

Canine compatibility: Leashed dogs permitted
Fees and permits: None
Schedule: Year-round, 24 hours per day
Maps: USGS Boulder Mountain AZ and Mine Mountain AZ; National Geographic/Trails Illustrated Superstition and Four Peaks Wilderness map; Tonto National Forest map
Trail contact: Mesa Ranger District, Tonto National Forest, 5140 E. Ingram St., Mesa, AZ 85205; (480) 610-3300; www.fs.usda.gov/tonto

Finding the trailhead: This is the easiest trailhead to reach in the Four Peaks region. You can avoid the shuttle to the Cline Trailhead if you do a shorter, out-and-back hike.

To reach the Ballantine Trailhead, at the start of the hike, drive north on AZ 87 from Mesa. Note your mileage at Shea Boulevard; drive about 21 miles north on AZ 87 from the Shea Boulevard interchange to the signed trailhead on the right side of the highway. GPS: N33 45.87' / W111 29.60'

To reach the Cline Trailhead, at the end of the hike, from Mesa, drive north on AZ 87. Note your mileage at Shea Boulevard, then drive 14 miles farther. Turn right on FR 143 and continue 11.2 miles to the Cline Trailhead, on the left. The last 5 miles of this seldom-maintained dirt road may require a high-clearance vehicle. GPS: N33 43.681' / W111 24.128'

The Hike

Follow Ballantine Trail as it climbs east away from the highway for a short distance, then swings northeast onto the ridge north of Camp Creek. As the trail swings back to the east, it drops into Camp Creek itself, then follows the creek (which has seasonal water) generally east.

Near the headwaters of Camp Creek, the trail crosses a flat and enters Ballantine Canyon. This is a good goal for an out-and-back hike from the Ballantine Trailhead, for those who wish to avoid driving the rough road to the Cline Trailhead.

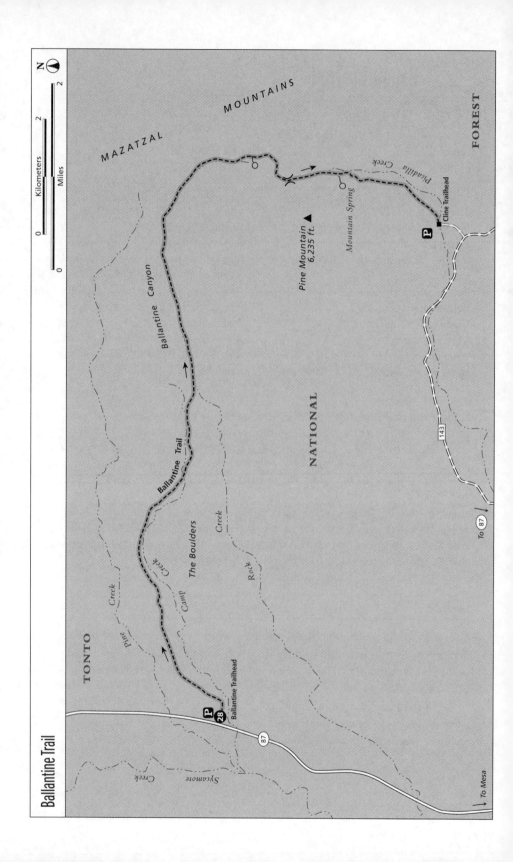

Ballantine Trail

The trail climbs steadily east up Ballantine Canyon and enters the chaparral zone. As it nears the crest of the Mazatzal Mountains, the canyon and trail veer south, and the trail tops out at a saddle just east of Pine Mountain.

From the saddle, the trail drops steeply into the headwaters of Picadilla Creek, passing Mountain Spring, then reaches Cline Trailhead, the end of the hike.

Miles and Directions

0.0   From the Ballantine Trailhead, hike east on Ballantine Trail.

4.6   The trail enters Ballantine Canyon. This is a good turnaround spot for out-and-back hikers.

8.5   Pass near Pine Mountain.

10.5   Arrive at the Cline Trailhead.

Sonoran Desert foothills along the Camp Creek Trail after a refreshing winter rain

29 Alder Creek Loop

This long loop backpack in the Four Peaks Wilderness takes you through a wide variety of country and features great views of Four Peaks from all sides. You'll also hike a section of the Arizona Trail.

Start: Mud Spring Trailhead
Distance: 24.7-mile loop
Hiking time: About 3 to 4 days
Difficulty: Strenuous due to distance, elevation change, and faint trails
Best seasons: Oct–Apr
Trail surface: Dirt trails, dirt roads
Land status: Tonto National Forest, Four Peaks Wilderness
Nearest town: Mesa
Water availability: Seasonally at Four Peaks Spring Number 1, Browns Cabin Spring, Cane Spring, Adams Camp Spring, Shake Spring, and Bear Spring

Other users: Horses; vehicles and mountain bikes on dirt roads
Canine compatibility: Leashed dogs permitted
Fees and permits: None
Schedule: Year-round, 24 hours per day
Maps: USGS Boulder Mountain AZ and Mine Mountain AZ; National Geographic/Trails Illustrated Superstition and Four Peaks Wilderness map; Tonto National Forest map
Trail contact: Mesa Ranger District, Tonto National Forest, 5140 E. Ingram St., Mesa, AZ 85205; (480) 610-3300. Tonto Basin Ranger District, Tonto National Forest, 28079 N. AZ 188, Roosevelt, AZ 85545; (928) 467-3200; www.fs.usda.gov/tonto

Finding the trailhead: From Mesa, drive north on AZ 87. Note your mileage at Shea Boulevard, then drive 14 miles farther. Turn right on FR 143, and continue 15.4 miles to the Mud Spring Trailhead, on the right. The last 9 miles of this seldom-maintained dirt road may require a high-clearance vehicle. GPS: N33 42.09' / W111 21.71'

The Hike

From the trailhead, take the Soldier Trail, which heads southeast, climbing steadily up the headwaters of Cottonwood Creek. The climb steepens as the trail passes through dense chaparral, passing Four Peaks Spring Number 1.

After the trail crosses Big Saddle at 1 mile, it starts down to Soldier Camp, steeply at first, but then the grade moderates. The open, grassy, south-facing slopes are a startling change from the first portion of the trail. At Soldier Camp, the trail crosses Boulder Creek and heads south. A short climb leads over a spur ridge, then the trail descends to cross an unnamed tributary of Boulder Creek. Finally, the trail works its way onto another ridge. Here you'll turn left on Cane Spring Trail, which descends into Cane Spring Canyon and turns south.

Turn left onto FR 401, a four-wheel-drive road, and continue south to Cane Springs Trailhead. From the trailhead, go east on Alder Creek Trail, which heads southeast at first and then climbs over a low saddle. The route then climbs gradually

Lower Alder Creek

east, up a drainage and over a second saddle, into the Long Canyon drainage. It descends southeast to the site of Adams Camp, then contours east along the benches above the confluence of Long Canyon and Alder Creek. When it reaches Alder Creek, the trail turns north up its namesake creek and climbs gradually. Near the head of the canyon the trail veers east of Alder Creek for the final, steep climb to Black Bear Saddle.

Turn left onto Four Peaks Trail (Arizona Trail), and follow this good trail as it contours north. You'll be in and out of ponderosa pine stands, the few that survived the

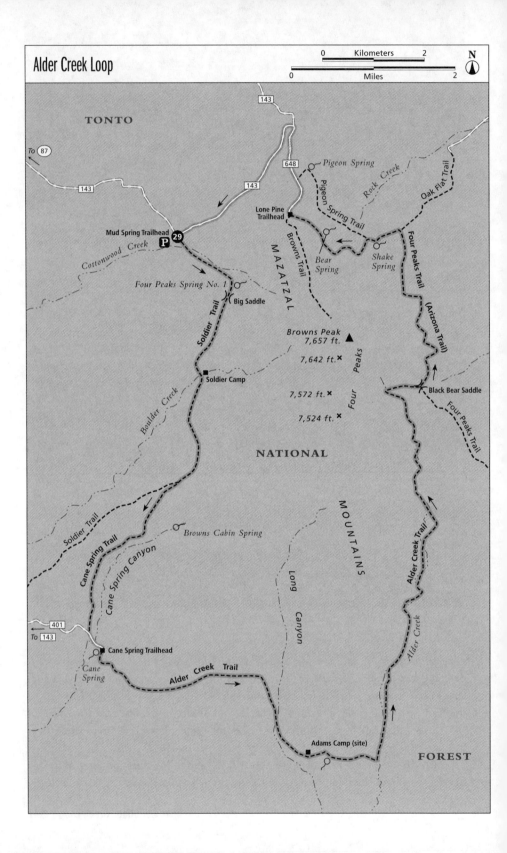

Alder Creek Loop

Kilometers 0 — 2
Miles 0 — 2

N

TONTO

To 87

143

143

143

648

Pigeon Spring

Rock Creek

Oak Flat Trail

Lone Pine Trailhead

Pigeon Spring Trail

Mud Spring Trailhead

P 29

Cottonwood Creek

Four Peaks Spring No. 1

Big Saddle

Bear Spring

Shake Spring

Browns Trail

MAZATZAL

Four Peaks Trail (Arizona Trail)

Soldier Trail

Browns Peak 7,657 ft.

7,642 ft. ✕

7,572 ft. ✕

7,524 ft. ✕

Four Peaks

Boulder Creek

Soldier Camp

Black Bear Saddle

Four Peaks Trail

NATIONAL

MOUNTAINS

Soldier Trail

Cane Spring Trail

Cane Spring Canyon

Browns Cabin Spring

Long Canyon

Alder Creek Trail

Alder Creek

401

To 143

Cane Spring Trailhead

Cane Spring

Alder Creek Trail

Adams Camp (site)

FOREST

Lone Fire in 1996. Four Peaks Trail contours north for a while, then starts to descend into a drainage. The trail veers west out of the drainage, then meets Oak Flat Trail at a low saddle; stay left on Four Peaks Trail. A gradual climb leads to the junction with Pigeon Spring Trail in a ravine. Continue on Four Peaks Trail as it turns left and climbs steeply up this ravine, then turns right out of the ravine. It contours northwest to Lone Pine Trailhead.

From the Lone Pine Trailhead, walk north on FR 648 north, then turn left on FR 143 to return to the Mud Spring Trailhead and your vehicle.

Option: The last 4.3 miles of the loop are on dirt roads. If you want to avoid the dirt road hiking, you can shuttle a vehicle to the Lone Pine Trailhead. To reach the Lone Pine Trailhead rom Mud Spring Trailhead, drive 2.1 miles east on FR 143, then turn right onto FR 648 and continue 1 mile south to the Lone Saddle Trailhead at the end of the road. GPS: N33 42.338' / W111 20.291'

Miles and Directions

0.0 Start at the Mud Spring Trailhead, and hike southeast on Soldier Trail.

1.2 Cross Big Saddle.

2.3 Pass Soldier Camp.

4.0 Turn left onto Cane Spring Trail and descend into Cane Spring Canyon.

6.2 Turn left onto FR 401.

6.5 Arrive at the Cane Spring Trailhead. Continue southeast on Alder Creek Trail.

8.2 Cross an unnamed pass.

10.0 Pass the site of Adams Camp.

11.1 Reach Alder Creek; follow Alder Creek Trail north (upstream).

17.0 At Black Bear Saddle, turn left on Four Peaks Trail.

19.4 At the junction with Oak Flat Trail, stay left on Four Peaks Trail.

19.9 At the junction with Pigeon Spring Trail, stay left on Four Peaks Trail.

21.4 Reach Lone Pine Trailhead; follow FR 648 north.

22.6 Turn left onto FR 143.

24.7 Arrive back at the Mud Spring Trailhead.

30 Lower Soldier Trail

This loop hike in the Four Peaks foothills takes you along ridges with superb views of Four Peaks and the Superstition Mountains. It's a good midwinter hike, when the high country is snow-covered.

Start: Cottonwood Camp
Distance: 5.6-mile loop
Hiking time: About 4 hours
Difficulty: Moderate due to elevation change
Best seasons: Oct–Apr
Trail surface: Dirt trails, dirt roads
Land status: Tonto National Forest, Four Peaks Wilderness
Nearest town: Mesa
Other users: Horses; vehicles and mountain bikes on dirt roads
Water availability: None

Canine compatibility: Leashed dogs permitted
Fees and permits: None
Schedule: Year-round, 24 hours per day
Maps: USGS Boulder Mountain AZ and Mormon Flat Dam AZ; National Geographic/Trails Illustrated Superstition and Four Peaks Wilderness map; Tonto National Forest map
Trail contact: Mesa Ranger District, Tonto National Forest, 5140 E. Ingram St., Mesa, AZ 85205; (480) 610-3300; www.fs.usda.gov/tonto

Finding the trailhead: From Mesa, drive north on AZ 87. Note your mileage at Shea Boulevard, then drive 14 miles farther. Turn right on FR 143, drive 2.1 miles, then turn right on FR 401 and continue 4.3 miles to Cottonwood Camp and the end of the maintained road. GPS: N33 37.37' / W111 26.87'

The Hike

From Cottonwood Camp, follow Soldier Trail east. It starts a gradual climb along a ridge. After a mile or so the grade steepens, and the trail ends at Cane Spring Road (FR 401). Turn right on this four-wheel-drive road, and follow it down the ridge to the southwest and south. A switchback takes the road off the ridge, where it turns southwest and crosses a drainage. Turning west, the road works its way down a ridge to Cottonwood Creek (a normally dry wash), then turns north and follows the wash a short distance back to the trailhead.

Mohave rattlesnake

Miles and Directions

0.0 From the Cottonwood Camp Trailhead, hike east on Soldier Trail.

2.2 Turn right on Cane Spring Road (FR 401).

5.6 Arrive back at Cottonwood Camp Trailhead.

Lower Soldier Trail

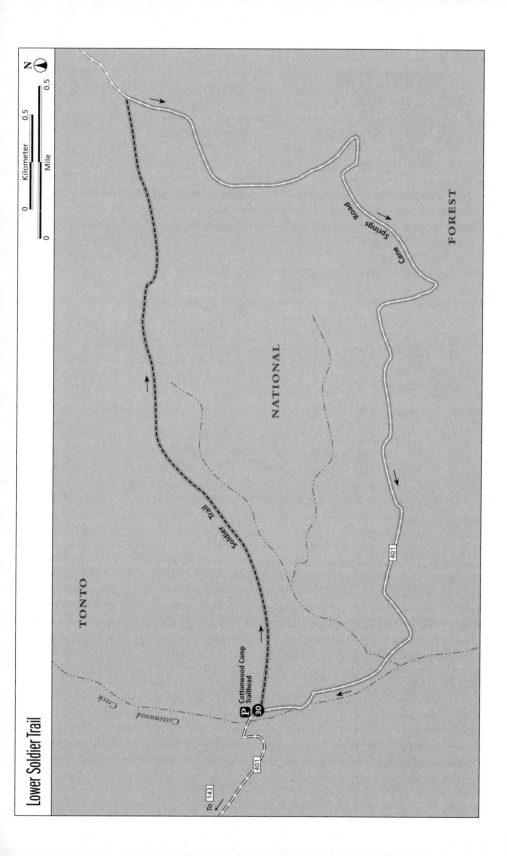

31 Browns Peak

This hike, part of which travels cross-country, leads to the top of the highest summit of the Four Peaks Wilderness and southern Mazatzal Mountains. And as you would expect, the views are stunning.

Start: Lone Pine Trailhead
Distance: 3.8 miles out and back
Hiking time: About 4 hours
Difficulty: Moderate due to cross-country hiking, rock scrambling, and elevation gain
Best seasons: Spring through fall;Oct–Apr
Trail surface: Dirt trails, cross-country terrain, rock scrambling
Land status: Tonto National Forest, Four Peaks Wilderness
Nearest town: Mesa
Other users: Horses
Water availability: None

Canine compatibility: Leashed dogs permitted
Fees and permits: None
Schedule: Year-round, 24 hours per day
Maps: USGS Four Peaks AZ; National Geographic/Trails Illustrated Superstition and Four Peaks Wilderness map; Tonto National Forest map
Trail contact: Mesa Ranger District, Tonto National Forest, 5140 E. Ingram St., Mesa, AZ 85205; (480) 610-3300; www.fs.usda.gov/tonto

Finding the trailhead: From Mesa, drive northeast on AZ 87. At Shea Boulevard note your mileage, and continue 14 miles to FR 143. Turn right onto this maintained dirt road, which becomes unmaintained and much rougher after 6.7 miles. When you are 18.3 miles from AZ 87, turn right onto FR 648 and continue 1 mile south to the Lone Pine Trailhead at the end of the road. GPS: N33 42.338' / W111 20.291'

The Hike

Start on Browns Trail, which climbs south from the trailhead and soon enters a stand of ponderosa pine and Gambel oak. Luckily, this stand was nearly untouched by the Lone Fire of 1996. The trail swings southwest and passes through a broad saddle, then turns southeast, back toward the main ridge, and enters an area where the Lone Fire destroyed nearly all the trees. Be alert for falling trees, which can topple at any time. Windy and wet weather is especially hazardous. As consolation, the distant view is better without the forest.

After crossing the main ridge, the trail works its way up the northeast slopes, using an occasional switchback. A slight descent leads to the end of the trail in Browns Saddle.

Although you can reach the summit by several different routes, the following is one of the easiest. Continue cross-country south up the ridge toward Browns Peak. Though the craggy peak looks impressive, it's actually easy to climb and you'll only need your hands in a few places. Note the prominent ravine that splits the north face

Most trailheads in the Superstition and Mazatzal Mountains are accessed via long dirt roads. Here, Browns Peak towers above the road to Lone Pine Trailhead.

of the peak. This is your goal, but you won't be able to see it when you get closer. When you reach the first rock outcrops, turn right and work your way into the main gully that drains the prominent ravine. If you stay high, right at the base of the rock, you'll avoid the worst of the brush. Then head directly up the ravine. There's one spot in the ravine where you'll need your hands. The ravine tops out on the west shoulder of the peak, and then it is a short scramble to the left (east) to reach the summit.

From this lofty vantage point you can see much of the country covered by this guide. Though the bulk of the three other peaks in the Four Peaks group block some of the view to the south, you can still see much of the Superstition Mountains. To the west lies the Valley of the Sun, containing Phoenix and its sister cities. The desert plain is dotted with low mountain ranges that seem to recede into the distance. On a clear day you can see the McDowell Mountains and, far to the west, the Harquahala Mountains. To the northwest, the bulk of the Bradshaw Mountains looms above the lower-elevation New River Mountains. The Mazatzal Mountains run north-northwest from your perch—the rounded summit of Mount Ord, crowned with radio towers and a fire lookout, is clearly visible. The rugged peaks of the Mazatzal

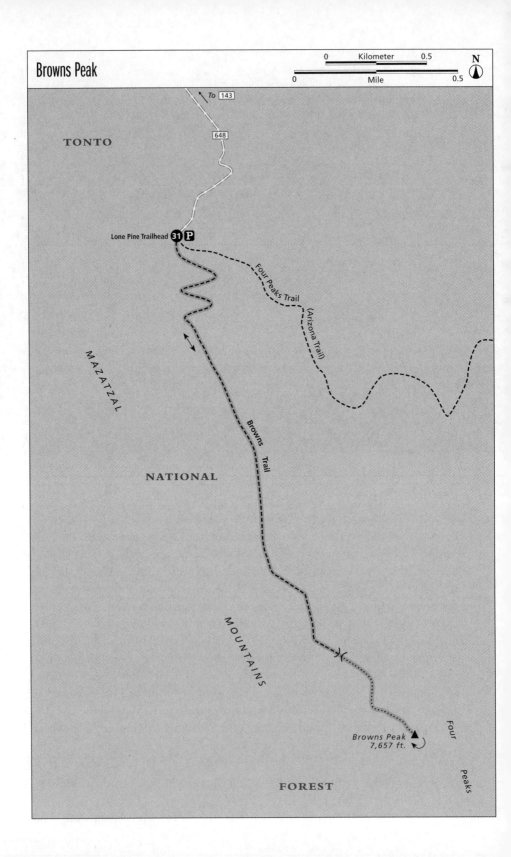

Browns Peak

To 143

648

TONTO

Lone Pine Trailhead 31 P

Four Peaks Trail

(Arizona Trail)

MAZATZAL

Browns Trail

NATIONAL

MOUNTAINS

Browns Peak
7,657 ft.

Four

Peaks

FOREST

0   Kilometer   0.5

0   Mile   0.5

N

Wilderness form the backdrop for Mount Ord. North and eastward, the clean line of the Mogollon Rim slices across the horizon near Payson, and to the east the wide bulk of the Sierra Ancha dominates the skyline. To the southeast, you can see Pinal Peak, rising above the town of Globe.

Miles and Directions

0.0 From the Lone Pine Trailhead, hike south on Browns Trail.

1.5 Reach Browns Saddle. Leave the trail and hike south toward Browns Peak.

1.9 Reach the top of Browns Peak. Retrace your steps.

3.8 Arrive back at the trailhead.

32 Pigeon Spring Loop

This easy loop hike on the north slopes of Four Peaks passes through the remains of a large stand of ponderosa pine burned in the 60,000-acre Lone Fire in 1996. Although most of the big trees are gone, many other plants are making a comeback.

Start: Pigeon Trailhead
Distance: 3.4-mile loop
Hiking time: About 2 hours
Difficulty: Easy
Best seasons: Oct–Apr
Trail surface: Dirt trails, dirt roads
Land status: Tonto National Forest, Four Peaks Wilderness
Nearest town: Mesa
Other users: Horses on trails; vehicles and moutnain bikes on FR 648
Water availability: Seasonally at Pigeon Spring and Bear Spring
Canine compatibility: Leashed dogs permitted

Fees and permits: None
Schedule: Year-round, 24 hours per day
Maps: USGS Four Peaks AZ; National Geographic/Trails Illustrated Superstition and Four Peaks Wilderness map; Tonto National Forest map
Trail contact: Mesa Ranger District, Tonto National Forest, 5140 E. Ingram St., Mesa, AZ 85205; (480) 610-3300. Tonto Basin Ranger District, Tonto National Forest, 28079 N. AZ 188, Roosevelt, AZ 85545; (928) 467-3200; www.fs.usda.gov/tonto

Finding the trailhead: From Mesa, drive northeast on AZ 87. At Shea Boulevard note your mileage, and continue 14 miles to FR 143. Turn right onto this maintained dirt road, which becomes unmaintained and much rougher after 6.7 miles. When you are 18.3 miles from AZ 87, turn right onto FR 648 and continue 0.6 mile south to Pigeon Trailhead. GPS: N33 42.65' / W111 20.19'

The Hike

This is an interesting hike on a short segment of the Arizona Trail through the heart of the Lone Fire burn. Watch out for unstable trees, which can fall at any time.

From the trailhead, follow Pigeon Spring Trail, an old road, downhill to Pigeon Spring, which is in a masonry box. From the spring, the trail turns southerly and climbs over an unnamed saddle that is strewn with granite boulders. Thanks to the fire, there's a great view of Four Peaks from this minor pass. From the pass, the trail drops slightly and crosses a drainage, then begins to climb gradually along the slopes at the head of Rock Creek. There's seasonal water in the drainage below Bear Spring, which sometimes forms a small cascade over the granite cliffs below the trail.

As the trail crosses ravines and climbs around ridges, you'll pass though stands of pines that were mostly untouched by the Lone Fire, and then back into areas where every scrap of vegetation was burned. Pigeon Spring Trail ends at the junction with Four Peaks Trail (Arizona Trail), just after crossing a ravine.

Yuccas are common throughout the Mazatzal Mountains.

Turn right and follow Four Peaks Trail as it climbs steeply up the ravine. Abruptly the trail swings west and levels off. Continue to contour on Four Peaks Trail past Bear Spring. The trail ends at Lone Pine Trailhead. Walk north on FR 648 to reach Pigeon Trailhead and your vehicle.

The early summer of 1996 was extremely dry, and when a careless, ignorant camper abandoned a campfire near Pigeon Spring, it soon exploded into a raging wildfire that incinerated 60,000 acres. The fire burned out of control for six days, and it took the efforts of hundreds of firefighters to contain. It's humbling to realize that

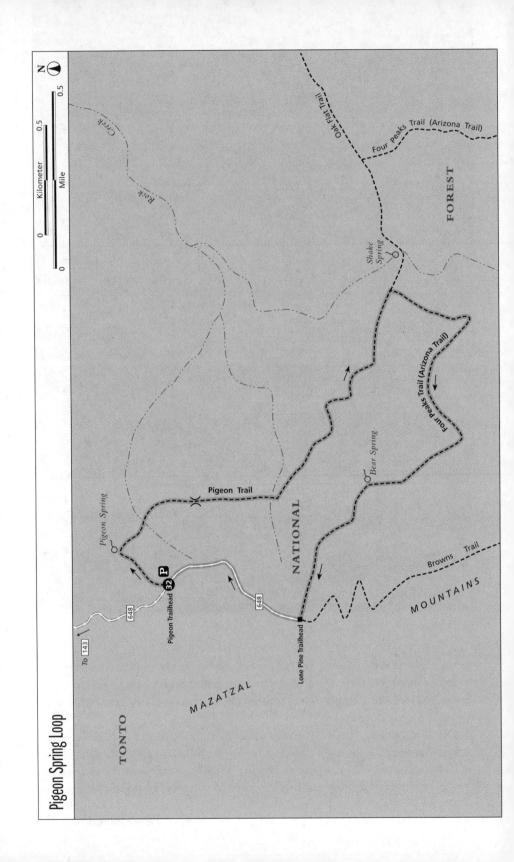

Pigeon Spring Loop

a few coals from a campfire grew to become Arizona's largest wildfire. Though the Lone Fire is certainly the most devastating wildfire to occur in the Four Peaks area, the steep, dry mountains, rising directly out of the desert, have always had serious wildfires. Amazingly, pockets of Douglas fir and ponderosa pine have survived all of the fires. And, within the heavily burned areas, vegetation is rapidly making a comeback, aided by a couple of wet winters and several very wet summers. Although the tall ponderosa pines will not return for hundreds of years, the open slopes left by the burn are often a riot of colorful wildflowers after a wet winter.

Miles and Directions

0.0 From the Pigeon Trailhead, start on Pigeon Trail (Arizona Trail).
0.2 Pass Pigeon Spring.
0.5 Cross through an unnamed saddle.
1.1 Cross the drainage below Bear Spring.
1.5 Turn right onto Four Peaks Trail (Arizona Trail).
2.5 Pass Bear Spring.
3.0 Reach the Lone Pine Trailhead. Walk north on FR 648.
3.4 Arrive back at the Pigeon Spring Trailhead.

33 Rock Creek Loop

This excellent long day hike or overnight trip leads from the eastern foothills through rugged canyons on the northeast slopes of Four Peaks. Part of the hike follows the Arizona Trail along a high, scenic ridge.

Start: Rock Creek Trailhead
Distance: 14.4-mile loop
Hiking time: About 10 hours or 2 days
Difficulty: Strenuous due to distance and elevation change
Best seasons: Fall through spring;Oct–Apr
Trail surface: Dirt
Land status: Tonto National Forest, Four Peaks Wilderness
Nearest town: Globe
Other users: Horses on trails; vehicles and mountain bikes on FR 445 and FR 445A

Water availability: Seasonally in Rock Creek and at Chillicut Spring, Shake Spring, Oak Flat Spring, and Fox Gulch Spring
Canine compatibility: Leashed dogs permitted
Fees and permits: None
Schedule: Year-round, 24 hours per day
Maps: USGS Four Peaks AZ; National Geographic/Trails Illustrated Superstition and Four Peaks Wilderness map; Tonto National Forest map
Trail contact: Tonto Basin Ranger District, Tonto National Forest, 28079 N. AZ 188, Roosevelt, AZ 85545; (928) 467-3200; www .fs.usda.gov/tonto

Finding the trailhead: From Mesa, drive north on AZ 87. Note your mileage at the junction with Shea Boulevard. Continue another 48 miles, then turn right onto AZ 188. Continue about 24 miles to Three Bar Road (FR 445), and turn right. Continue 3.2 miles to a T intersection, then turn left on FR 445A. Go less than 0.1 mile, then turn right on the spur road to Rock Creek Trailhead. GPS: N33 43.26' / W111 16.04'

The Hike

From the trailhead, Chillicut Trail, a former jeep road, climbs gradually southwest up an unnamed tributary of Rock Creek onto a ridge. The climb steepens as the trail swings south toward a low pass. After crossing through the unnamed pass, the trail contours into Baldy Canyon, then starts a steep climb up a ridge. After the trail crosses a spur ridge, the climb moderates and the trail returns to the bed of Baldy Canyon. The climb steepens again in the upper part of the canyon.

After passing Chillicut Spring, the trail veers onto a ridge to the east and climbs steeply to the top of Buckhorn Mountain and meets Four Peaks Trail (Arizona Trail).

Turn right, and follow Four Peaks Trail northwest along Buckhorn Ridge toward Four Peaks. This section of the trail offers spectacular views of the Four Peaks area, the Superstition Mountains, and Tonto Basin and Roosevelt Lake. The most scenic campsites are along the ridge, though you'll have to carry water for a dry camp. Camping is limited along much of the loop due to steep slopes and narrow canyons.

Agave is not something to tangle with.

Just before the ridge starts climbing steeply again, you'll pass through Black Bear Saddle, where the Alder Creek Trail joins from the left. Remain on Four Peaks Trail through Black Bear Saddle, where the trail turns right, contours around a steep hillside, then starts a steep descent down a northeast-facing drainage.

Just after the trail veers out of the drainage to the west, it meets Oak Flat Trail in a saddle (Shake Spring is 0.3 mile west on the Four Peaks Trail on Oak Flat Trail).

Turn right on Oak Flat Trail, and follow it down a ridge to the northeast. The trail turns north for the final descent to Big Oak Flat and the Oak Flat Trailhead, both located along Rock Creek. Oak Flat Spring is 0.1 mile south of the trailhead.

From the trailhead, follow FR 445 down Rock Creek. Bear right on FR 445A to return to the Rock Creek Trailhead and your vehicle.

Miles and Directions

0.0 From the Rock Creek Trailhead, start on Chillicut Trail.

2.1 Cross an unnamed pass.

2.7 Descend into Baldy Canyon and follow Chillicut Trail southwest up a ridge.

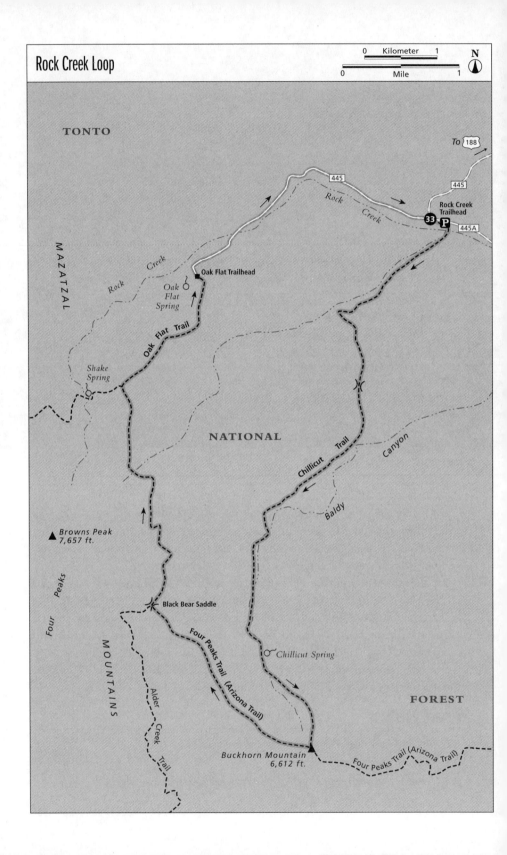

TONTO

To 188

445

445

Rock   Creek

Rock Creek Trailhead

33 P

445A

MAZATZAL

Rock   Creek

Oak Flat Trailhead

Oak Flat Spring

Oak   Flat   Trail

Shake Spring

NATIONAL

Chillicut   Trail

Canyon

Baldy

Browns Peak
7,657 ft.

Four   Peaks

Black Bear Saddle

Four Peaks Trail (Arizona Trail)

Chillicut Spring

MOUNTAINS

FOREST

Alder   Creek   Trail

Buckhorn Mountain
6,612 ft.

Four Peaks Trail (Arizona Trail)

6.1 Arrive at Buckhorn Mountain; turn right on Four Peaks Trail (Arizona Trail).

8.1 Reach the Alder Creek Trail junction at Black Bear Saddle. Descend northeast from the saddle on Four Peaks Trail (Arizona Trail).

10.3 Turn right onto Oak Flat Trail.

11.8 Reach the Oak Flat Trailhead; walk east on FR 445.

14.3 Bear right onto FR 445A.

14.4 Arrive back at the Rock Creek Trailhead.

34 Four Peaks Trail

This hike takes you along the southern end of Four Peaks Trail, which is also the route of the Arizona Trail at the south end of the Mazatzal Mountains passage. The hike culminates at 6,612-foot Buckhorn Mountain, which has a commanding view of the Four Peaks Wilderness, the southern Mazatzal Mountains, the Superstition Mountains, the Sierra Ancha, Roosevelt Lake, and Tonto Basin.

Start: Mills Ridge Trailhead
Distance: 7.8 miles out and back
Hiking time: About 6 hours
Difficulty: Moderate due to elevation change
Best seasons: Oct–Apr
Trail surface: Dirt
Land status: Tonto National Forest, Four Peaks Wilderness
Nearest town: Globe
Other users: Horses
Water availability: Seasonal at Granite Spring

Canine compatibility: Leashed dogs permitted
Fees and permits: None
Schedule: Year-round, 24 hours per day
Maps: USGS Four Peaks AZ and Theodore Roosevelt Dam AZ; National Geographic/Trails Illustrated Superstition and Four Peaks Wilderness map; Tonto National Forest map
Trail contact: Tonto Basin Ranger District, Tonto National Forest, 28079 N. AZ 188, Roosevelt, AZ 85545; (928) 467-3200; www.fs.usda.gov/tonto

Finding the trailhead: From Mesa, drive north on AZ 87. Note your mileage at the junction with Shea Boulevard. Continue another 48 miles, then turn right onto AZ 188. Continue about 30.3 miles, then turn right on FR 429. Drive 4.3 miles to the Mills Ridge Trailhead. A four-wheel-drive vehicle is recommended for FR 429. GPS: N33 40.29' / W111 14.57'

The Hike

Four Peaks Trail climbs steadily southwest up the ridge north of Buckhorn Creek, then leaves the ridge at a saddle and turns south to cross Buckhorn Creek. South of the crossing, the trail climbs steeply for a while, then veers west above Hackberry Creek. Beyond the creek, the climb moderates a bit. The trail passes Granite Spring at the head of Hackberry Creek, then climbs to the top of the ridge to the west. It follows the ridge to the summit of Buckhorn Mountain.

This rounded peak is the highest point on Buckhorn Ridge, which is the southernmost portion of the Mazatzal Mountains. The ridge runs several miles northwest and culminates at Browns Peak, the highest of the Four Peaks. Buckhorn Ridge slopes gently to the southeast for about 2 miles before suddenly plunging into the depths of the Salt River Canyon, now filled with Apache Lake. The views from this lofty vantage point are tremendous.

Browns Peak, on the left, is the highest of the Four Peaks at 7,641 feet. ▶

Four Peaks Trail

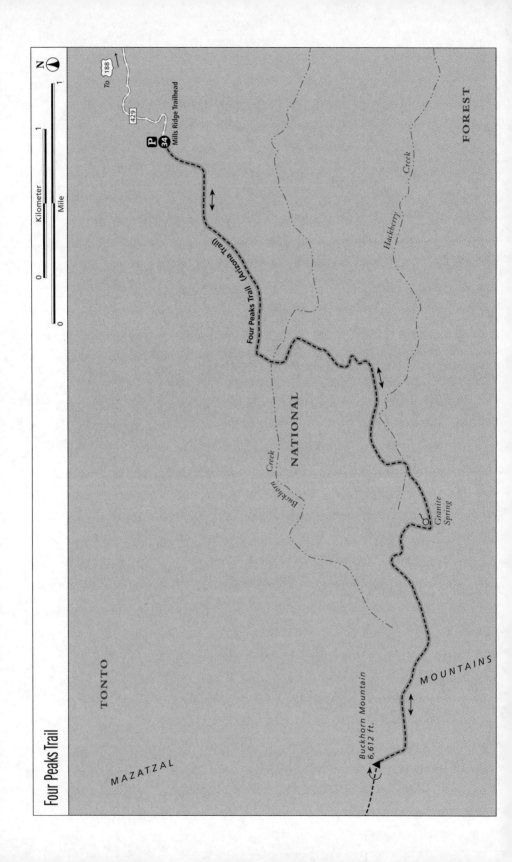

N

To (188)

(429)

P (34) Mills Ridge Trailhead

Four Peaks Trail (Arizona Trail)

Hackberry Creek

TONTO

MAZATZAL

NATIONAL

Buckhorn Creek

Granite Spring

FOREST

Buckhorn Mountain
6,612 ft.

MOUNTAINS

Kilometer

Mile

Miles and Directions

0.0 From the Mills Ridge Trailhead, hike southwest on Four Peaks Trail (Arizona Trail).

1.2 Cross Buckhorn Creek.

2.6 Pass Granite Spring.

3.9 Arrive at the summit of Buckhorn Mountain. Return the way you came.

7.8 Arrive back at the trailhead.

Mazatzal Wilderness

North of Slate Creek Divide (the pass used by AZ 87), the Mazatzal Mountains increase in elevation. The northern Mazatzal Mountains are largely within the Mazatzal Wilderness—one of Arizona's most remote wild areas, despite lying only 50 airline miles northeast of greater Phoenix. The south boundary of the wilderness is west of Sunflower and west of AZ 87. The east boundary runs along the eastern foothills of the range. On the north, the wilderness includes part of the mesa country below the Mogollon Rim. The western boundary of the wilderness lies west of the Verde River for about half its length, and thus includes part of Arizona's only designated Wild and Scenic River. The wilderness boundary crosses to the east side of the river north of Horseshoe Lake; the boundary runs several miles east of the reservoir but still includes most of the desert foothills.

The northern Mazatzal Mountains encompass a wild variety of terrain, from desert plains to pine-forested mountains to rocky peaks, but deep, rugged canyons are the dominant feature of the landscape. From the Verde River on the west, the terrain rises eastward, at first gradually, then more abruptly as the Precambrian rock backbone of the range is exposed. Numerous deep, rough canyons carve up the western mesas and rugged peaks. As the terrain rises, the low desert cactus and shrubs give way to high desert grasses and diminutive pinyon pines and juniper trees. The range culminates in the 7,000-foot crest; several peaks reach just less than 8,000 feet. Outcrops of Precambrian Mazatzal quartzite, Maverick shale, and other rocks have been twisted and warped by the titanic mountain-building forces that created these mountains, at the same time the Rocky Mountains were lifted.

Vegetation in the Mazatzal Wilderness is a mix of chaparral and ponderosa pines. There are even a few Douglas fir, white fir, and quaking aspen trees mixed in on the cooler, north-facing slopes. The eastern slopes are quite abrupt, falling rapidly, sometimes in spectacular cliffs, to the desert valley of the Tonto Basin. On the north, the Mazatzal Mountains abruptly terminate at the East Verde River, a westward-flowing tributary of the Verde River. The Mazatzal Wilderness north of the East Verde River is quite different in character from what is south of the river. Here, broad volcanic mesas covered with pinyon-juniper forest are cut by several deep gorges.

Most of the high country in the Mazatzal Wilderness was burned by the Willow Fire in 2004. While the Mazatzal Mountains have a long history of wildfire, this fire took place during an extended drought and killed large areas of ponderosa pine and Douglas fir forest at the higher elevations and on north-facing slopes. Still, pockets of forest survived the fire, and lower-elevation stands of chaparral always recover quickly from fire.

Access

The easiest access to the Mazatzal Wilderness is from AZ 87 along the east side of the mountains. Cross F, Mormon Grove, and Mount Peeley Trailheads allow access to the southeast portion of the wilderness and are reached from FR 201, which leaves AZ 87 just south of Slate Creek Divide.

Deer Creek Trailhead, at the junction of AZ 88 and AZ 188, provides access to some of the eastern canyons and is one of the only Mazatzal Wilderness trailheads accessible by paved road. A few miles north on AZ 88, FR 419, though dirt, is well maintained and can be driven by normal cars. It provides access to the Barnhardt Trailhead, the most popular Mazatzal trailhead.

Farther north, near the hamlet of Rye on AZ 87, FR 414 gives access to the Rock Creek and Mineral Creek Trailheads, at the foot of the eastern slopes. Rock Creek Trailhead requires a four-wheel-drive vehicle to reach. From AZ 87 in Payson, go west on Main Street, which becomes FR 406, as an alternate route to Mineral Creek Trailhead. This is also the road to City Creek and Doll Baby Trailheads, which provide access to the north end of Mazatzal Divide Trail and the East Verde River. Normally, low-clearance vehicles can reach these three trailheads by this route.

From the town of Strawberry on AZ 87 north of Payson, FR 708 and FR 194 can be used to reach the Twin Buttes Trailhead, which provides access to the portion of the wilderness north of the East Verde River. Using FR 708 and FR 502, you can reach the site of the decommissioned Childs Power Plant on the Verde River, at the north edge of the wilderness.

West-side trailheads are more difficult to reach. Sheep Bridge Trailhead, on the Verde River, is the primary west-side access and can be reached from I-17 and the Bloody Basin Road (FR 269). Sheep Bridge can also be reached from the town of Carefree (north of Phoenix) via Seven Springs Road (FR 24). Both roads are long and remote and can be rough—a high-clearance vehicle is recommended. The southwest corner of the wilderness can be reached from Carefree via FR 24, FR 19, and FR 205 to Horseshoe Dam. The vehicle crossing at the dam is closed to the public, so hikers have to cross the dam via the pedestrian walkway under the spillway lip, then walk FR 205 for several miles to the Davenport Wash Trailhead.

Camping

There are few public campgrounds near the Mazatzal Wilderness. Houston Mesa Campground is located at the north end of Payson, off AZ 87. Cave Creek Recreation Area is west of the town of Carefree on Carefree Highway, off I-17. There are three Tonto National Forest campgrounds located together along FR 24 (the southern access to Sheep Bridge Trailhead); these are Cave Creek, CCC, and Seven Springs Campgrounds. Horseshoe Campground is located just below Horseshoe Dam, reached via FR 19, FR 24, and FR 205. Dispersed camping away from developed sites is generally allowed in the Tonto National Forest, except where posted otherwise. Please respect all such closures, as well as all posted private land.

Services

Full services are available in Mesa, south of the wilderness on AZ 87, and Payson, east of the wilderness on AZ 87. Limited services are available in the settlements of Sunflower, Rye, Pine, and Strawberry, located along AZ 87 east of the wilderness. Outdoor specialty shops are located in Payson, Tempe, Scottsdale, and Phoenix.

Permits and Restrictions

In the Mazatzal Wilderness, group size is limited to fifteen people, and the stay limit is fourteen days. Permits are not required, though this may change in the future. Check with the trail contact listed with each hike for current information.

35 Marion Spring

This is a good day hike on a section of the Arizona Trail in the southeast corner of the Mazatzal Wilderness. It can be combined with Squaw Flat to make a much longer day hike or an overnight trip. The trail starts from the Cross F Trailhead, one of the few Mazatzal trailheads that can be reached from a paved road.

Start: Cross F Trailhead
Distance: 6.8 miles out and back
Hiking time: About 5 hours
Difficulty: Moderate due to elevation change
Best seasons: Oct–Apr
Trail surface: Dirt
Land status: Tonto National Forest, Mazatzal Wilderness
Nearest town: Payson
Other users: Horses
Water availability: Seasonal at Marion Spring
Canine compatibility: Leashed dogs permitted

Fees and permits: None
Schedule: Year-round, 24 hours per day
Maps: USGS Reno Pass AZ and Lion Mountain AZ; National Geographic/Trails Illustrated Mazatzal and Pine Mountain Wilderness Areas map; USFS Mazatzal Wilderness map; Tonto National Forest map
Trail contact: Mesa Ranger District, Tonto National Forest, 5140 E. Ingram St., Mesa, AZ 85205; (480) 610-3300; www.fs.usda.gov/tonto

Finding the trailhead: From Mesa, drive about 50 miles north on AZ 87, then turn left on FR 627 just before crossing Slate Creek Divide (this turnoff is 27 miles south of Payson). Drive 1.2 miles, then turn left at the FR 201 junction to remain on FR 627 Drive 2.3 miles to the Cross F Trailhead, which is on the right where a power line crosses the road. GPS: N33 54.52' / W111 29.18'

The Hike

Little Saddle Trail (Arizona Trail) starts on the west side of the highway and can be difficult to locate. It crosses under the power line, then heads west up an unnamed tributary of Sycamore Creek. It follows this tributary as it turns north and enters a canyon. The trail turns northwest, climbs through a low saddle, and then follows a ridge northwest. At the point the Arizona Trail turns northeast and starts to traverse the slopes south of Potato Patch, turn left and hike northwest to Marion Spring, the goal of the hike. You're on the south slopes of Saddle Mountain, which is visible to the north. To the south, you can see much of the rugged country west of Sycamore Creek.

Arizona has quite a few "Sycamore Creeks," and when you see the namesake tree, you'll understand why. The Arizona sycamore is a massive, spreading, streamside tree with mottled greenish-brown bark. Its large leaves usually have five points and resemble a maple's, while the seeds are found in fuzzy "buttonballs" that swing from slender stems. Arizona sycamore is a water-loving tree that grows along drainages,

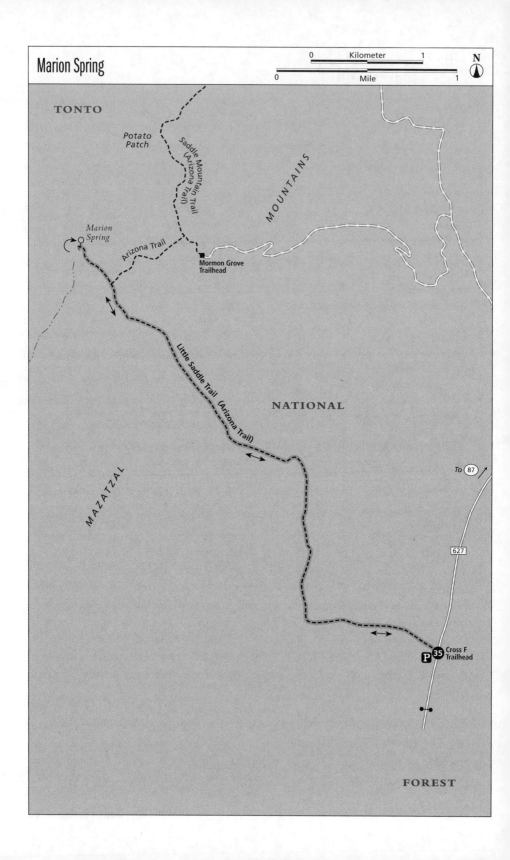

An aerial view of the southern Mazatzal Wilderness after the Willow Fire of 2002 burned most of the area. Wildfires have always been common in the Mazatzal Mountains.

and its presence means water is not far below the surface. If you're in need of water, look carefully as you hike along the streambed, because there are likely to be surface pools somewhere.

Miles and Directions

0.0 From the Cross F Trailhead, hike west, up the canyon.

3.2 Stay left at the Arizona Trail junction.

3.4 Reach Marion Spring. Return the way you came.

6.8 Arrive back at the trailhead.

36 Squaw Flat

This day hike leads through the rugged country in the Saddle Mountain area at the southern end of the Mazatzal Wilderness.

Start: Squaw Flat Trailhead
Distance: 9.4 miles out and back
Hiking Time: About 6 hours
Difficulty: Moderate due to distance and elevation change
Best seasons: Oct–Apr
Trail surface: Dirt
Land status: Tonto National Forest, Mazatzal Wilderness
Nearest town: Payson
Other users: Horses
Water availability: Seasonal at Squaw Flat Spring

Canine compatibility: Leashed dogs permitted
Fees and permits: None
Schedule: Year-round, 24 hours per day
Maps: USGS Reno Pass AZ and Lion Mountain AZ; National Geographic/Trails Illustrated Mazatzal and Pine Mountain Wilderness Areas map; USFS Mazatzal Wilderness map; Tonto National Forest map
Trail contact: Mesa Ranger District, Tonto National Forest, 5140 E. Ingram St., Mesa, AZ 85205; (480) 610-3300; www.fs.usda.gov/tonto

Finding the trailhead: From Mesa, drive about 50 miles north on AZ 87, then turn left on FR 627 just before crossing Slate Creek Divide (this turnoff is 27 miles south of Payson). Drive 1.2 miles, then turn right onto FR 201. Continue 1.3 miles, then turn left on FR 25. After 2.7 miles, turn left on FR 25A. Continue 5 miles to Mormon Grove Trailhead. FR 25 and FR 25A are dirt and may require a high-clearance vehicle. GPS: N33 56.34' / W111 30.13'

The Hike

Start the hike on Saddle Mountain Trail, an old mining road that climbs the ridge west of the trailhead, then passes through a saddle and swings north to another saddle, passing the junction with the Little Saddle Trail. The old road contours north along the east slopes of a ridge, which are covered with dense chaparral. Due to recent brush fires, you'll have some good views into Sycamore Canyon to the east.

The old road passes through another saddle on the southeast slopes of Saddle Mountain. The gently sloping semidesert grassland you see to the west is called Potato Patch. Follow the trail around the east side of Saddle Mountain; it soon turns more to the northeast and descends toward McFarland Canyon. A spur trail (also a former mining road) branches right to the old Story Mine. Continue on the main trail to the bottom of McFarland Canyon.

Here, Thicket Spring Trail (Arizona Trail) goes right; turn left onto Copper Camp Trail and follow it west up McFarland Canyon. The head of McFarland Canyon is thickly forested with Arizona cypress, which is fairly common in the northern Mazatzal Mountains. There should be water at Squaw Flat Spring, which is in the bed of McFarland Canyon.

Mount Peeley dominates the southern Mazatzal Wilderness.

Just beyond the spring, turn right onto Sheep Creek Trail. The trail climbs out of the bed, then heads northwest across Squaw Flat, which is actually the hilly basin at the head of McFarland Canyon. The trail reaches the rim at the head of Sheep Creek, the destination of the hike. This vantage point offers sweeping views of the southern portion of the Mazatzal Wilderness. The saddle-shaped peak to the south is the appropriately named Saddle Mountain. The bulk of Sheep Mountain looms to the northeast, and the steep canyons that form the head of Sheep Creek dominate the view to the north and northwest.

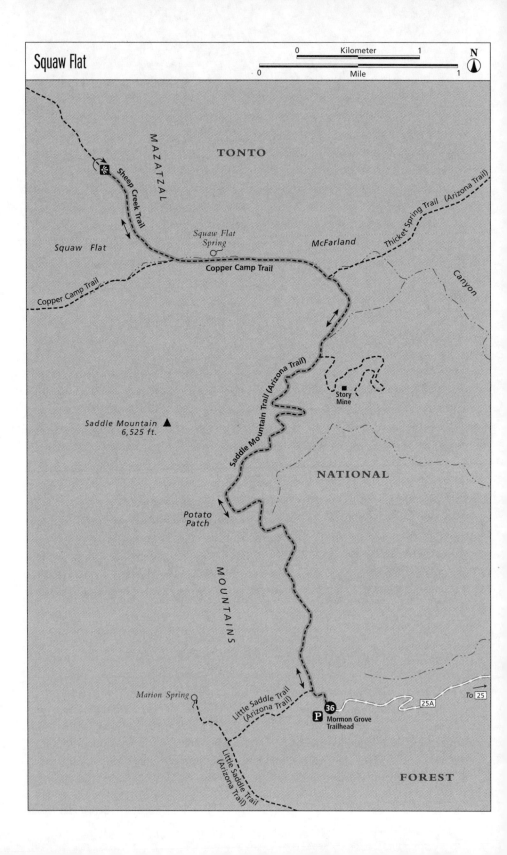

Miles and Directions

0.0 From the Mormon Grove Trailhead, hike northwest on Saddle Mountain Trail.

0.2 At the Little Saddle Trail junction, stay right on Saddle Mountain Trail.

1.4 Pass the Potato Patch.

2.8 Pass the Story Mine Trail; stay left on Saddle Mountain Trail.

3.3 At the junction with Thicket Spring Trail (Arizona Trail), turn left onto Copper Camp Trail.

4.1 Turn right onto Sheep Creek Trail.

4.7 Reach the viewpoint on the rim. Return the way you came.

9.4 Arrive back at the trailhead.

37 Copper Camp Creek

This challenging trail and cross–country backpack leads through beautiful and seldom
-visited country in the southern portion of the Mazatzal Wilderness.

Start: Mormon Grove Trailhead
Distance: 18.8-mile lollipop
Hiking time: About 2 to 3 days
Difficulty: Strenuous due to distance and
elevation change
Best seasons: Oct–Apr
Trail surface: Dirt trails, old dirt roadway
Land status: Tonto National Forest, Mazatzal
Wilderness
Nearest town: Payson
Other users: Horses
Water availability: Seasonal at Squaw Flat
Spring and Sheep Creek Seep

Canine compatibility: Leashed dogs permitted
Fees and permits: None
Schedule: Year-round, 24 hours per day
Maps: USGS Reno Pass AZ and Lion Moun-
tain AZ; National Geographic/Trails Illustrated
Mazatzal and Pine Mountain Wilderness Areas
map; USFS Mazatzal Wilderness map; Tonto
National Forest map
Trail contact: Mesa Ranger District, Tonto
National Forest, 5140 E. Ingram St., Mesa, AZ
85205; (480) 610-3300; www.fs.usda.gov/
tonto

Finding the trailhead: From Mesa, drive about 50 miles north on AZ 87, then turn left on FR
627, just before crossing Slate Creek Divide (this turnoff is 27 miles south of Payson). Drive 1.2
miles, then turn right onto FR 201. Continue 1.3 miles, then turn left onto FR 25. After 2.7 miles,
turn left onto FR 25A. Continue 5 miles to Mormon Grove Trailhead. FR 25 and FR 25A are dirt
and may require a high-clearance vehicle. GPS: N33 56.34' / W111 30.13'

The Hike

Some of the trails on this hike get very little use and can be difficult to find. You
should have both the wilderness map and the USGS maps, and be skilled in map
reading and cross–country travel, before attempting this hike.

Start on Saddle Mountain Trail, an old mining road that climbs the ridge west of
the trailhead, then passes through a saddle and swings north to another saddle, passing
the junction with the Little Saddle Trail (Arizona Trail). The old road contours north
along the east slopes of a ridge, which are covered with dense chaparral. Due to recent
brush fires, you'll have some good views into Sycamore Canyon to the east.

The old road passes through another saddle on the southeast slopes of Saddle
Mountain. The gently sloping desert grassland you see to the west is called Potato
Patch. Follow the trail around the east side of Saddle Mountain; it soon turns more
to the northeast and descends toward McFarland Canyon. A spur trail (also a former
mining road) branches right to the old Story Mine. Continue on the main trail to the
bottom of McFarland Canyon.

The southern Mazatzal Wilderness before several wildfires burned through the area

Here, Thicket Spring Trail (Arizona Trail) goes right; turn left onto Copper Camp Trail and follow it west up McFarland Canyon. The head of McFarland Canyon is thickly forested with Arizona cypress, which is fairly common in the northern Mazatzal Mountains. There is seasonal water at Squaw Flat Spring, which is in the bed of McFarland Canyon. Just beyond the spring, stay left on Copper Camp Trail. Sheep Creek Trail, which goes right, is the return of the loop section of the route.

Copper Camp Trail continues a gradual climb west to the head of McFarland Canyon, then heads out onto a brushy ridge. This trail gets very little use and can be hard to find. It is shown on the USFS wilderness map, but not on the USGS topo.

Soon the trail descends steeply down a ridge to the southwest. Copper Camp Trail then turns northwest, then west, and works its way toward Copper Camp Creek

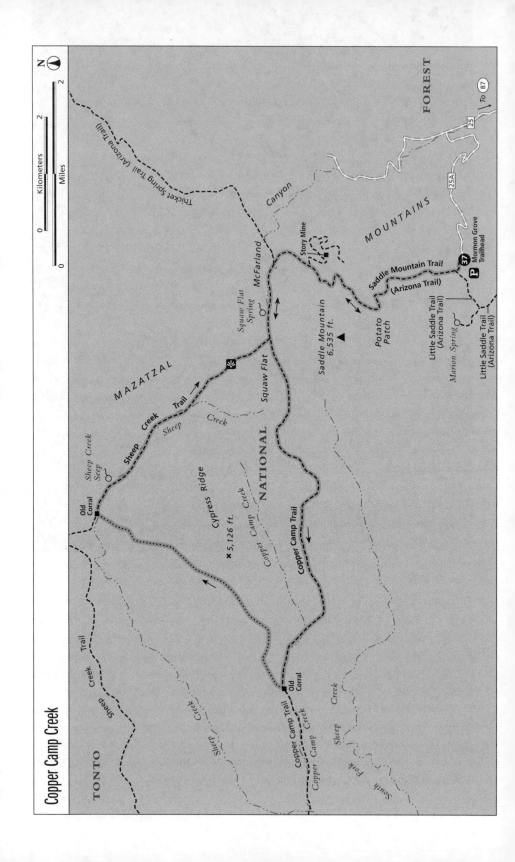

Copper Camp Creek

N

Kilometers
0   1   2

Miles
0   1   2

TONTO

NATIONAL

FOREST

MAZATZAL

MOUNTAINS

Sheep Creek Trail

Sheep Creek Seep

Old Corral

Sheep Creek Trail

Sheep Creek

Cypress Ridge

× 5,126 ft.

Copper Camp Creek

Copper Camp Trail

Old Corral

Copper Camp Trail

Copper Camp Creek

Sheep Creek

South Fork

Squaw Flat Spring

Squaw Flat

McFarland Canyon

Story Mine

Saddle Mountain
6,535 ft.

Potato Patch

Saddle Mountain Trail
(Arizona Trail)

Thicket Spring Trail (Arizona Trail)

Marion Spring

Little Saddle Trail
(Arizona Trail)

Little Saddle Trail
(Arizona Trail)

Mormon Grove
Trailhead

P

37

25A

25

To 87

through a complex of ridges and small canyons. After skirting a low ridge on the south, it drops into the Copper Camp Creek bed and stays there. Watch for an old corral about 0.6 mile downstream from the point where the trail meets the bed. This is the lowest point of the hike and the start of the cross-country portion. There are small campsites along the creek.

Leave the trail at the corral and follow an old route northeast onto the west end of Cypress Ridge (some maps show a trail here, but there is no trace of one now). Generally, work your way east-northeast, staying on the ridge just north of Copper Camp Creek, toward the crest of Cypress Ridge, which is clearly visible above. You should reach the crest at a point about 0.3 mile west of Point 5,126 on the USGS Lion Mountain topo.

After the steep climb, the gentle north slopes of Cypress Ridge are a welcome relief. Work your way northeast toward Sheep Creek Seep, which is shown correctly on the Lion Mountain topo, but not on the USFS wilderness map. Much of the plateau is open grassland, although there are some large areas of dense chaparral to avoid. The route drops into Sheep Creek at another old corral, just northwest of Sheep Creek Seep. There is seasonal water in Sheep Creek and at the seep, and a few small campsites.

Turn right onto Sheep Creek Trail, a little-used but easy-to-follow trail, and follow it southeast up Sheep Creek. The grade is moderate for a while, but then steepens as the trail leaves the creek and climbs directly to the rim of Squaw Flat. Your reward for all the hard work is tremendous views of much of the country you've just hiked. Continue southeast down gently sloping Squaw Flat into McFarland Canyon, then turn left on the Copper Camp Trail to complete the loop. Return to the Mormon Grove Trailhead as you came, via the Copper Camp and Saddle Mountain Trails.

Miles and Directions

0.0   From the Mormon Grove Trailhead, hike northwest on Saddle Mountain Trail.

0.2   At the Little Saddle Trail junction, stay right on Saddle Mountain Trail.

1.4   Pass the Potato Patch.

2.8   At the junction with Story Mine Trail, stay left on Saddle Mountain Trail.

3.3   At the junction with Thicket Spring Trail (Arizona Trail), turn left onto Copper Camp Trail.

4.1   At the junction with Sheep Creek Trail, stay left on Copper Camp Trail.

8.7   Reach the old corral; leave the trail and hike northeast onto Cypress Ridge.

10.2   At the west end of Cypress Ridge, head northeast toward Sheep Creek.

11.9   Turn right onto Sheep Creek Trail.

14.3   Cross the ridge north of Squaw Flat.

14.9   Turn left onto Copper Camp Trail, closing the loop.

15.7   At the junction with Thicket Spring Trail, turn right on Saddle Mountain Trail.

18.8   Arrive back at the Mormon Grove Trailhead.

38 Mazatzal Divide Trail

The Mazatzal Divide Trail is the premier backpack in the Mazatzal Wilderness and runs nearly the entire length of the northern Mazatzal Mountains, staying on or near the crest. The Arizona Trail follows the Mazatzal Divide Trail for most of its Mazatzal Mountain passage.

Start: Mount Peeley Trailhead
Distance: 28.3 miles point to point with shuttle
Hiking time: About 3 to 4 days
Difficulty: Strenuous due to length and elevation change
Best seasons: Oct–Nov and Mar–Apr
Trail surface: Dirt
Land status: Tonto National Forest, Mazatzal Wilderness
Nearest town: Payson
Other users: Horses
Water availability: Seasonal at Fisher Spring, Bear Spring, Windsor Spring, Brody Seep, Chilson Spring, Horse Camp Seep, and Hopi Spring

Canine compatibility: Leashed dogs permitted
Fees and permits: None
Schedule: Year-round, 24 hours per day
Maps: USGS Mazatzal Peak AZ, North Peak AZ, Cypress Butte AZ; National Geographic/Trails Illustrated Mazatzal and Pine Mountain Wilderness Areas map; USFS Mazatzal Wilderness map; Tonto National Forest map
Trail contact: Mesa Ranger District, Tonto National Forest, 5140 E. Ingram St., Mesa, AZ 85205; (480) 610-3300. Tonto Basin Ranger District, Tonto National Forest, 28079 N. AZ 188, Roosevelt, AZ 85545; (928) 467-3200. Payson Ranger District, Tonto National Forest, 1009 E. AZ 260, Payson, AZ 85541; (928) 474-7900; www.fs.usda.gov/tonto

Finding the trailhead: From Mesa, drive about 50 miles north on AZ 87, then turn left on FR 627 just before crossing Slate Creek Divide (this turnoff is 27 miles south of Payson). Drive 1.2 miles, then turn right onto FR 201. Continue 1.3 miles, then turn right to remain on FR 201. Follow this graded dirt road 8 miles north and west to its end at Mount Peeley Trailhead. GPS: N34 0.29' / W111 28.28'

To reach the end of the hike at City Creek Trailhead from AZ 87 in Payson, drive west on Main Street. Stay on the main road past a golf course, where the pavement ends and the road becomes FR 406. City Creek Trailhead is 10 miles from Payson on FR 406. (If you reach the Doll Baby Ranch, you've gone 0.3 mile too far.) GPS: N34 13.06' / W111 27.92'

The Hike

Because the Mazatzal Divide Trail stays high on ridges most of the way, water can be a problem. None of the springs on or near the trail are reliable. It's best to do this hike in the spring after snowmelt, or in the fall after a wet summer. Don't depend on any single water source. The trail is not always shown correctly on the USGS maps; the wilderness map and the National Geographic/Trails Illustrated map show it correctly. This description follows the trail from south to north, which avoids the long, steep climb from the north trailhead.

Backpacking the Mazatzal Divide south of Mazatzal Peak

From the trailhead, hike west on Mazatzal Divide Trail, which begins as an old mining road. Follow the trail as it winds west along the ridge dividing the Deer Creek and Sycamore Creek drainages, then turns south along the east slopes of Mount Peeley. Turn sharply right on Mazatzal Divide Trail (Arizona Trail) and follow it west up a brushy slope. After a couple of switchbacks, the trail swings around the north side of Mount Peeley and levels off.

The trail contours west around the head of one of the many forks of Deer Creek, and then reaches a saddle on the crest of the Mazatzal Mountains. The trail now heads north along the crest. After a fairly level section, Mazatzal Divide Trail starts to climb gradually and turns eastward. The trail reaches its highest point just south of Peak 7,221, then descends east to Fisher Saddle. Bear Spring is located about 0.3 mile south on a spur trail, and Fisher Spring about the same distance north on the

Mazatzal Divide and Fisher Trails, but 450 feet lower than the saddle. There are small campsites in the saddle, and better ones farther on where the trail tops out on the ridge above Y Bar Basin.

Continue north on Mazatzal Divide Trail to the junction with Fisher Trail. Stay right to remain on Mazatzal Divide Trail, which climbs gradually through the scorched remains of the beautiful ponderosa pine and Douglas fir forest at the head of South Fork Deadman Creek. The trail then passes through a saddle onto the upper slopes of Y Bar Basin. Here the trail turns more to the north and descends gradually through pine-oak forest to Windsor Saddle and the junction with Y Bar Trail. Windsor Spring, which flows only in wet weather, is located about 100 yards south.

Stay left on Mazatzal Divide Trail as it contours the steep western slopes of Mazatzal Peak, at the headwaters of South Fork Deadman Creek. The west-facing slopes are drier, so the trail makes an abrupt transition from pine forest to chaparral, but the views of the rocky summit of Mazatzal Peak are spectacular, especially around sunset. You'll pass Brody Trail (Brody Seep is about 0.2 mile down this trail); stay right on Mazatzal Divide Trail and contour through occasional stands of ponderosa pine to the saddle at the head of Barnhardt Canyon. Barnhardt Trail goes right from this saddle. Stay left on Mazatzal Divide Trail, and descend gradually across grassy pinyon-juniper slopes to the northern end of Brody Trail. You can optionally turn left here and hike 0.1 mile south to Chilson Camp, an old cowboy line camp in a scenic meadow overlooking the west face of Mazatzal Peak. You should avoid camping at this overused site. Water used to be piped down to the camp from Chilson Spring, but unfortunately the spring is no longer reliable.

Back on Mazatzal Divide Trail, continue north as the trail contours brushy slopes into the North Fork Deadman Creek drainage. Pass the Sandy Saddle Trail; stay left on Mazatzal Divide Trail. The USGS North Peak map shows Mazatzal Divide Trail passing Horse Camp Seep, but the current line of the trail takes it east of the seep. There is a signed spur trail to the seep, and it's worth the short side trip to see the dramatic cliffs at the head of North Fork Deadman Creek. You can hike cross-country to a scenic overlook about 0.3 mile down the north fork, at the point where it drops into a deep canyon. There are good campsites near the seep.

Mazatzal Divide Trail continues north to Rock Creek Trail. Hopi Spring is located a few yards east on the Rock Creek Trail.

Stay left on Mazatzal Divide Trail and climb gradually up the broad forested basin at the head of the North Fork, then swing west to cross a ridge above Maverick Basin. The trail swings north again and descends gradually to The Park, a small pine flat at the head of Wet Bottom Creek. There are good campsites here but no water. Stay right at Willow Spring Trail, and then left at North Peak Trail.

In this area, the crest of the range consists of rolling hills covered with a mix of pinyon pine–juniper–Arizona cypress forest, chaparral, and occasional stands of ponderosa pine. The trail works generally north, contouring around the head of City Creek, then crossing the east slopes of Knob Mountain. North of Knob Mountain, the trail starts to descend and passes Red Hills Trail (Arizona Trail). Stay right on Mazatzal Divide Trail as it turns east briefly and then drops into City Creek. The descent continues steadily to the trail's end at City Creek Trailhead.

Option 1: From the point where the trail first enters the pine forest on the north slopes of Mount Peeley, you can easily hike cross-country about 0.5 mile to the summit. It's about 500 feet of climbing, but the going is easy and the views of the southern portion of the wilderness from the rounded, rocky summit of this 7,030-foot peak are worth it.

Option 2: Just north of Fisher Saddle, you can turn left onto Fisher Trail, an alternative route to Chilson Camp. This is a scenic but seldom-used trail that is difficult to find in places. You should have both the USGS Mazatzal Peak quad and the USFS Mazatzal Wilderness map. From the trail junction, Fisher Trail drops rapidly down a ridge to the head of South Fork Deadman Creek. This entire canyon head is covered with the remains of a dense Douglas fir and ponderosa pine forest that burned in the 2004 Willow Fire. The trail passes Fisher Spring, then continues down the bed of the drainage. It crosses a tributary canyon, then climbs onto a low ridge. The transition to a drier, pinyon-juniper forest is sudden as you cross the drainage. After passing through a broad saddle on the ridgecrest, Fisher Trail heads down a spur ridge running generally northwest, and reaches its lowest point as it crosses the canyon that drains the west face of Mazatzal Peak. You'll get occasional glimpses of the peak towering above you to the east.

From this point, Fisher Trail turns east and follows the north side of the drainage for about 0.2 mile before switching back to the northwest and climbing out of the canyon. This section is badly overgrown and is easy to lose. Watch for the old tree blazes and the large cairns to be certain you're on the trail. Once you climb out of the drainage, the slopes are less brushy and the trail is easier to follow. After climbing over a low ridge, the trail climbs onto a second ridge, then heads northeast, climbing steadily to the northwest shoulder of Peak 5,929. From this point, you'll have a sweeping view of South Fork Deadman Creek—a good excuse for a rest stop. The trail continues through a small stand of ponderosa pine, then climbs gradually to a saddle and the junction with Brody Trail.

Stay left and follow Brody Trail as it drops into another forested drainage. After crossing the bed, a signed spur trail leads a few yards to Brody Seep, a marginal spring located east of the bed (not actually in the bed, as the USGS map shows). The Brody Trail contours across open pinyon-juniper woodland, then drops into another small canyon (the Club Trail shown on the USGS map is overgrown and no longer in use). A short climb up the north side of this canyon takes you to Chilson Camp, the junction with the Davenport Trail, and Chilson Spring. Brody Trail can be difficult to locate as it heads north out of the camp area—it's about 100 yards northwest of the old wooden spring box.

This option is 0.9 mile shorter than Mazatzal Divide Trail, but adds 1,600 feet of elevation change. It will take you longer than staying on Mazatzal Divide Trail.

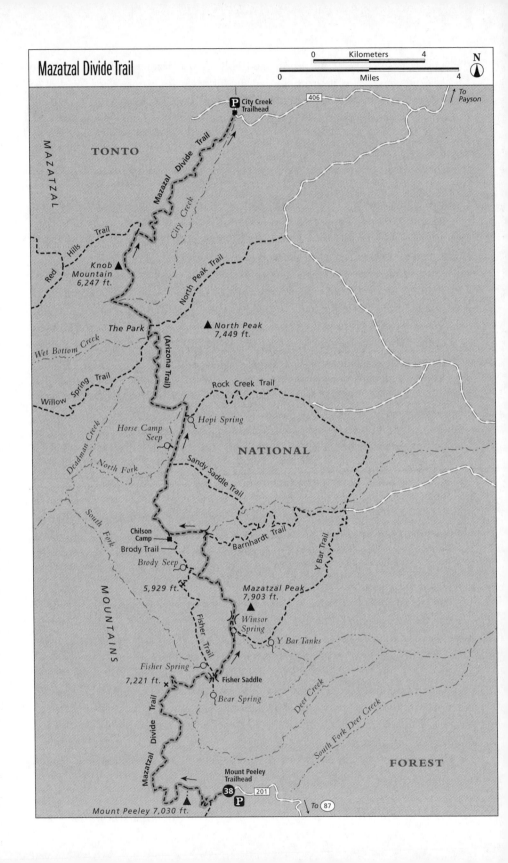

Mazatzal Divide Trail

0 Kilometers 4
0 Miles 4

N

To Payson

406

City Creek Trailhead

MAZATZAL

TONTO

Mazatzal Divide Trail

City Creek

Red Hills Trail

Knob Mountain 6,247 ft.

North Peak Trail

The Park

North Peak 7,449 ft.

(Arizona Trail)

Wet Bottom Creek

Willow Spring Trail

Deadman Creek

North Fork

Rock Creek Trail

Hopi Spring

Horse Camp Seep

NATIONAL

Sandy Saddle Trail

South Fork

Chilson Camp

Brody Trail

Barnhardt Trail

Y Bar Trail

Brody Seep

5,929 ft.

Mazatzal Peak 7,903 ft.

MOUNTAINS

Fisher Trail

Winsor Spring

Y Bar Tanks

Fisher Spring

7,221 ft.

Fisher Saddle

Bear Spring

Deer Creek

South Fork Deer Creek

Mazatzal Divide Trail

Mount Peeley Trailhead

38   201

To 87

FOREST

Mount Peeley 7,030 ft.

Option 3: If you want just a short taste of a less-used Mazatzal trail, turn left onto Brody Trail after contouring below Mazatzal Peak. The Brody Trail drops down a brushy ridge to the junction with Fisher Trail; turn right here. Then follow the description under Option 2 to reach Chilson Camp and Mazatzal Divide Trail. This option is 0.5 mile shorter than Mazatzal Divide Trail and adds 500 feet of elevation change. It'll take about the same amount of time as staying on Mazatzal Divide Trail.

The densely forested upper reaches of South Fork Deadman Creek were a mixed pine-fir forest before the Willow Fire. Most of the firs are Douglas fir, which is not a true fir. Douglas fir cones hang down, but the cones on true firs point straight up. White fir is mixed with the Douglas fir, and you can recognize it not only by its upright cones but also by its beautiful blue-green color. This graceful conifer is one of the prettiest trees in North America. There are also a few pockets of quaking aspen in this area, a deciduous tree that is the most widespread on the continent. In the Mazatzal Mountains, aspen is found only in the coolest, most favorable spots on north-facing slopes.

Miles and Directions

0.0 From the Mount Peeley Trailhead, hike west on Mazatzal Divide Trail.

0.4 Turn right to remain on Mazatzal Divide Trail.

6.9 Reach the high point of the hike.

8.3 Reach Fisher Saddle.

8.4 At the junction with Fisher Trail, stay right on Mazatzal Divide Trail.

9.8 Reach Windsor Saddle and the Y Bar Trail junction; stay left on Mazatzal Divide Trail.

11.4 At the junction with Brody Trail. stay right on Mazatzal Divide Trail.

12.6 Reach the Barnhardt Trail junction; stay left on Mazatzal Divide Trail.

13.5 At the Brody Trail junction, stay right on Mazatzal Divide Trail.

15.4 At the Sandy Saddle Trail junction, stay left on Mazatzal Divide Trail.

16.5 Reach Rock Creek Trail; stay left on Mazatzal Divide Trail.

19.6 Reach The Park and Willow Spring Trail; stay right on Mazatzal Divide Trail.

19.9 At the North Peak Trail junction, stay left on Mazatzal Divide Trail.

22.9 At the junction with Red Hills Trail, stay right on Mazatzal Divide Trail.

28.3 Arrive at City Creek Trailhead.

39 Deer Creek

This long loop day hike or backpack travels through several deep canyons in the eastern portion of the Mazatzal Wilderness, with several options for exploring the forks of Deer Creek.

Start: Deer Creek Trailhead
Distance: 16-mile loop
Hiking time: About 10 hours or 2 days
Difficulty: Strenuous due to distance and elevation change
Best seasons: Oct–Apr
Trail surface: Dirt trails, dirt roads
Land status: Tonto National Forest, Mazatzal Wilderness
Nearest town: Payson
Other users: Horses on trails; mountain bikes and vehicles on dirt road
Water availability: Seasonal in Deer Creek and at Maple and Pigeon Springs
Canine compatibility: Leashed dogs permitted
Fees and permits: None
Schedule: Year-round, 24 hours per day
Maps: USGS Mazatzal Peak AZ; National Geographic/Trails Illustrated Mazatzal and Pine Mountain Wilderness Areas map; USFS Mazatzal Wilderness map; Tonto National Forest map
Trail contact: Tonto Basin Ranger District, Tonto National Forest, 28079 N. AZ 188, Roosevelt, AZ 85545; (928) 467-3200; www .fs.usda.gov/tonto

Finding the trailhead: From Mesa, drive about 63 miles north on AZ 87. Turn left into the Deer Creek Trailhead, just south of the junction with AZ 188. GPS: N34 2.22' / W111 22.18'

The Hike

From the trailhead, start northwest on Deer Creek Trail (Forest Trail 45) as it climbs onto a low ridge. At the junctions with Gold Ridge Trail (which is the return route) and South Fork Trail, stay right on Deer Creek Trail.

Deer Creek Trail crosses South Fork Deer Creek, then swings into Deer Creek just upstream of a ranch (please respect the private land). Deer Creek Trail follows the creek west toward the mountains. Although the stream flow is seasonal, depending on recent rain and snow, the canyon bottom is always shady, graced by Arizona sycamores and other streamside trees. There are occasional small campsites along the canyon bottom.

When Deer Creek starts a turn to the southwest, Bars Canyon joins from the right. As you continue upstream along Deer Creek, the trail becomes fainter, but always stays near the bottom of the canyon. The appearance of the first ponderosa pines along the north-facing slopes signals that you're reaching the head of the canyon. After an unnamed tributary canyon comes in from the northwest, Deer Creek swings to the south briefly before resuming its southwesterly direction. You'll hike through a brushy meadow, then meet Davey Gowan Trail (FT 48).

Windmill in lower Deer Creek

Turn left and follow Davey Gowan Trail as it climbs east out of the canyon, then swings south onto a ridge and climbs to meet the Mount Peeley Road (FR 201) at 8.6 miles. This entire section was covered with a fine ponderosa pine and Douglas fir forest, but it was mostly burned in the Willow Fire.

Turn left onto the road, and hike east to a spur road branching left and downhill. Follow this road northeast to the start of Gold Ridge Trail (FT 47). The trail, an old jeep road, drops off the northwest side of the ridge, then swings east to follow the

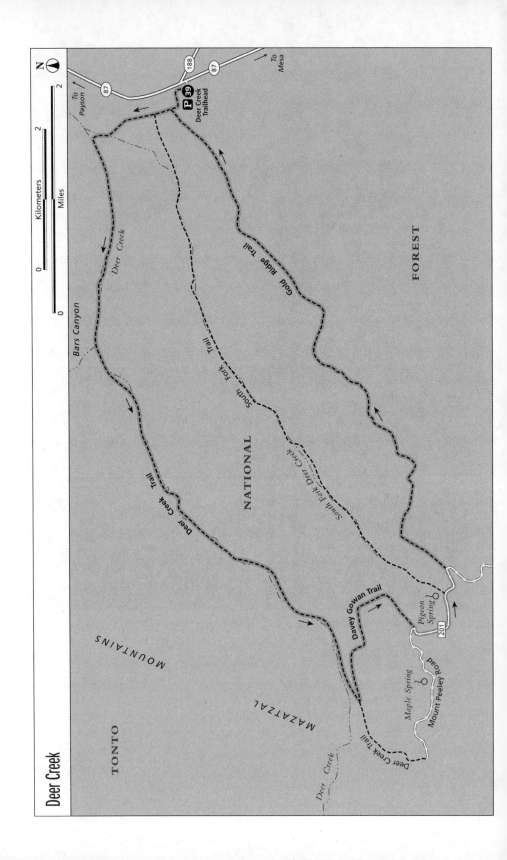

Deer Creek

general ridge system. You'll leave the pine forest behind as the trail descends onto lower, drier slopes. Watch for the point where the old jeep road veers north and Gold Ridge Trail becomes a foot trail, heading east for a short distance before turning northeast again. It descends a ridge that gives you great views to the northeast, then emerges onto gentler slopes covered with high desert grasses. Continue to Deer Creek Trail, then turn right to return to Deer Creek Trailhead.

Watch for mountain lion tracks along the dusty sections of the trail, especially early in the morning. The prints are larger than those of any dog, and a lack of claw marks confirms that the track was made by a large cat. Bobcat tracks are much smaller. The remote canyons of the Mazatzal Mountains are favored terrain for these large cats. Mountain lions, also known as cougars, require large amounts of territory remote from human influence. You may see their tracks, but you'll be very lucky to see the actual animal.

Bobcats are more common, though still rare. They occasionally jump in front of a vehicle on a dirt road and run for a few dozen yards before vanishing into the underbrush. In the backcountry, you'll be lucky to have a fleeting glimpse. Bobcats resemble a large house cat, except for their short "bobbed" tail.

Option: Instead of leaving Deer Creek on Davey Gowan Trail, stay right and follow Deer Creek Trail southwest as it climbs through the burnt remains of pine-fir forest to the Mount Peeley Trailhead. Turn left and walk the Mount Peeley Road east to Gold Ridge Trail. This option gets you into the head of Deer Creek, though it involves a little more road-walking. It adds 0.7 mile and less than an hour to the loop.

Miles and Directions

0.0 From the Deer Creek Trailhead, start on Deer Creek Trail.

0.3 Reach Gold Ridge Trail; stay right on Deer Creek Trail.

0.5 At the South Fork Trail junction, stay right on Deer Creek Trail.

1.1 Arrive at Deer Creek.

7.3 Turn left onto Davey Gowan Trail.

9.0 Turn left onto Mount Peeley Road.

9.7 Pass South Fork Trail; continue on Mount Peeley Road.

10.0 Turn left on spur road to Gold Ridge Trail.

10.1 Reach the start of Gold Ridge Trail.

15.7 Turn right onto Deer Creek Trail.

16.0 Arrive back at the Deer Creek Trailhead.

40 South Fork of Deer Creek

This hike features easy access into a deep canyon system at the southeast corner of the Mazatzal Wilderness. The trail starts in Sonoran Desert grassland and takes you through the chaparral and pinyon pine–juniper zone into lush pine-fir forest (though much of this forest was burned in the 2004 Willow Fire). Although the entire route makes for a long day hike, you can hike just a portion of the trail and turn back when ready, or do the trip as an overnight backpack. The South Fork is only a couple of miles shorter than the main fork of Deer Creek, and heads into equally interesting country.

Start: Deer Creek Trailhead
Distance: 12 miles out and back
Hiking time: About 8 hours or 2 days
Difficulty: Strenuous due to distance and elevation change
Best seasons: Oct–Apr
Trail surface: Dirt
Land status: Tonto National Forest, Mazatzal Wilderness
Nearest town: Payson
Other users: Horses

Water availability: Seasonal along South Fork Deer Creek and at Pigeon Spring
Canine compatibility: Leashed dogs permitted
Fees and permits: None
Schedule: Year-round, 24 hours per day
Maps: USGS Mazatzal Peak AZ; National Geographic/Trails Illustrated Mazatzal and Pine Mountain Wilderness Areas map; USFS Mazatzal Wilderness map; Tonto National Forest map
Trail contact: Tonto Basin Ranger District, Tonto National Forest, 28079 N. AZ188, Roosevelt, AZ 85545: (928) 467-3200; www.fs.usda.gov/tonto

Finding the trailhead: From Mesa, drive about 63 miles north on AZ 87. Turn left into the Deer Creek Trailhead, just south of the junction with AZ 188. GPS: N34 2.22' / W111 22.18'

The Hike

From the trailhead, start on Deer Creek Trail (Forest Trail 45). Hike past Gold Ridge Trail (FT 47), then turn left on South Fork Trail (FT 46). The trail soon drops into the streambed. At first, the South Fork is fairly open, but within a mile the canyon deepens. Arizona sycamores, cottonwoods, and other riparian (stream-loving) trees shade the trail as it follows the canyon southwest into the mountains. The creek itself may or may not be flowing, depending on recent weather.

As you progress farther up the canyon, the trail becomes fainter. About 4 miles from the trailhead, the first ponderosa pines appear on north-facing slopes, though the opposite canyon wall is still covered with chaparral, scattered juniper trees, and pinyon pines. Near the head of the canyon, the trail swings more to the south and climbs steeply. The South Fork Trail ends at the Mount Peeley Road. This is the turn-around point; retrace your steps to the trailhead.

Old stone cabin in Deer Creek

A few black bears are still found in the Mazatzal Mountains. Because they were hunted heavily for many years, the survivors are reclusive. You're more likely to see their tracks and their scat than the animal. Another sign of their presence is chewed-up trail signs.

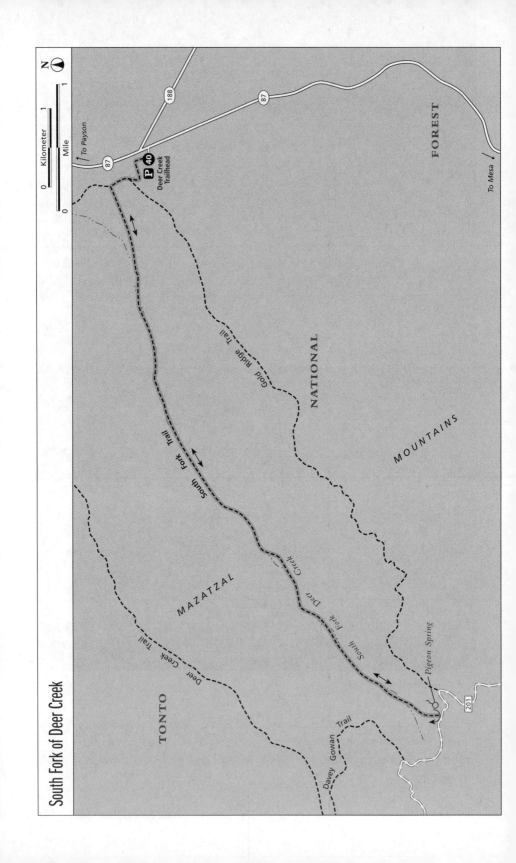

South Fork of Deer Creek

To Payson

87 188

87

P 40
Deer Creek Trailhead

FOREST

To Mesa

NATIONAL

MOUNTAINS

Gold Ridge Trail

South Fork Trail

MAZATZAL

Deer Creek

South Fork Deer Creek

Pigeon Spring

201

TONTO

Deer Creek Trail

Davey Gowan Trail

N

0   Kilometer   1
0   Mile   1

Miles and Directions

0.0   From the Deer Creek Trailhead, start on Deer Creek Trail.

0.3   At the Gold Ridge Trail junction, stay right on Deer Creek Trail.

0.5   Turn left onto South Fork Trail.

6.0   South Fork Trail ends at Mount Peeley Road (FR 201). Return the way you came.

12.0 Arrive back at the trailhead.

41 Y Bar Basin

This is a classic route around the range's highest peak and through a remarkable variety of terrain in the Mazatzal Wilderness; the trails are better maintained and easier to find than most of the trails in the wilderness. Part of the hike follows the Arizona Trail.

Start: Barnhardt Trailhead
Distance: 13.6-mile loop
Hiking time: About 10 hours or 2 days
Difficulty: Strenuous due to distance and elevation change
Best seasons: Oct–Apr
Trail surface: Dirt
Land status: Tonto National Forest, Mazatzal Wilderness
Nearest town: Payson
Other users: Horses
Water availability: Seasonal at Y Bar Tanks and Windsor Spring

Canine compatibility: Leashed dogs permitted
Fees and permits: None
Schedule: Year-round, 24 hours per day
Maps: USGS Mazatzal Peak AZ; National Geographic/Trails Illustrated Mazatzal and Pine Mountain Wilderness Areas map; USFS Mazatzal Wilderness map; Tonto National Forest map
Trail contacts: Payson Ranger District, Tonto National Forest, 1009 E. AZ 260, Payson, AZ 85541; (928) 474-7900; www.fs.usda.gov/tonto

Finding the trailhead: From Mesa, drive about 67 miles north on AZ 87, then turn left on the Barnhardt Road (FR 419). (This turnoff is just south of the Gisela turnoff.) Continue 5 miles to the trailhead, at the end of the maintained dirt road. GPS: N34 5.58' / W111 25.30'

The Hike

Start on Y Bar Trail and follow it up a series of broad switchbacks, climbing southwest onto a ridge covered with grass and pinyon–juniper woodland. As Y Bar Trail reaches the foot of the steeper slopes, it turns more to the south and climbs along the east slopes of Mazatzal Peak, crossing numerous small canyons. The trail crosses onto the west side of Shake Tree Canyon. Below and to the east, Shake Tree Canyon cuts through a spectacular area of cliffs and rock fins.

The trail continues up Shake Tree Canyon, crossing a pine-forested, northeast-facing slope, then works its way across the slopes west of the canyon's bed. The climb ends as the trail reaches Cactus Saddle, between Mazatzal Peak and Cactus Ridge. From the saddle, Y Bar Trail descends southwest, then levels out and contours across a small drainage. A small seep spring in this drainage sometimes has water. If not, follow the drainage downstream a hundred yards to Y Bar Tanks, a more reliable water source.

Beyond the seep, the trail contours westward, then turns northwest and climbs to Windsor Saddle. Windsor Spring, a small pool next to the trail about 0.1 mile south of the saddle, has water only in wet weather. There is a small campsite on the saddle.

Spring wildflowers along Y Bar Trail

Turn right onto Mazatzal Divide Trail (Arizona Trail), which heads north and contours along the west slopes of Mazatzal Peak. You'll have fine views of the rocky summit, as well as the head of South Fork Deadman Creek to the west. The

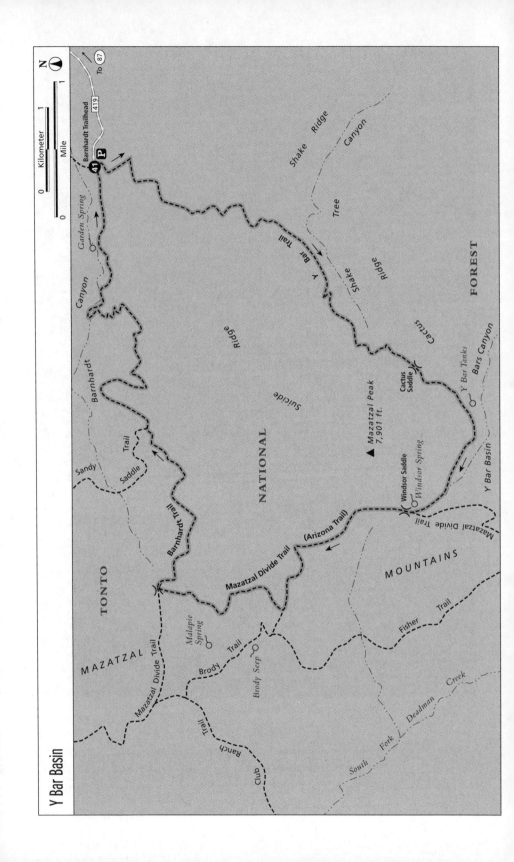

Y Bar Basin

well-constructed trail descends gradually northwest as it works its way around ridges and ravines. At Brody Trail (Brody Seep is 0.7 mile northwest), stay right on Mazatzal Divide Trail. You'll turn northward again and pass through several small stands of ponderosa pine as the trail contours to the saddle at the head of Barnhardt Canyon.

Turn right on Barnhardt Trail and follow it generally east. The trail traverses the south slopes of the broad basin at the head of Barnhardt Canyon, passing through chaparral and occasional stands of ponderosa pines. There are a few campsites along this section. At Sandy Saddle Trail, stay right on Barnhardt Trail. Casterson Seep, shown on the maps where the Sandy Saddle Trail crosses Barnhardt Creek, only flows during wet weather.

The trail swings around a ridge, where you can leave the trail momentarily and walk a few yards north to a viewpoint overlooking the impressive gorge of Barnhardt Canyon. The trail swings south beyond this point and crosses a drainage where there may be seasonal pools a few yards upstream from the trail. In cold weather the waterfall above the upper pool is often graced with a beautiful tapestry of icicles.

The trail descends eastward along the south slopes of Barnhardt Canyon, skirting some impressive cliffs. Note the bent and twisted layers of metamorphic rock—mute testimony to the incredible forces that created these mountains. The trail turns north and descends a steep ridge in a series of switchbacks until it is close to the canyon bottom, then heads east again and stays just above the bed all the way back to the Barnhardt Trailhead.

The twisted rocks so evident in Barnhardt Canyon are schist and quartzite, metamorphic rocks that were subjected to tremendous pressure and heat while still buried deep underground. Originally, these rocks were deposited as sediments in the form of shale and sandstone, but the forces associated with mountain-building completely changed their character. Imagine the amount of force required to make these hard rocks flow like toothpaste squeezed from a tube.

Miles and Directions

0.0 From the Barnhardt Trailhead, start on Y Bar Trail.

3.9 Cross Cactus Saddle.

4.2 Y Bar Tanks is 100 yards down the drainage.

5.5 Reach Windsor Saddle; turn right onto Mazatzal Divide Trail (Arizona Trail).

7.2 At the Brody Trail junction, stay right on Mazatzal Divide Trail.

8.4 Turn right onto Barnhardt Trail.

10.1 At the junction with Sandy Saddle Trail, stay right on Barnhardt Trail.

13.6 Arrive back at the Barnhardt Trailhead.

42 Mazatzal Peak

This hike takes you to the summit of Mazatzal Peak, the highest point in the Mazatzal Mountains.

Start: Barnhardt Trailhead
Distance: 8.2-mile loop
Hiking time: About 7 hours
Difficulty: Strenuous due to cross-country hiking, brush, and elevation change
Best seasons: Apr–May and Oct–Nov
Trail surface: Dirt trails, cross-country terrain
Land status: Tonto National Forest, Mazatzal Wilderness
Nearest town: Payson
Other users: Horses on the trails
Water availability: None

Canine compatibility: Leashed dogs permitted
Fees and permits: None
Schedule: Year-round, 24 hours per day
Maps: USGS Mazatzal Peak AZ; National Geographic/Trails Illustrated Mazatzal and Pine Mountain Wilderness Areas map; USFS Mazatzal Wilderness map, Tonto National Forest map
Trail contact: Payson Ranger District, Tonto National Forest, 1009 E. AZ 260, Payson, AZ 85541; (928) 474-7900; www.fs.usda.gov/tonto

Finding the trailhead: From Mesa, drive about 67 miles north on AZ 87, then turn left onto the Barnhardt Road (FR 419). (This turnoff is just south of the Gisela turnoff). Continue 5 miles to the trailhead at the end of the maintained dirt road. GPS: N34 5.58' / W111 25.30'

The Hike

You'll encounter some brush along the route up Mazatzal Peak, and should have the USGS Mazatzal Peak map and skill in cross-country route finding before attempting this hike.

Start on Y Bar Trail and follow it up a series of broad switchbacks, climbing southwest onto a ridge covered with grass and pinyon-juniper woodland. As Y Bar Trail reaches the foot of the steeper slopes, it turns more to the south and climbs along the east slopes of Mazatzal Peak, crossing numerous small canyons.

The trail crosses onto the west side of Shake Tree Canyon. Below and to the east, Shake Tree Canyon cuts through a spectacular area of cliffs and rock fins. The trail continues up Shake Tree Canyon, crossing a pine-forested, northeast-facing slope, then works its way across the slopes west of the canyon's bed. The climb ends as the trail reaches Cactus Saddle, between Mazatzal Peak and Cactus Ridge.

At Cactus Saddle, leave the trail and head west-northwest up the ridge, directly toward Barnhardt Peak. This ridge is moderately brushy, but the worst can be avoided by sticking to rock outcrops as much as possible. The Willow Fire helped clear the brush in 2004.

The steep climb moderates as you approach the summit of Mazatzal Peak. Views to the east are somewhat limited, but westward the view encompasses much of the

Descending the Barnhardt Trail

western slopes of the range. The steep west face of Mazatzal Peak drops dramatically into the headwaters of South Fork Deadman Creek.

The descent follows Suicide Ridge to the northeast. Walk a short distance east from the summit, but turn northeast before reaching the steeper slopes and cliffs near the ascent route. The idea is to stay on the crest of Suicide Ridge, which slopes gradually and runs parallel to the Y Bar Trail. Though the ridge is brushy, the crest is broad enough to allow you to avoid the worst of the brush. Near the end, the ridge drops steeply into Barnhardt Canyon. Be sure to stay far enough east to avoid the cliffs above the Barnhardt Trail west of Garden Spring. You should reach Barnhardt Trail just west of Barnhardt Trailhead. Once on the trail, turn right to return to your vehicle.

The rocky slopes of the Mazatzal Mountains are home to Mojave rattlesnakes, which occur in a variety of colors, depending on their habitat. Their venom is one of most dangerous of all rattlesnake venoms, but fortunately Mojaves are very assertive and won't hesitate to warn you with a strident rattle if you encroach on their territory. They sometimes rattle at you from more than a hundred feet away. Rattlesnakes don't range very far during their hunt for mice and other small rodents, so if you encounter one in an area, you may see the same snake again if you return at a later

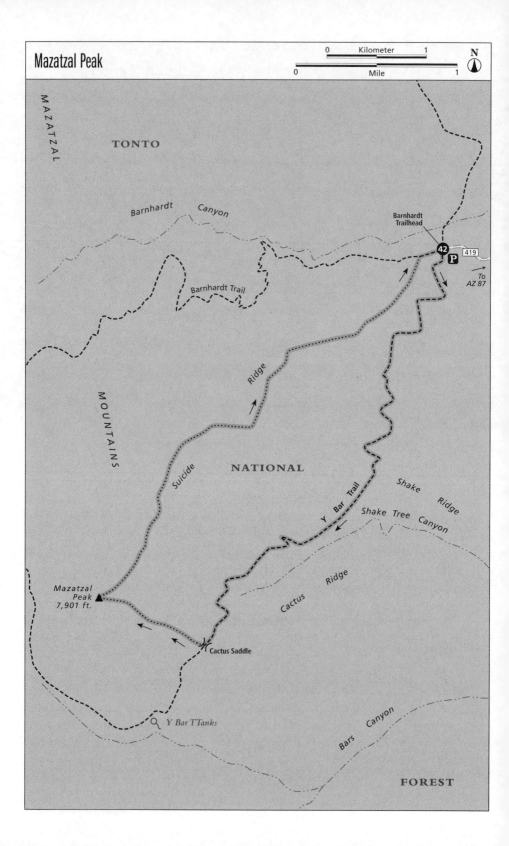

Mazatzal Peak

MAZATZAL

TONTO

Barnhardt Canyon

Barnhardt Trailhead

42 419

To AZ 87

Barnhardt Trail

MOUNTAINS

Ridge

Suicide

NATIONAL

Y Bar Trail

Shake Ridge

Shake Tree Canyon

Mazatzal Peak 7,901 ft.

Cactus Ridge

Cactus Saddle

Y Bar T Tanks

Bars Canyon

FOREST

0   Kilometer   1

0   Mile   1

N

time. You can avoid unpleasant rattlesnake encounters by always watching where you place your hands and feet, and by being aware of likely locations for snakes.

Option: From the summit of Mazatzal Peak, you can return the way you came if you want less cross-country hiking.

Miles and Directions

0.0 From the Barnhardt Trailhead, start on Y Bar Trail.

3.9 Reach Cactus Saddle. Head cross-country to the northwest, directly toward Mazatzal Peak.

4.7 Reach the summit of Mazatzal Peak. To descend, head northwest down Suicide Ridge.

7.9 Turn right onto Barnhardt Trail.

8.2 Arrive back at the Barnhardt Trailhead.

43 Rock Creek

This scenic loop uses two of the most spectacular trails in the Mazatzal Mountains to take you through an excellent variety of terrain. Part of the hike follows the Arizona Trail near the crest of the range.

Start: Barnhardt Trailhead
Distance: 16.3-mile loop
Hiking time: About 10 hours or 2 days
Difficulty: Strenuous due to distance and elevation change
Best seasons: Oct–Nov, Apr–May
Trail surface: Dirt
Water availability: Seasonal at Chilson Spring, Horse Camp Seep, Hopi Spring, and in Rock Creek
Other users: Horses
Canine compatibility: Leashed dogs permitted
Land status: Tonto National Forest, Mazatzal Wilderness

Nearest town: Payson
Fees and permits: None
Schedule: Year-round, 24 hours per day
Maps: USGS Mazatzal Peak AZ and North Peak AZ; National Geographic/Trails Illustrated Mazatzal and Pine Mountain Wilderness Areas map; USFS Mazatzal Wilderness map; Tonto National Forest map
Trail contact: Payson Ranger District, Tonto National Forest, 1009 E. AZ 260, Payson, AZ 85541; (928) 474-7900; www.fs.usda.gov/tonto

Finding the trailhead: From Mesa, drive about 67 miles north on AZ 87, then turn left onto the Barnhardt Road (FR 419). (This turnoff is just south of the Gisela turnoff.) Continue 5 miles to the Barnhardt Trailhead at the end of the maintained dirt road. GPS: N34 5.58' / W111 25.30'

The Hike

Start off by hiking west on Barnhardt Trail. This well-constructed, popular trail climbs gradually into lower Barnhardt Canyon, then switchbacks south up a steep ridge, away from the canyon bottom. The trail then swings westward, working its way up through several cliffs.

Beyond the cliffs, the trail crosses a small, rocky drainage, which sometimes hosts pools of water just above the trail, and occasionally flowing water. The trail then swings around a ridge into the brushy basin at the headwaters of Barnhardt Canyon—walk north a few yards from the ridge for a great view of upper Barnhardt Canyon.

At Sandy Saddle Trail, stay left and continue on Barnhardt Trail as it climbs gradually around the basin. At the saddle at the head of Barnhardt Canyon, turn right on Mazatzal Divide Trail (Arizona Trail), and follow the divide trail west across an open, grassy slope. The trail passes above a meadow in the pygmy forest of pinyon pines and junipers and meets the Brody Trail. You can go left here and walk about 0.1 mile to Chilson Camp, a historic line camp used by cowboys. The old cabin is long gone,

Pools at Horse Camp Seep

and Chilson Spring, which used to supply the camp, is no longer reliable, but it's still a scenic spot.

Back on Mazatzal Divide Trail, continue north as the trail climbs gradually along the west-facing slopes at the head of North Fork Deadman Creek. At the second junction with Sandy Saddle Trail, stay left on Mazatzal Divide Trail. A bit farther on, a

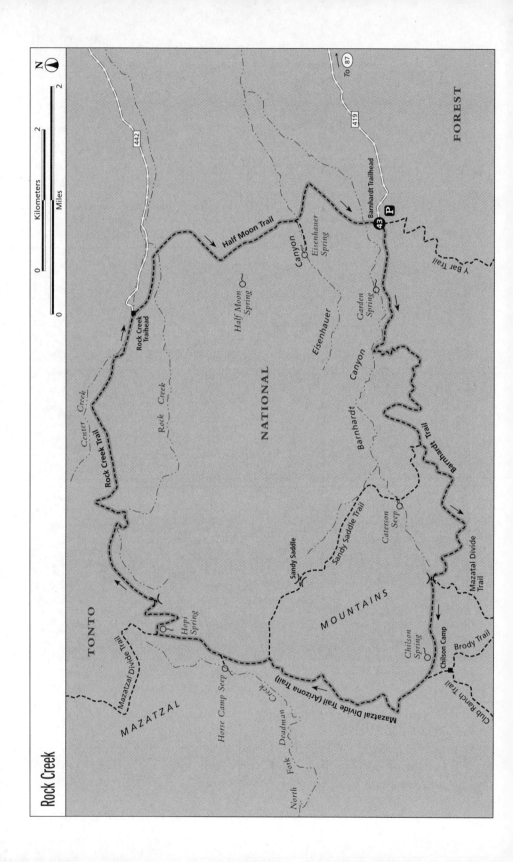

Rock Creek

spur trail heads left to Horse Camp Seep, a seasonal water source with some excellent campsites. You may also find water in stone tanks in the bedrock nearby.

Mazatzal Divide Trail climbs more steeply to reach Hopi Spring. Turn right onto Rock Creek Trail. The Rock Creek Trail climbs east in a series of switchbacks, finally reaching a pass on the crest of the range and the highest point of the hike. You can take a break and enjoy great views of much of the northern Mazatzal Mountains at this point.

From the pass the trail descends northeast, staying above the canyon bottom. Just when the cliffs begin to hem in the route, the trail abruptly turns east, then south, and descends a steep ridge into Rock Creek. There are often pools in this section of the creek, and during the spring snowmelt delightful cascades fill the canyon. The trail follows the creek a short distance, then crosses it again and heads down the steep, rocky slopes north of the creek. An impressive amount of trail construction was done here to get through several cliffs, and, of course, you have expansive views to the east. The trail emerges onto less steep but brushy slopes and descends a long ridge into Center Creek. Follow the trail a short distance east to the Rock Creek Trailhead.

At the trailhead, turn right onto Half Moon Trail, which is not shown on the USGS maps but is shown on the USFS wilderness map. The trail contours onto a ridge, then follows the ridge east before turning south to cross Rock Creek. It crosses a flat, then turns southwest and climbs gradually toward Half Moon Spring. Before reaching the spring (a spur trail continues to the spring), the trail turns southeast and contours the base of the brushy hills. It crosses Eisenhauer Canyon, then swings around a ridge into Barnhardt Canyon. A short climb brings you to Barnhardt Trailhead.

New Mexico locust, a member of the pea family, is common along Mazatzal Divide Trail. This plant has very sharp spines that are about 0.5 to 1 inch long, and it tends to overgrow the trail. As compensation, it often puts on a fine spring display of pale pink to rose-colored flowers in droopy clusters. Native Americans ate the flowers, and quail and squirrels love the seeds. New Mexico locust is also a favorite browse plant for mule deer and domestic cattle.

Option: You can use the seldom-traveled Sandy Saddle Trail as an optional way to reach the Mazatzal Divide Trail, bypassing the Chilson Camp area. This route is 1.3 miles shorter.

Miles and Directions

0.0   From the Barnhardt Trailhead, start on Barnhardt Trail.

3.3   At the junction with Sandy Saddle Trail, stay left on Barnhardt Trail.

5.0   Turn right onto Mazatzal Divide Trail (Arizona Trail).

6.0   At the Brody Trail junction, stay right on Mazatzal Divide Trail.

7.8   Reach the second junction with Sandy Saddle Trail; stay left on Mazatzal Divide Trail.

9.0   Turn right onto Rock Creek Trail.

9.6   Pass the highest point of the hike.

13.0   Reach the Rock Creek Trailhead; turn right onto Half Moon Trail.

16.3   Arrive back at Barnhardt Trailhead.

44 North Peak

This strenuous but rewarding hike takes you to the top of seldom-climbed North Peak, the aptly named northernmost summit of the Mazatzal Mountains. Your reward for all the hard work is a panoramic view of the northern Mazatzal Mountains and the Mogollon Rim.

Start: Mineral Creek Trailhead
Distance: 7.2 miles out and back
Hiking time: About 6 hours
Difficulty: Strenuous due to elevation change and cross-country travel
Best seasons: Oct–Apr
Trail surface: Dirt trails, cross-country terrain
Land status: Tonto National Forest, Mazatzal Wilderness
Nearest town: Payson
Other users: Horses on trails
Water availability: Seasonal at Mineral Spring
Canine compatibility: Leashed dogs permitted

Fees and permits: None
Schedule: Year-round, 24 hours per day
Maps: USGS Mazatzal Peak AZ and North Peak AZ; National Geographic/Trails Illustrated Mazatzal and Pine Mountain Wilderness Areas map; USFS Mazatzal Wilderness map; Tonto National Forest map
Trail contact: Payson Ranger District, Tonto National Forest, 1009 E. AZ 260, Payson, AZ 85541; (928) 474-7900; www.fs.usda.gov/tonto

Finding the trailhead: From AZ 87 in Payson, drive west on Main Street. Stay on the main road past a golf course, where the pavement ends and the road becomes FR 406. About 5.2 miles from AZ 87, turn left onto FR 414 and go another 5.2 miles. Turn right and continue 0.1 mile to the Mineral Creek Trailhead. GPS: N34 10.69' / W111 26.87'

The Hike

North Peak Trail initially follows an old, closed road up Mineral Creek. When the old road ends, the trail turns south and starts a steep, sustained climb up chaparral-covered slopes. After passing Mineral Spring, the trail reaches a steep ridge and turns west. The climb moderates as the ridge turns southwest and then comes out onto gentler slopes covered with a mix of pinyon pine, juniper, and ponderosa pine.

Just as the mountainside becomes steeper, leave the trail and climb cross-country directly up the shallow ridge to the southeast, toward the summit of North Peak. A bit of oak brush is easily avoided, and the ridge leads directly to the rounded summit. From the top, you can see the northern Mazatzal Mountains and much of the western Mogollon Rim, which forms the skyline to the north and northeast.

The Mogollon Rim is a major physiographic boundary that runs more than 200 miles across Arizona. It separates the Colorado Plateau to the north from the basin-and-range province to the south. In the basin and range, mountain ranges that trend north–south are separated by intervening valleys. The Mazatzal Mountains, bounded

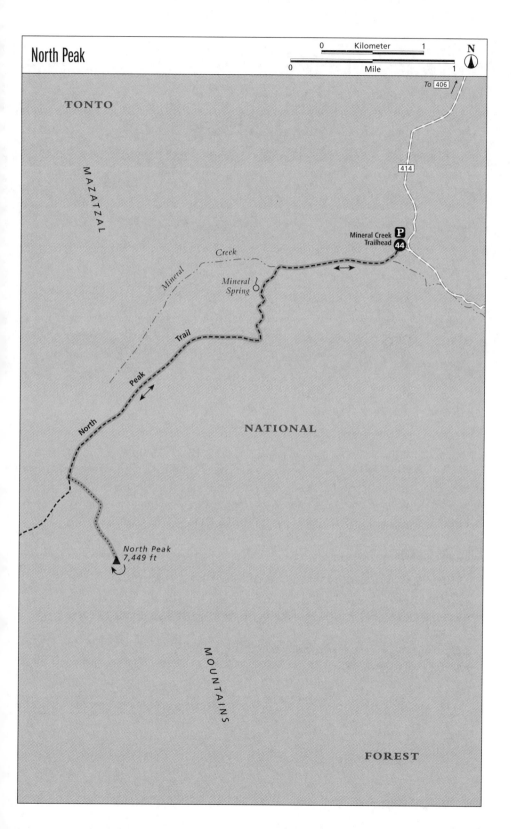

North Peak

TONTO

MAZATZAL

To 406

414

Mineral Creek Trailhead P 44

Mineral *Creek*

Mineral Spring

Trail

Peak

North

NATIONAL

North Peak 7,449 ft

MOUNTAINS

FOREST

Kilometer

Mile

N

An aerial view of the south ridge of North Peak five years after the Willow Fire burned most of the Mazatzal high country. Brush and grass have already returned.

on the west by the Verde River valley and the New River Mountains, and on the east by Tonto Basin and the Sierra Ancha, is a classic example. As mountain-building stresses acted on the region, faults formed and large blocks of bedrock were lifted upward to form the mountains. Other blocks dropped to form the valleys. In Arizona, all of the basin-and-range country is part of the Colorado River drainage.

Miles and Directions

0.0 From the Mineral Creek Trailhead, hike south and west on North Peak Trail.

1.0 Pass Mineral Spring.

3.0 Leave the trail and hike cross-country to the southeast, up the ridge, directly toward the summit.

3.6 Arrive on the summit of North Peak. Return the way you came.

7.2 Arrive back at the trailhead.

45 Knob Mountain Loop

This fine backpacking loop takes you on a section of Mazatzal Divide Trail, across the pine-forested slopes of Knob Mountain at the north end of the Mazatzal Mountains, along a portion of the Arizona Trail, and through a scenic canyon on the East Verde River.

Start: City Creek Trailhead
Distance: 18.9-mile loop
Hiking time: About 2 to 3 days
Difficulty: Strenuous due to distance, elevation change, and cross-country hiking
Best seasons: Oct–Apr
Trail surface: Dirt trails, dirt roads, cross-country terrain
Land status: Tonto National Forest, Mazatzal Wilderness
Nearest town: Payson
Other users: Horses on trails, vehicles and mountain bikes on roads
Water availability: East Verde River; seasonal

at Brush Spring and Bullfrog Spring
Canine compatibility: Leashed dogs permitted
Fees and permits: None
Schedule: Year-round, 24 hours per day
Maps: USGS North Peak AZ and Cypress Butte AZ; National Geographic/Trails Illustrated Mazatzal and Pine Mountain Wilderness Areas map; USFS Mazatzal Wilderness map; Tonto National Forest map
Trail contact: Payson Ranger District, Tonto National Forest, 1009 E. AZ 260, Payson, AZ 85541: (928) 474-7900; www.fs.usda.gov/tonto

Finding the trailhead: From AZ 87 in Payson, drive west on Main Street. Stay on the main road past a golf course, where the pavement ends and the road becomes FR 406. Continue 10 miles to the City Creek Trailhead. (If you reach the Doll Baby Ranch, you've gone 0.3 mile too far.) GPS: N34 13.06' / W111 27.92'

The Hike

Start the loop by hiking the well-graded Mazatzal Divide Trail, which climbs steadily southwest along City Creek. When the trail reaches the northeast ridge of Knob Mountain, turn right onto Red Hills Trail. (This trail is shown correctly on the USFS Mazatzal Wilderness map but incorrectly on the USGS maps.) The trail drops into a beautiful pine-forested drainage at the head of Boardinghouse Canyon, follows it west, then climbs up another tributary on the west end of Knob Mountain.

Turn right onto Brush Trail, which wanders northwest across gentle terrain before dropping down to a saddle and turning north into the head of Houston Creek. Brush Spring is just off the trail in one of the unnamed tributaries of Houston Creek, and there is a large campsite there.

Brush Trail continues north through a mix of chaparral, pinyon pines, and juniper trees.

Pockets of ponderosa pine survived the Willow Fire in this aerial view of the Knob Mountain area, creating a mosaic of forest, chaparral brush, and grassland that is especially favorable to wildlife.

At the head of Houston Creek, Brush Trail swings west, crosses a saddle, then drops into the head of Bullfrog Canyon. Turn right on Bull Spring Trail just before a saddle, and follow the trail down into Bullfrog Canyon. The trail, an old mining road, drops steeply northeast down the brushy slopes and finally comes out onto gentler terrain. The trail turns east and crosses a saddle just south of Copper Mountain before ending at FR 406.

Cross the road and walk cross-country to the east, to the East Verde River. Follow the river upstream. The East Verde is usually a small stream, but can run high during snowmelt or after wet weather. If the river is running too high to safely walk along the banks, then follow FR 406 back to the City Creek Trailhead.

After hiking through a short but narrow canyon, you emerge into an open valley and meet FR 406 again at the wilderness boundary and the Doll Baby Trailhead. Walk east on the forest road to return the City Creek Trailhead.

The pine-oak forest on the upper slopes of Knob Mountain is dominated by two trees, the tall ponderosa pine and the much smaller Gambel oak. These deciduous oaks usually grow about 10 to 20 feet tall, with slender trunks, and they tend to form dense clumps, which provide cover for wildlife. Deer feed on the leaves and shoots, and Native Americans ground the acorns into a meal. After leaching out the bitter tannin, the meal was made into mush, soup, and pancakes.

Other oaks found in the ponderosa forest include the massive Emory oak and Arizona white oak. Both grow to be large, spreading trees. They are both evergreen,

Knob Mountain Loop

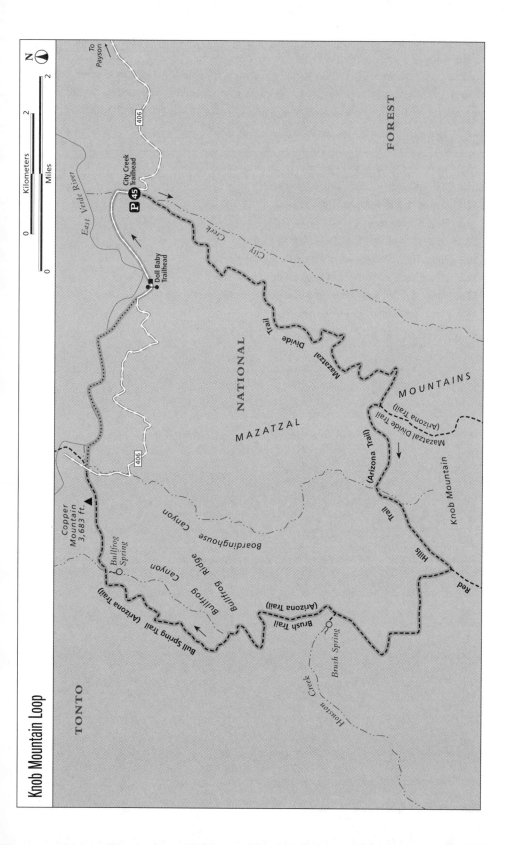

in that dropped leaves are quickly replaced. The alligator juniper is unmistakable. Its scored, gray bark strongly resembles alligator hide. It too is a massive tree, often more than 4 feet in diameter at the base. Alligator juniper is very resistant to wildfire—often parts of the tree will be scarred from old fires while the remainder lives on.

Miles and Directions

0.0 From the City Creek Trailhead, start on Mazatzal Divide Trail.

5.4 Turn right onto Red Hills Trail (Arizona Trail).

7.7 Turn right onto Brush Trail (Arizona Trail).

9.9 Pass Brush Spring.

12.1 Turn right onto Bull Spring Trail (Arizona Trail).

15.1 Cross FR 406 and descend east to the East Verde River.

15.5 At the East Verde River, turn right and head upstream.

17.6 Reach the Doll Baby Trailhead; follow FR 406 east.

18.9 Arrive back at the City Creek Trailhead.

46 White Rock Spring

The Mazatzal Wilderness extends north of the Mazatzal Mountains to include the lower portion of the East Verde River and the mesa country north of the river. This long day hike or backpack takes you along a portion of the Arizona Trail to a small spring located on the rim of one of these mesas and involves less elevation change than most trails in the wilderness.

Start: Doll Baby Trailhead
Distance: 15.8 miles out and back
Hiking time: About 10 hours or 2 days
Difficulty: Strenuous due to distance and elevation gain
Best seasons: Oct–Apr
Trail surface: Dirt trails, dirt roads
Land status: Tonto National Forest, Mazatzal Wilderness
Nearest town: Payson
Other users: Horses on trails, vehicles and mountain bikes on roads

Water availability: East Verde River, seasonal at White Rock Spring
Canine compatibility: Leashed dogs permitted
Fees and permits: None
Schedule: Year-round, 24 hours per day
Maps: USGS North Peak AZ, Cypress Butte AZ, Cane Springs Mountain AZ; National Geographic/Trails Illustrated Mazatzal and Pine Mountain Wilderness Areas map; USFS Mazatzal Wilderness map; Tonto National Forest map
Trail contact: Payson Ranger District, Tonto National Forest, 1009 E. AZ 260, Payson, AZ 85541; (928) 474-7900; www.fs.usda.gov/tonto

Finding the trailhead: From AZ 87 in Payson, drive west on Main Street. Stay on the main road past a golf course, where the pavement ends and the road becomes FR 406. Continue 11.4 miles to the Doll Baby Trailhead at the wilderness boundary. GPS: N34 12.88' / W111 28.86'

The Hike

From the Doll Baby Trailhead, continue beyond the locked gate on FR 406 (this portion of the road lies within the wilderness and is open by permit for access to private land). The road switchbacks a couple of times to gain the top of a ridge just south of the East Verde River gorge, then descends west into Boardinghouse Canyon.

The trail turns north and goes to LF Ranch. At Bull Spring Trailhead, turn right onto Saddle Ridge Trail, which is also the Arizona Trail. The trail skirts the ranch on the east, then crosses the East Verde River.

On the north side of the river, the trail crosses Rock Creek. After passing the short spur trail to Polk Spring, Saddle Ridge Trail climbs onto the southern tip of Polles Mesa, west of Rock Creek. The trail wanders north through pinyon-juniper forest across the volcanic mesa. You'll pass Red Saddle Tank in a meadow. The trail continues north to the foot of a low rim, then turns east along its base and passes White Rock Spring. The trail then climbs to the edge of the rim, east of the spring. This spot

The East Verde River divides the northern Mazatzal Mountains from the volcanic mesas at the north end of the Mazatzal Wilderness.

on the edge of White Rock Mesa is the goal and turnaround point, because it offers good views of Polles Mesa and the north end of the Mazatzal Mountains. Those who are backpacking can find several scenic campsites along the rim.

In contrast to the fault-block mountains that make up most of the Mazatzal Wilderness, the northern section of the wilderness consists of broad mesas cut by a few deep canyons. These mesas slope southward from the Mogollon Rim. Their surface is mostly formed of volcanic basalt rocks, the remnants of massive lava flows that covered the area. An open pinyon pine–juniper forest covers the mesas, tending to become thicker at higher elevations to the north.

Option 1: Instead of hiking the road from the trailhead, you can follow the East Verde River downstream 2.2 miles to Saddle Ridge Trail. This option is 1.1 miles shorter than the road, but the cross-country hike down the river may not be passable in spring or at other times when the river is high.

Option 2: An option for a shorter day hike is to walk the river to Saddle Ridge Trail, then return on the road. This is an easy 5.5-mile loop, with just 600 feet of elevation change. The East Verde River is an easy cross-country walk if the river is low, and you'll hike through a small but pretty canyon.

Miles and Directions

0.0 From the Doll Baby Trailhead, hike west on FR 406.

3.5 Turn right onto Saddle Ridge Trail (Arizona Trail).

4.0 Cross East Verde River.

4.5 Pass Polk Spring.

7.4 Pass White Rock Spring.

7.9 Reach the rim of White Rock Mesa. Return the way you came.

15.8 Arrive back at the trailhead.

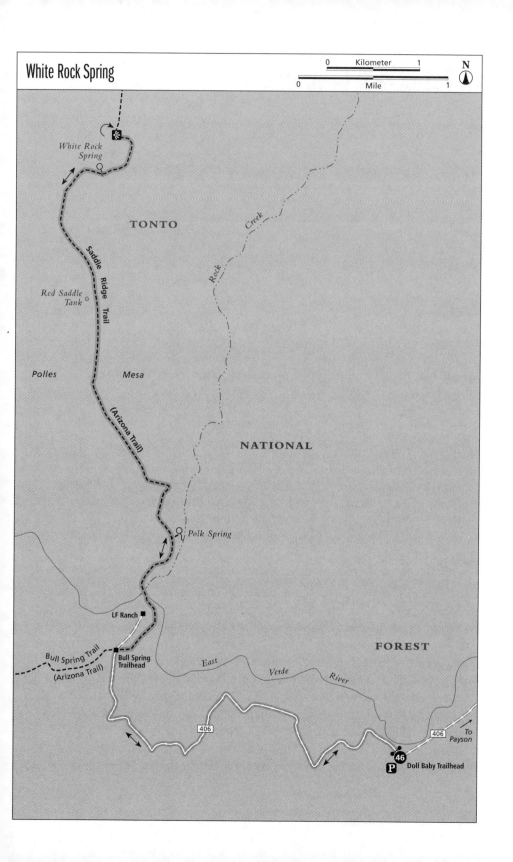

0   Kilometer   1

0   Mile   1

N

White Rock Spring

TONTO

Rock   Creek

Saddle Ridge Trail

Red Saddle Tank

Polles   Mesa

(Arizona Trail)

NATIONAL

Polk Spring

LF Ranch

FOREST

Bull Spring Trail

Bull Spring Trailhead

(Arizona Trail)

East   Verde   River

406

406

To Payson

46

P   Doll Baby Trailhead

47 East Verde Confluence

This trek uses a seldom-hiked trail through remote country to reach the confluence of the East Verde and Verde Rivers. The section of the Verde River at the end of this hike is part of Arizona's only federally designated Wild and Scenic River, and it's one of the last free-flowing rivers left in the state. It flows through a beautiful sampling of the Sonoran Desert.

Start: Deadman Trailhead
Distance: 13.2 miles out and back
Hiking time: About 9 hours
Difficulty: Strenuous due to distance, elevation change, and faint trails
Best seasons: Oct–Apr
Trail surface: Dirt trails
Land status: Tonto National Forest, Mazatzal Wilderness
Nearest town: Payson
Other users: Horses

Water availability: Fossil Creek, East Verde, and Verde Rivers
Canine compatibility: Leashed dogs permitted
Fees and permits: None
Schedule: Year-round, 24 hours per day
Maps: USGS Verde Hot Springs AZ; National Geographic/Trails Illustrated Mazatzal and Pine Mountain Wilderness Areas map; USFS Mazatzal Wilderness map; Tonto National Forest map
Trail contact: Payson Ranger District, Tonto National Forest, 1009 E. AZ 260, Payson, AZ 85541; (928) 474-7900; www.fs.usda.gov/tonto

Finding the trailhead: From Payson, drive 19 miles north on AZ 87 to Strawberry, then turn left onto Fossil Creek Road at Strawberry Lodge. This road continues west through the village and becomes FR 708. Go 5 miles, then turn left on FR 591. Go 5.6 miles to the Deadman Trailhead, near Deadman Tank at the end of the road. This road is impassable in wet weather and may require four-wheel drive at any time. GPS: N34 21.89' / W111 38.82'

The Hike

The Deadmans Mesa Trail heads south across the broad tip of Deadman Mesa, passing through open pinyon pine–juniper forest. At the southern rim of Deadman Mesa, the trail drops steeply down a ridge. Just before the end of the ridge, the trail veers west and drops into Fossil Creek.

Continue on Deadman Mesa Trail down Fossil Creek past the confluence with Hardscrabble Creek. Before Fossil Creek meets the Verde River, the trail crosses the creek and climbs southwest. The trail is obvious where it climbs away from the creek, but becomes faint on the open, grassy slopes above. If you lose it, just head cross-country uphill toward the pass, where you'll intercept Verde River Trail.

Turn right onto Verde River Trail and follow it south over a ridge to the Verde River. The confluence of the East Verde and Verde Rivers, the destination for the hike,

Solo camp in a grassy meadow, Mazatzal Wilderness

is just to the south. This section of the Verde River Trail is frequently destroyed by floods—just pick the least brushy route.

The Verde and East Verde Rivers are rare examples of permanent Arizona streams. Most stream courses in this region are dry much of the time. The few permanent streams provide a riparian habitat that is home to plants and animals that are

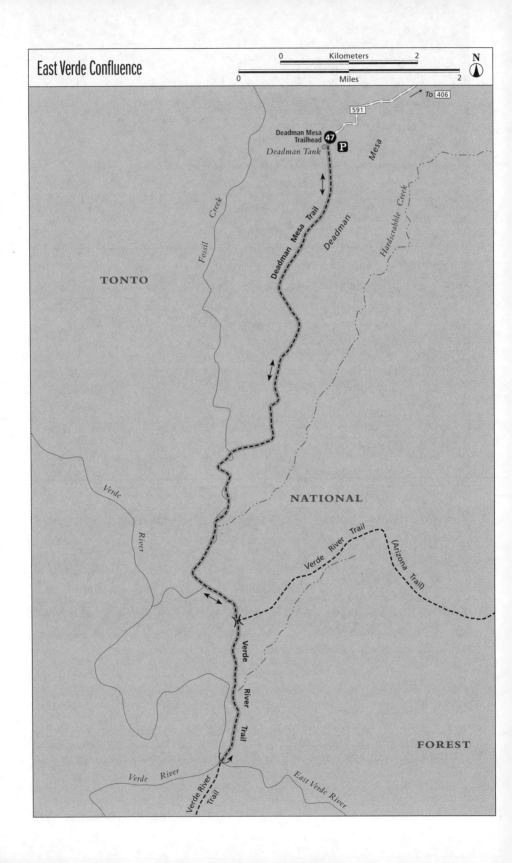

completely dependent on it. Water-loving trees such as Fremont cottonwood, Arizona walnut, Arizona ash, and Arizona sycamore grow only along streams where water is on or near the surface.

Miles and Directions

0.0 From Deadman Mesa Trailhead, start on Deadman Mesa Trail.

1.9 Reach the rim of Deadman Mesa.

3.4 Arrive at Fossil Creek; follow the trail left (downstream).

5.3 Turn right onto Verde River Trail.

5.9 Reach the Verde River.

6.6 Arrive at the confluence with East Verde River. Return the way you came.

13.2 Arrive back at the trailhead.

48 Red Creek

Red Creek is a tributary of the Verde River featuring a perennial stream and easy hiking. Since it's outside the wilderness, you may encounter off-road vehicles on the weekends. During the week it's a very pleasant hike.

Start: 2.3 miles north of FR 269 on FR 18
Distance: 8 miles out and back
Hiking time: About 5 hours
Difficulty: Easy
Best seasons: Oct–Apr
Trail surface: Two-track road
Land status: Tonto National Forest
Nearest town: Carefree
Other users: Horses, motor vehicles, mountain bikes
Water availability: Red Creek, Verde River

Canine compatibility: Leashed dogs permitted
Fees and permits: None
Schedule: Year-round, 24 hours per day
Maps: USGS Bloody Basin AZ and Wet Bottom Mesa AZ; USFS Mazatzal Wilderness map; Tonto National Forest map
Trail contact: Cave Creek Ranger District, Tonto National Forest, 40202 N. Cave Creek Rd., Scottsdale, AZ 85262; (480) 595-3300; www .fs.usda.gov/tonto

Finding the trailhead: From the junction of Cave Creek Road and Scottsdale Road in Carefree, drive 35 miles northeast on Cave Creek Road; after the pavement ends, it becomes FR 24, a maintained dirt road. Turn right onto FR 269, go 2.8 miles, then turn left onto FR 18, an unmaintained road that is passable for most vehicles. Continue 2.3 miles to the top of the final, steep descent into Red Creek. GPS: N34 9.97' / W111 46.11'

Another way to reach the junction of FR 24 and 269 is to exit I-17 at the Bloody Basin interchange, just south of Cordes Junction. Go east on Bloody Basin Road, which becomes FR 269 at the national forest boundary. You'll reach the FR 24 junction 25 miles from I-17. Bloody Basin Road fords the Agua Fria River, which may be impassable when the river is high from snowmelt or after a storm.

The Hike

Walk down the steep, rough jeep road into Red Creek, then turn right and walk downstream. Although this non-wilderness canyon is sometimes used as a four-wheel-drive route to the Verde River, the route lies in the streambed for much of the way, and tracks soon wash out. Except on busy weekends, following Red Creek makes for an enjoyable and easy hike, and the creek flows year-round.

The canyon soon narrows and winds between reddish rock walls. A jeep road crosses the alluvial flat south of the creek—you can either walk the road across this pleasant flat or stay in the creekbed. The canyon walls close in a bit beyond the flat, and the creek makes its way around several sharp bends before emerging from the canyon a final time.

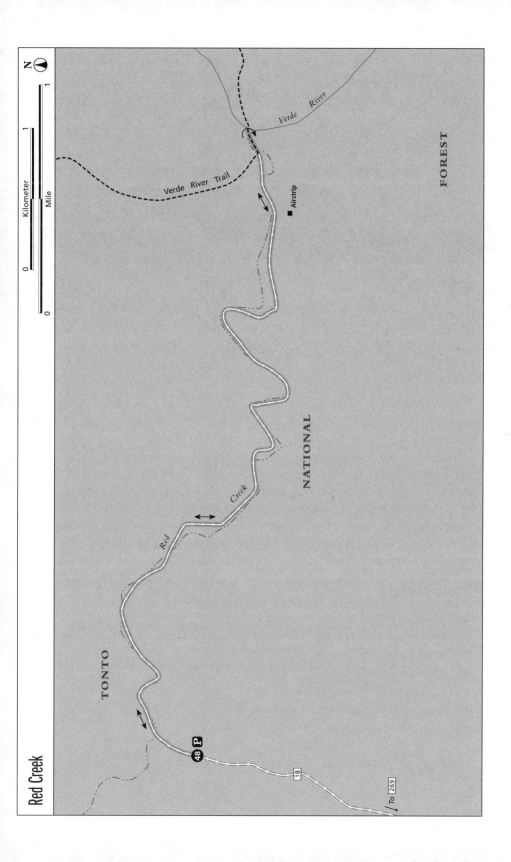

Red Creek

Both rare and protected, Gila monsters appear to be sluggish, but they will move fast and bite if disturbed.

Where Red Creek meets Verde River Trail, turn right and follow the trail a short distance to the low-water ford where the Verde River Trail crosses the river. This is the turnaround.

Options: You can do a longer hike by exploring either up- or downstream on the Verde River Trail. The Wet Bottom Trail can be reached from a junction a short distance south on the Verde River Trail. Another possibility is to hike cross-country up Wet Bottom Creek from the point where the Verde River Trail crosses it.

Use caution if you plan to cross the Verde River. During low water, fording is easy, but after storms or during spring snowmelt the river may be running too high to cross.

Miles and Directions

0.0 Walk down to Red Creek from the trailhead.

0.2 Turn right and follow Red Creek downstream.

0.8 Reach the end of the narrows.

3.1 Reach the end of the canyon.

3.9 Turn right (east) on Verde River Trail.

4.0 Reach the Verde River. Return the way you came.

8.0 Arrive back at the trailhead.

49 Verde River Trail

This unique and historic trail follows the Verde River along the west side of the Mazatzal Wilderness, and was originally built by shepherds to move their stock from winter pastures in the desert north of Scottsdale to summer pastures high on the Mogollon Rim north of Payson.

Start: Twin Buttes Trailhead
Distance: 29.3 miles point to point with shuttle
Hiking time: About 4 days
Difficulty: Strenuous due to distance and elevation gain
Best seasons: Oct–Apr
Trail surface: Dirt
Land status: Tonto National Forest, Mazatzal Wilderness
Nearest towns: Carefree, Payson
Other users: Horses
Water availability: Verde River; seasonal in lower Wet Bottom Creek. There is no water along the trail from Twin Buttes Trailhead to the river, and portions of the southern third of the trail are often a mile or more from the river.

Canine compatibility: Leashed dogs permitted
Fees and permits: None
Schedule: Year-round, 24 hours per day
Maps: USGS Cane Springs Mountain Verde Hot Springs AZ, Wet Bottom Mesa AZ, Chalk Mountain AZ; National Geographic/Trails Illustrated Mazatzal and Pine Mountain Wilderness Areas map; USFS Mazatzal Wilderness map; Tonto National Forest map
Trail contact: Payson Ranger District, Tonto National Forest, 1009 E. AZ 260, Payson, AZ 85541; (928) 474-7900. Cave Creek Ranger District, Tonto National Forest, 40202 N. Cave Creek Rd., Scottsdale, AZ 85262; (480) 595-3300; www.fs.usda.gov/tonto

Finding the trailhead: To reach the south trailhead from the junction of Cave Creek Road and Scottsdale Road in Carefree, drive 35 miles northeast on Cave Creek Road; after the pavement ends this becomes FR 24, a maintained dirt road. Turn right onto FR 269, and go 10 miles to the Sheep Bridge Trailhead at the end of the road. FR 269 is usually passable for ordinary cars, but may become impassable, even for high-clearance, four-wheel-drive vehicles, after a major storm. GPS: N34 4.77' / W111 42.46'

Another way to reach the junction of FR 24 and FR 269 is to exit I-17 at the Bloody Basin interchange, just south of Cordes Junction. Go east on Bloody Basin Road, which becomes FR 269 at the national forest boundary. You'll reach the FR 24 junction 25 miles from I-17. Bloody Basin Road fords the Agua Fria River, which may be impassable when the river is high from snowmelt or after a storm.

The north trailhead can be reached from the Bloody Basin exit on I-17 by continuing 28 miles north, then exiting at AZ 260. Go 27 miles east on AZ 260, then turn right on AZ 87. Drive south 8 miles to Strawberry, then turn left onto Fossile Creek Road at Strawberry Lodge, and continue west 2.7 miles (this road becomes FR 708). Turn left onto FR 428, go 0.7 mile, then turn right onto FR 194. Drive 4.2 miles to the Twin Buttes Trailhead. This road is impassable in wet weather and may require a four-wheel-drive vehicle. GPS: N34 21.17' / W111 34.21'

The Hike

This long trail follows the Verde River for much of its length, and was built to move sheep from summer pastures high on the Mogollon Rim to winter grazing in the desert north of Phoenix. It's an all-downhill shuttle hike if you start from the north end, at Twin Buttes Trailhead.

The Verde River is a federally designated Wild and Scenic River, and the segment followed by this hike is entirely within the Mazatzal Wilderness. The river is home to a population of endangered desert bald eagles. The trail fords the river in two places, which is easily done at low water; at high water you can use the aptly named Highwater Trail to avoid both fords. The final crossing at Sheep Bridge Trailhead is bridged. You'll also have to cross the East Verde River and Wet Bottom Creek; both are easy at low water but may be impossible during spring snowmelt or after a major storm. There are numerous campsites along the trail—the most pleasant are along the section where the trail is close to the river.

The trail, a closed jeep trail built for access to stock tanks, heads southwest through the low saddle between Twin Buttes. It descends very gradually along Road Ridge, one of many volcanic, pinyon and juniper-covered mesas in the northern section of the wilderness. The trail turns to the west and crosses Camp Gulch before climbing a couple of hundred feet onto Cedar Bench. Turning to the northwest to reach the edge of the mesa, the trail then drops southwest down a ridge and passes the junction with the Deadman Mesa Trail at a saddle. A further descent takes you to the Verde River bottom.

After crossing the East Verde River, the trail cuts across a bend, then returns to the river to pass Goat Camp Canyon and Petes Cabin Mesa. Highwater Trail forks left (east); stay right, following the Verde River Trail to the crossing north of Canoe Mesa. Because the river swings wide around Canoe Mesa, the trail takes a shortcut directly south, passing west of Table Mountain, and doesn't return to the riverbank until the next crossing at Red Creek.

After crossing to the east side of the Verde River after Red Creek, you'll meet Wet Bottom Trail. Stay right and follow Verde River Trail south to cross Wet Bottom Creek, which has a seasonal flow at the trail crossing. The trail wanders up to a mile east of the river as it makes its way through the low hills. The river finally bends east toward the trail, and you'll hike along a bluff with a sweeping view of the desert waterway. The trail drops off the bluff to cross Dry Wash; the river is close by and easily accessible. Again, the trail climbs away from the river to cross H K Mesa (stay right at the junction with Dutchman Grave Trail), then descends into Sycamore Creek. Willow Spring Trail joins from the left; stay right once again and cross Sheep Bridge to the trailhead on the west bank of the river.

The foot-and-stock suspension bridge was built by the USDA Forest Service to replace a dangerously deteriorated historic structure. A plaque on the original west abutment describes how shepherds built the old bridge so their animals could safely cross the Verde River during the spring high water.

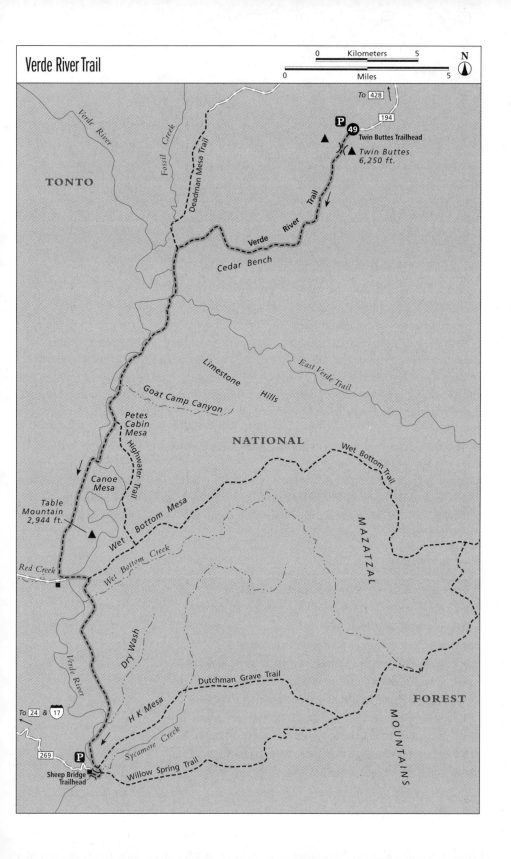

Verde River Trail

To 428

194

P **49** Twin Buttes Trailhead

▲ Twin Buttes
6,250 ft.

TONTO

Verde River

Fossil Creek

Deadman Mesa Trail

Verde River Trail

Cedar Bench

Limestone Hills

East Verde Trail

Goat Camp Canyon

Petes Cabin Mesa

Highwater Trail

NATIONAL

Wet Bottom Trail

Canoe Mesa

Table Mountain 2,944 ft.
▲

Wet Bottom Mesa

Wet Bottom Creek

Red Creek
■

M A Z A T Z A L

Dry Wash

Verde River

Dutchman Grave Trail

FOREST

To 24 & 17

269

H K Mesa

Sycamore Creek

M O U N T A I N S

P
Sheep Bridge Trailhead
■

Willow Spring Trail

Verde River near the confluence of the East Verde River

Coyotes are common throughout the west, and you're likely to hear their unique yipping song anywhere in Arizona, especially at dawn or dusk. These small, brownish-gray members of the dog family are extremely intelligent and have actually thrived in the presence of encroaching civilization. Once humans exterminated wolves from the Southwest, coyotes starting hunting in packs just like their former competitors. Coyotes mostly feed on rabbits and small rodents. They are not a danger to hikers, though their song can be startling, especially if they suddenly start to yip close by your camp. Usually other members of the pack will join in, and the coyote chorus can continue for some time.

Option: You can avoid both river fords by turning left on the Highwater Trail, then right on the Wet Bottom Trail. This option is 0.1 mile shorter than the Verde River Trail and adds no elevation change. It also keeps you away from the river for several miles; the next easy access is at Dry Wash.

Miles and Directions

0.0 From the Twin Buttes Trailhead, start on Verde River Trail.

9.1 At the junction with Deadman Mesa Trail, stay left on Verde River Trail.

9.8 Reach the Verde River.

10.4 Reach the confluence with the East Verde River.

15.3 At the Highwater Trail junction, stay right on Verde River Trail.

16.7 Cross the Verde River at the ford north of Canoe Mesa.

21.2 Cross the Verde River at the ford at the mouth of Red Creek.

21.7 At the Wet Bottom Trail junction, stay right on Verde River Trail.

28.6 At the Dutchman Grave Trail junction, stay right on Verde River Trail.

28.9 At the Willow Spring Trail junction, stay right on Verde River Trail.

29.3 Arrive at the Sheep Bridge Trailhead.

50 Wet Bottom Mesa

This is one of several excellent loop backpacks that start from Sheep Bridge Trailhead. This hike starts in the classic Sonoran Desert foothills at the Verde River and loops through the pinyon–juniper woodland on the west side of the Mazatzal Mountains, then crosses the dramatic gorge carved by Wet Bottom Creek. The loop finishes along the Verde River.

Start: Sheep Bridge Trailhead
Distance: 33.5-mile loop
Hiking time: About 4 to 5 days
Difficulty: Strenuous due to distance, elevation change, and cross-country terrain
Best seasons: Oct–Apr
Trail surface: Dirt trails
Land status: Tonto National Forest, Mazatzal Wilderness
Nearest town: Carefree
Other users: Horses
Water availability: Verde River, Sycamore Creek; seasonal at Dutchman Grave Spring,

Wet Bottom Creek, and Bull Spring
Canine compatibility: Leashed dogs permitted
Fees and permits: None
Schedule: Year-round, 24 hours per day
Maps: USGS Chalk Mountain AZ, Wet Bottom Mesa AZ, Cypress Butte AZ; National Geo-graphic/Trails Illustrated Mazatzal and Pine Mountain Wilderness Areas map; USFS Mazat-zal Wilderness map; Tonto National Forest map
Trail contact: Cave Creek Ranger District, Tonto National Forest, 40202 N. Cave Creek Rd., Scottsdale, AZ 85262; (480) 595-3300; www .fs.usda.gov/tonto

Finding the trailhead: To reach the south trailhead from the junction of Cave Creek Road and Scottsdale Road in Carefree, drive 35 miles northeast on Cave Creek Road; after the pavement ends this becomes FR 24, a maintained dirt road. Turn right onto FR 269, and go 10 miles to the Sheep Bridge Trailhead at the end of the road. FR 269 is usually passable for ordinary cars but may become impassable, even for high-clearance, four-wheel-drive vehicles, after a major storm. GPS: N34 4.77' / W111 42.46'

Another way to reach the junction of FR 24 and FR 269 is to exit I-17 at the Bloody Basin interchange, just south of Cordes Junction. Go east on Bloody Basin Road, which becomes FR 269 at the national forest boundary. You'll reach the FR 24 junction 25 miles from I-17. Bloody Basin Road fords the Agua Fria River, which may be impassable when the river is high from snowmelt or after a storm.

The Hike

This route features a section of cross–country hiking, and some of the trails are faint and may be difficult to find in places. You should have the USGS topographic maps, the Mazatzal Wilderness map, and cross–country navigation skills before attempting this hike.

Start by crossing Sheep Bridge, then stay left on Verde River Trail at the Willow Spring Trail junction. After crossing Sycamore Creek, turn right onto Dutchman

Wet Bottom Creek drains the northwest slopes of the Mazatzal Mountains through an impressive granite canyon.

Grave Trail (the Verde River Trail is the return route). Follow Dutchman Grave Trail northeast up onto H K Mesa. Dutchman Grave Trail continues across the mesa, paralleling Sycamore Creek (the creek is always about 0.5 miles south and has a permanent flow). After the trail swings around the east side of a small hill, it climbs over a saddle and drops into a basin.

Turn left onto Red Hills Trail (Dutchman Grave Spring is 0.4 mile east on the Dutchman Grave Trail). Red Hills Trail heads north and climbs over a saddle just east of a rocky hill. It stays east of a major tributary of Sycamore Creek, then turns northeast and climbs steeply up a ravine containing an old mine. Once it gains the crest at the head of the ravine, the trail swings sharply southeast and wanders across the broad mesa. The trail is faint and easy to lose in the high desert grassland but is marked with cairns.

After about a mile the trail turns north and climbs a drainage. The first juniper trees appear in this area. The trail passes over two low saddles before descending northeast into a canyon. It follows the drainage northeast (upstream), climbing along its north side, and reaches a saddle on the ridge overlooking Wet Bottom Creek.

At this point Red Hills Trail turns sharply south along the ridge. Leave the trail and descend north-northeast, hiking cross-country, into Wet Bottom Creek. From the trail, contour northeast along the hillside, cross an east-trending ridge, then descend to a small saddle. Descend north along a ridge to Wet Bottom Creek. This is the route of an old trail, but little trace remains.

Once in the Wet Bottom drainage, head north (downstream). Wet Bottom Creek is very scenic and has seasonal water—sometimes a lot of water! Just upstream of the mouth of Bull Spring Canyon, climb north up a brushy slope, parallel to the canyon. There are traces of the old trail here. Climb over the low ridge, marked "4325" on the USGS topographic map, then contour above the bed of the canyon until it's possible to descend to the bed. The trail, now more distinct, follows the bed north to Bull Spring and an old rancher's line cabin set in the pinyon pines and junipers.

Turn left on Wet Bottom Trail, which heads northwest and climbs out of the Bull Spring basin. After crossing a saddle, it turns west and crosses a tributary of Wet Bottom Creek before gaining the crest of the ridge to the west. The trail turns southwest and descends, gradually at first, then more steeply, working its way down the slopes above Canyon Creek. Eventually it emerges onto Wet Bottom Mesa and meets the Highwater Trail.

Stay left on Wet Bottom Trail and continue southwest across Wet Bottom Mesa, then down toward the Verde River. Turn left onto Verde River Trail and hike south, crossing Wet Bottom Creek near its confluence with the Verde River. There is seasonal water in the creek.

Continue south on Verde River Trail as it works its way through low hills. For several miles the trail stays about a mile east of the river. Stay right at Dutchmans Grave Trail and again at Willow Spring Trail to return to the Sheep Bridge Trailhead.

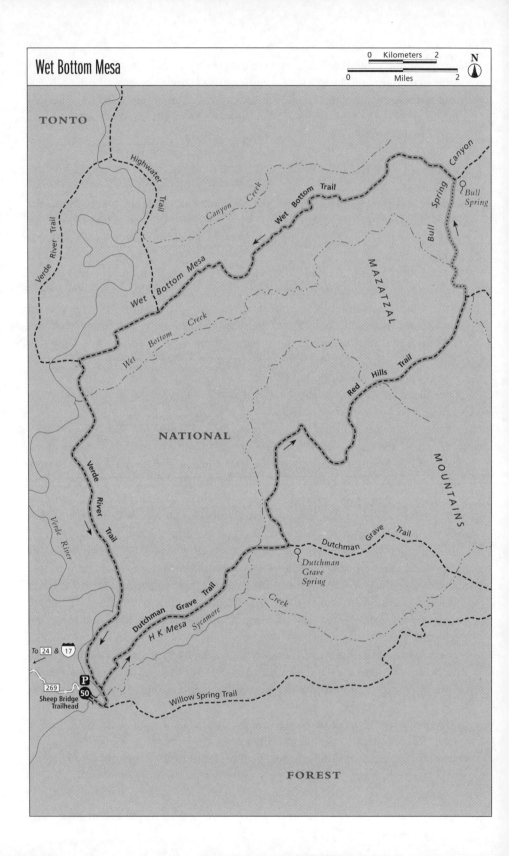

Wet Bottom Mesa

TONTO

Highwater Trail

Verde River Trail

Wet Bottom Mesa

Canyon Creek

Wet Bottom Trail

MAZATZAL

Bull Spring Canyon

Bull Spring

Wet Bottom Creek

Red Hills Trail

NATIONAL

MOUNTAINS

Verde River Trail

Verde River

Dutchman Grave Trail

Dutchman Grave Spring

Dutchman Grave Trail

H K Mesa

Sycamore Creek

To 24 & 17

269

P
50

Sheep Bridge
Trailhead

Willow Spring Trail

FOREST

N

Miles and Directions

0.0 From the Sheep Bridge Trailhead, cross Sheep Bridge on Verde River Trail.

0.4 At the Willow Spring Trail junction, stay left on Verde River Trail.

0.7 Turn right onto Dutchman Grave Trail.

5.6 Turn left onto Red Hills Trail.

12.8 Leave the formal trail and descend north, hiking cross-country, into Wet Bottom Creek.

14.0 Turn left (north) and hike downstream along Wet Bottom Creek.

14.8 Cross Wet Bottom Creek just downstream of Bull Spring Canyon and climb up the slope to the north.

16.7 Pass Bull Spring and turn left onto Wet Bottom Trail.

23.9 At the Highwater Trail junction, stay left on Wet Bottom Trail.

25.9 Turn left onto Verde River Trail.

32.8 At the Dutchman Grave Trail junction, stay right on Verde River Trail.

33.1 At the Willow Spring Trail junction, stay right on Verde River Trail.

33.5 Arrive back at the Sheep Bridge Trailhead.

51 Mountain Spring Loop

This fine backpacking loop travels through the beautiful Sonoran Desert foothills and pinyon pine–juniper forests on the west slopes of the Mazatzal Mountains.

Start: Sheep Bridge Trailhead
Distance: 21.2-mile loop
Hiking time: About 3 days
Difficulty: Strenuous due to distance and elevation change
Best seasons: Oct–Apr
Trail surface: Dirt
Land status: Tonto National Forest, Mazatzal Wilderness
Nearest town: Carefree
Other users: Horses
Water availability: Verde River, and seasonally at Willow, Mountain, and Dutchmans Grave springs

Canine compatibility: Leashed dogs permitted
Fees and permits: None
Schedule: Year-round, 24 hours per day
Maps: USGS Chalk Mountain AZ and Table Mountain AZ; National Geographic/Trails Illustrated Mazatzal and Pine Mountain Wilderness Areas map; USFS Mazatzal Wilderness map; Tonto National Forest map
Trail contact: Cave Creek Ranger District, Tonto National Forest, 40202 N. Cave Creek Rd., Scottsdale, AZ 85262; (480) 595-3300; www .fs.usda.gov/tonto

Finding the trailhead: To reach the south trailhead from the junction of Cave Creek Road and Scottsdale Road in Carefree, drive 35 miles northeast on Cave Creek Road; after the pavement ends this becomes FR 24, a maintained dirt road. Turn right onto FR 269, and go 10 miles to the Sheep Bridge Trailhead at the end of the road. FR 269 is usually passable for ordinary cars, but may become impassable, even for high-clearance, four-wheel-drive vehicles, after a major storm. GPS: N34 4.77' / W111 42.46'

Another way to reach the junction of FR 24 and 269 is to exit I-17 at the Bloody Basin interchange, just south of Cordes Junction. Go east on Bloody Basin Road, which becomes FR 269 at the national forest boundary. You'll reach the FR 24 junction 25 miles from I-17. Bloody Basin Road fords the Agua Fria River, which may be impassable when the river is high from snowmelt or after a storm.

The Hike

To begin, cross Sheep Bridge, then turn right onto Willow Spring Trail. This distinct and easy-to-follow trail crosses the gentle foothills north of Horse Creek, heading east toward the distant mountains. This is an especially delightful walk after a wet winter, when the desert flowers bloom in wild profusion.

About a mile before the foothills, Willow Spring Trail skirts just north of Horse Creek; during the cool season there is usually water in the creek, a couple hundred yards south of the trail. This is a good place to pick up water for camp, as the trail soon starts a long climb with no water available until you reach Mountain Spring. You can camp along the ridge or ahead near Willow Spring Basin.

Spring flowers on the Mountain Spring Loop

After another mile of gentle terrain, the trail climbs gradually up the ridge just north of Horse Creek, drops back alongside the creek temporarily, then abruptly veers north and climbs steeply onto a ridge. It turns east again, crossing a saddle on the edge of Willow Spring Basin (Willow Spring is 0.3 mile southeast, in the bed of Horse Creek). The trail then turns north again and resumes climbing. By now you've gained enough elevation to leave the Sonoran Desert below and enter high desert grassland.

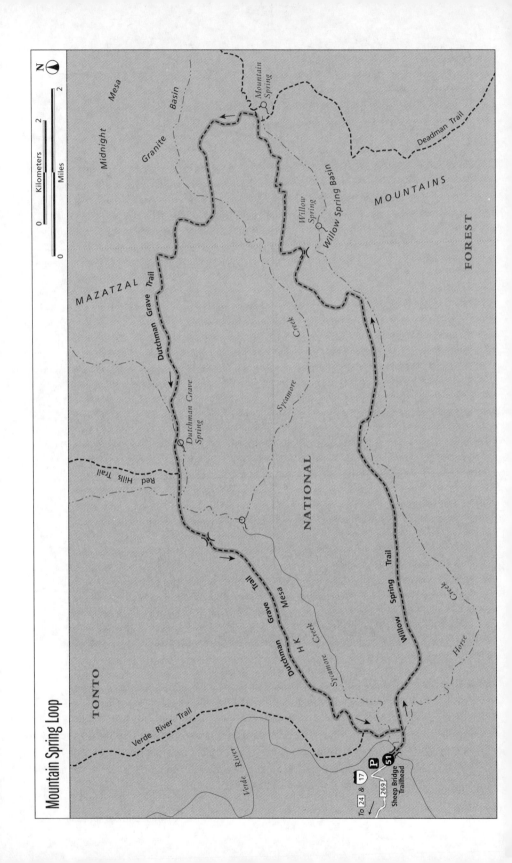

Mountain Spring Loop

N

Kilometers
0   2

Miles
0   2

TONTO

MAZATZAL

NATIONAL

FOREST

MOUNTAINS

Midnight Mesa

Granite Basin

Mountain Spring

Deadman Trail

Dutchman Grave Trail

Willow Spring

Willow Spring Basin

Dutchman Grave Spring

Red Hills Trail

Sycamore Creek

Dutchman Grave Trail

H K Mesa

Sycamore Creek

Willow Spring Trail

Verde River Trail

Horse Creek

Verde River

To 24 & 17

269

P

51

Sheep Bridge Trailhead

Once it regains the ridgecrest north of Horse Canyon, the Willow Spring Trail turns east and climbs up this ridge, gradually at first, then more steeply. The climb moderates as the trail approaches the basin at the head of Horse Creek. At Deadman Trail, stay left on Willow Spring Trail to Dutchman Grave Trail. Turn left here, onto Dutchman Grave Trail. (Mountain Spring is a few yards east, in the drainage at the head of Horse Creek.) There are small campsites in this area.

Head north on Dutchman Grave Trail, which contours until it reaches the ridge south of Granite Basin, where it turns west and descends to cross Sycamore Creek. At the top of the climb out of this small canyon, the trail turns northwest and skirts several drainages before turning west again. The trail then works its way west down the slope and reaches Dutchman Grave Spring, which is in an unnamed tributary of Sycamore Creek. There are campsites near the spring.

Continue west to the Red Hills Trail junction; stay left on Dutchman Grave Trail and follow it across the basin to the west. The Dutchman Grave Trail turns southwest and climbs over a saddle, then skirts a small hill and climbs onto H K Mesa. Follow the trail southwest as it skirts the southern edge of the mesa, just above Sycamore Creek (a reliable water source).

Eventually, the trail drops off the southwest end of the mesa and ends at the Verde River Trail. Turn left onto Verde River Trail, and stay right at Willow Spring Trail junction. Cross Sheep Bridge to return to the Sheep Bridge Trailhead.

Miles and Directions

0.0 From the Sheep Bridge Trailhead, cross Sheep Bridge and start on Verde River Trail.

0.4 Turn right onto Willow Spring Trail.

9.9 At the Deadman Trail junction, stay left on Willow Spring Trail.

10.0 Turn left onto Dutchman Grave Trail.

15.3 Pass Dutchman Grave Spring.

15.5 At the Red Hills Trail junction, stay left on Dutchman Grave Trail.

20.5 Turn left onto Verde River Trail.

20.8 At the Willow Spring Trail junction, stay right on Verde River Trail.

21.2 Arrive back at the Sheep Bridge Trailhead.

52 The Park

This is yet another fine backpacking loop that starts from Sheep Bridge Trailhead. This one takes you from Sonoran Desert foothills to the headwaters of Wet Bottom Creek in the pine-forested high country of the Mazatzal Mountains and back.

Start: Sheep Bridge Trailhead
Distance: 41.6-mile loop
Hiking time: About 5 to 7 days
Difficulty: Strenuous due to distance, elevation change, and faint trails
Best seasons: Oct–Nov and Apr–May
Trail surface: Dirt
Land status: Tonto National Forest, Mazatzal Wilderness
Nearest towns: Carefree
Other users: Horses
Water availability: Seasonal in Horse Creek and at Willow Spring, Lost Spring, Mountain Spring, Fuller Seep, and Dutchman Grave Spring. Sycamore Creek has a permanent flow.
Canine compatibility: Leashed dogs permitted
Fees and permits: None
Schedule: Year-round, 24 hours per day
Maps: USGS Chalk Mountain AZ, Table Mountain AZ, Cypress Butte AZ, North Peak AZ, Wet Bottom Mesa AZ; National Geographic/Trails Illustrated Mazatzal and Pine Mountain Wilderness Areas map; USFS Mazatzal Wilderness map; Tonto National Forest map
Trail contact: Cave Creek Ranger District, Tonto National Forest, 40202 N. Cave Creek Rd., Scottsdale, AZ 85262; (480) 595-3300; www .fs.usda.gov/tonto

Finding the trailhead: To reach the south trailhead from the junction of Cave Creek Road and Scottsdale Road in Carefree, drive 35 miles northeast on Cave Creek Road; after the pavement ends this becomes FR 24, a maintained dirt road. Turn right onto FR 269, and go 10 miles to the Sheep Bridge Trailhead at the end of the road. FR 269 is usually passable for ordinary cars but may become impassable, even for high-clearance, four-wheel-drive vehicles, after a major storm. GPS: N34 4.77' / W111 42.46'

Another way to reach the junction of FR 24 and FR 269 is to exit I-17 at the Bloody Basin interchange, just south of Cordes Junction. Go east on Bloody Basin Road, which becomes FR 269 at the national forest boundary. You'll reach the FR 24 junction 25 miles from I-17. Bloody Basin Road fords the Agua Fria River, which may be impassable when the river is high from snowmelt or after a storm.

The Hike

Although this entire loop is on trails, portions of the trails are very faint. You should have the USGS topographic maps, the USDA Forest Service wilderness map, and cross-country navigational skills before attempting this trip.

To begin, cross Sheep Bridge and turn right onto Willow Spring Trail. This distinct and easy-to-follow trail crosses the gentle foothills north of Horse Creek, heading east toward the distant mountains. This is an especially delightful walk after a wet winter, when the desert flowers bloom in wild profusion. About a mile before the

Mountain Spring is an important seasonal spring on the loop through The Park.

foothills, Willow Spring Trail skirts just north of Horse Creek; during the cool season there is usually water in the creek, a couple hundred yards south of the trail. This is a good place to pick up water for camp, as the trail soon starts a long climb with no water available until you reach Mountain Spring.

After a mile of gentle terrain, the trail climbs gradually up the ridge just north of Horse Creek, drops back alongside the creek temporarily, then abruptly veers north and climbs steeply onto a ridge. It turns east again, crossing a saddle on the edge of Willow Spring Basin (the spring is 0.3 mile southeast in the bed of Horse Creek). It then turns north again, and resumes climbing. By now you've gained enough elevation to leave the Sonoran Desert below and enter high desert grassland.

Once it regains the ridgecrest north of Horse Canyon, the Willow Spring Trail turns east and climbs up the ridge, gradually at first, then more steeply. The climb moderates as the trail approaches the basin at the head of Horse Creek. At Deadman Trail, stay left on Willow Spring Trail. Stay right again at the Dutchman Grave Trail junction (10.0 miles), remaining on the Willow Spring Trail. There are small campsites in this area.

You'll pass the short spur trail to Mountain Spring and then start climbing again. The trail leaves the high desert grassland and enters the pygmy pinyon–juniper forest. Another spur trail goes to Lost Spring, which is a seasonal water source (this spring is not shown on the USGS map). The trail turns north and runs along a ridge to the base of Midnight Mesa, then contours the slopes of the mesa just below its east rim. Shortly after passing through a saddle into the Wet Bottom Creek drainage, you'll meet Midnight Trail; stay right on Willow Spring Trail. The trail turns east and slowly descends into a tributary of Wet Bottom Creek. You may find water in the creek. There is a small campsite at the creek crossing.

Willow Spring Trail starts a steep climb to the northeast, finally contouring into a saddle above Maverick Basin. It then contours north another mile or so to end at Mazatzal Divide Trail (Arizona Trail). Turn left onto Mazatzal Divide Trail and walk through The Park, a small pine-forested basin at the head of Wet Bottom Creek. There is plenty of camping at The Park, but no water.

North Peak Trail branches right at the north side of The Park; stay left on the Mazatzal Divide Trail, which turns northwest to the head of a tributary of City Creek, then climbs over the east shoulder of Knob Mountain. This is the highest elevation point of the trip. The trail heads north (the trail shown going west over Knob Mountain on the Cypress Butte USGS topographic map no longer exists) and descends a ridge west of Hells Hole.

Turn left onto Red Hills Trail and follow the path as it drops into a very pretty basin filled with ponderosa pine on the north slopes of Knob Mountain. Red Hills Trail then climbs onto the west end of Knob Mountain and meets Brush Trail. Stay left on Red Hills Trail and follow it southwest to the rim of Knob Mountain.

The trail plunges into another tributary of Wet Bottom Creek via a series of steep and rocky switchbacks. The trail may be rough, but the views are good. After the steep descent the trail levels out into Fuller Seep basin, a fine spot with some nice campsites. Fuller Seep usually has water during the cool season.

Below the seep, the trail climbs away from the basin and meets the north end of the Midnight Trail, coming in from the left. Stay right on Red Hills Trail and follow it over a small saddle, then west to a ridge. The trail drops down this ridge to Wet Bottom Creek. Wet Bottom Creek usually flows at this delightful spot, which is a great lunch spot but no campsites.

A steep climb takes you out of the creek to the west and south, up a ridge thickly covered with Arizona cypress trees. After the trail tops out, it wanders west, then north to an unnamed saddle west of Wet Bottom Creek. The trail is faint here in many places, and your route-finding skills will get a workout. The trail is shown on the wilderness map but not on the USGS map. Although the trail heads generally west, it takes a very indirect route and it's easy to lose at unexpected turns. Watch for, and carefully follow, the rock cairns.

From the saddle, the trail turns west again and descends gradually into a tributary of Sycamore Creek. There is seasonal water here and a few campsites. The trail climbs over a couple of saddles, then swings northwest and descends a grassy ridge. Near the end of this ridge the trail abruptly turns southwest and descends a steep ravine past an old mine. The trail then turns south and descends along the east slopes of an unnamed tributary of Sycamore Creek. Eventually it crosses a low saddle and drops down to end at Dutchman Grave Trail. Dutchman Grave Spring is 0.4 mile east. There are several campsites in this area.

Turn right onto Dutchman Grave Trail and follow it across a basin, then southwest and over a saddle. The trail descends the slope, then skirts a small hill and climbs onto

The Park

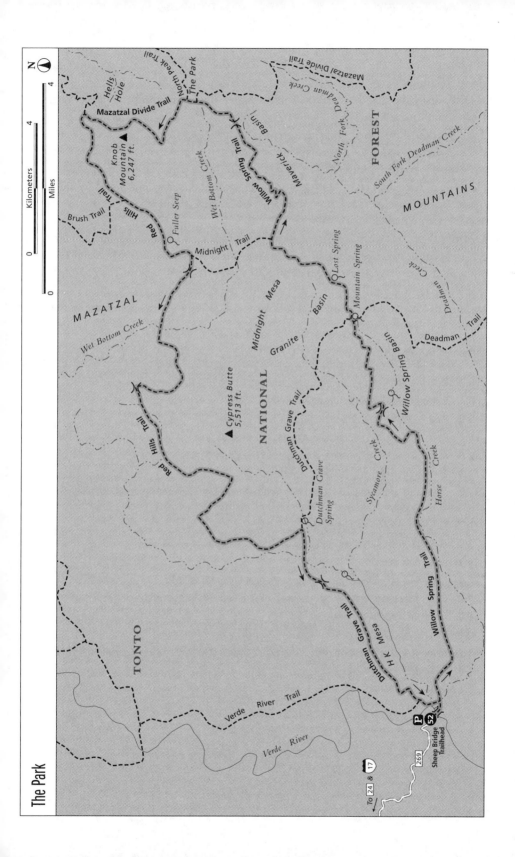

H K Mesa. Follow the trail southwest as it skirts the southern edge of the mesa, just above Sycamore Creek, a reliable water source.

Eventually, the trail drops off the southwest end of the mesa and ends at the Verde River Trail. Turn left onto Verde River Trail, and then stay right at the Willow Spring Trail junction. Cross Sheep Bridge to return to the Sheep Bridge Trailhead.

The Arizona cypress, a 20- to 40-foot-tall tree with distinctive, curly red bark, is a close relative of the famous Monterey cypress and Italian cypress. The needles resemble those of the junipers. In Arizona, the cypress is found in the central and southeast mountains. Some fine stands are found in the Mazatzal Mountains, especially in the Wet Bottom Creek drainage.

Option: You can take a significant shortcut by turning left on Midnight Trail. This 2.2-mile connector trail leaves Willow Spring Trail east of Midnight Mesa and takes you down across Wet Bottom Creek to join Red Hills Trail west of Fuller Seep. It makes the loop 9.6 miles shorter. Even if you do the full loop, you might consider taking a side hike on the Midnight Trail because it takes you to the scenic upper portion of Wet Bottom Creek.

Miles and Directions

0.0 From the Sheep Bridge Trailhead, cross Sheep Bridge and start on the Verde River Trail.

0.4 Turn right onto Willow Spring Trail.

9.9 Pass Deadman Trail; stay left on Willow Spring Trail.

10.0 Pass Dutchman Grave Trail; stay right on Willow Spring Trail.

12.5 At the Midnight Trail junction, stay right on Willow Spring Trail.

17.3 Turn left onto Mazatzal Divide Trail (Arizona Trail).

17.5 Arrive at The Park. At the junction with North Peak Trail, stay left on Mazatzal Divide Trail (Arizona Trail).

20.7 Turn left onto Red Hills Trail.

23.0 At the junction with Brush Trail, stay left on Red Hills Trail.

24.1 Pass Fuller Seep.

25.1 At the second Midnight Trail junction, stay right on Red Hills Trail.

29.2 Cross the saddle west of Wet Bottom Creek; the Red Hills Trail turns abruptly west.

36.0 Turn right onto Dutchmans Grave Trail.

40.9 Turn left onto Verde River Trail.

41.2 At the Willow Spring Trail junction, stay right on Verde River Trail and cross Sheep Bridge.

41.6 Arrive at the Sheep Bridge Trailhead.

53 Club Cabin

Yet another classic backpacking loop starts from Sheep Bridge and travels through the Sonoran Desert before hooking up through the pine-forested Mazatzal high country. Highlights include a historic rancher's line cabin and camp and stunning views of Mazatzal Peak.

Start: Sheep Bridge Trailhead
Distance: 45.6-mile lollipop
Hiking time: About 5 to 7 days
Difficulty: Strenuous due to distance, elevation change, and faint trails
Best seasons: Oct-Apr
Trail surface: Dirt
Land status: Tonto National Forest, Mazatzal Wilderness
Nearest town: Carefree
Other users: Horses
Water availability: Verde River; seasonal at Willow Spring, Mountain Spring, Mesquite Spring, Deadman Creek, Davenport Wash, Club Spring, Red Rock Spring, South Fork Deadman

Creek, Chilson Spring, Horse Camp Seep, Hopi Spring, Lost Spring
Canine compatibility: Leashed dogs permitted
Fees and permits: None
Schedule: Year-round, 24 hours per day
Maps: USGS Chalk Mountain AZ, Table Mountain AZ, Mazatzal Peak AZ, North Peak AZ, Cypress Butte AZ; National Geographic/Trails Illustrated Mazatzal and Pine Mountain Wilderness Areas map; USFS Mazatzal Wilderness map; Tonto National Forest map
Trail contact: Cave Creek Ranger District, Tonto National Forest, 40202 N. Cave Creek Rd., Scottsdale, AZ 85262; (480) 595-3300; www .fs.usda.gov/tonto

Finding the trailhead: To reach the south trailhead from the junction of Cave Creek Road and Scottsdale Road in Carefree, drive 35 miles northeast on Cave Creek Road; after the pavement ends this becomes FR 24, a maintained dirt road. Turn right onto FR 269, and go 10 miles to the Sheep Bridge Trailhead at the end of the road. FR 269 is usually passable for ordinary cars but may become impassable, even for high-clearance, four-wheel-drive vehicles, after a major storm. GPS: N34 4.77' / W111 42.46'

Another way to reach the junction of FR 24 and FR 269 is to exit I-17 at the Bloody Basin interchange, just south of Cordes Junction. Go east on Bloody Basin Road, which becomes FR 269 at the national forest boundary. You'll reach the FR 24 junction 25 miles from I-17. Bloody Basin Road fords the Agua Fria River, which may be impassable when the river is high from snowmelt or after a storm.

The Hike

Although the entire route is on trails, some of the trails are faint and hard to find. You should have the USGS topographic maps, the USFS wilderness map, and good route-finding skills before attempting this hike.

Begin by crossing Sheep Bridge, then turn right onto Willow Spring Trail. This distinct and easy-to-follow trail crosses the gentle foothills north of Horse Creek,

Club cabin is an old rancher's line cabin.

heading east toward the distant mountains. This is especially delightful after a wet winter, when the desert flowers bloom in wild profusion.

About a mile before the foothills, Willow Spring Trail skirts just north of Horse Creek; during the cool season there is usually water in the creek, a couple hundred yards south of the trail. This is a good place to pick up water for camp, as the trail soon starts a long climb, with no water available until you reach Mountain Spring. You can also camp right here, on the ridge.

After a mile of gentle terrain, the trail climbs gradually up the ridge just north of Horse Creek, drops back alongside the creek temporarily, then abruptly veers north and climbs steeply onto a ridge. It turns east again, crossing a saddle on the edge of Willow Spring Basin (the spring is 0.3 mile southeast in the bed of Horse Creek). The trail then turns north again and resumes climbing. By now you've gained enough elevation to leave the Sonoran Desert below and enter high desert grassland.

Once it regains the ridgecrest north of Horse Canyon, Willow Spring Trail turns east and climbs up the ridge, gradually at first, then more steeply. The climb moderates as the trail approaches the basin at the head of Horse Creek. Mountain Spring is nearby, and there are a few small campsites.

Turn right onto Deadman Trail, which climbs south onto the ridge above Deadman Creek, then drops west to a saddle. Now the trail turns south again and descends to Deadman Creek, staying just west of a drainage. The Table Mountain USGS quadrangle shows the trail swinging west before descending to Deadman Creek, but the present route follows a more direct, cairn-marked route south to the creek. Use care, because the route is easily lost in the grassy terrain, which is crisscrossed by cattle trails. Deadman Creek often has water, and there are small campsites

Directly south of the creek crossing, the flat-topped bulk of Table Mountain dominates the skyline. Deadman Trail climbs southeast over the saddle east of Table Mountain, passing Mesquite Spring along the way. From the saddle, the trail descends southeast down a drainage and ends at the junction with Davenport Trail, in Davenport Wash. There is seasonal water in Davenport Wash.

Turn left onto Davenport Trail, which climbs up a gentle ridge to the east. As the grasslands give way to diminutive juniper trees and chaparral, you'll reach a short spur trail to Club Cabin and Club Spring. The cabin is an old rancher's line cabin, used during cattle roundups and other work. The spring is behind the cabin. There are small campsites here.

From the cabin the trail swings north, climbing steadily to cross a couple of minor ridges. It then turns generally northeast, working its way across a complex of ridges and drainages to cross a ridge at 5,000 feet, then descending steeply to cross South Fork Deadman Creek. There is usually water at this very scenic spot. A steep climb east of the creek leads over a ridge, where the trail contours northeast to Chilson Camp.

Chilson Camp is another former line camp, but the old cabin is long gone. Chilson Spring, a few hundred yards up the hillside northeast of the camp, used to be piped down to the camp, but this water source is no longer reliable.

Turn left onto Brody Trail, and then onto Mazatzal Divide Trail (Arizona Trail), which heads north, contouring across brushy slopes into the North Fork Deadman Creek drainage. At Sandy Saddle Trail, stay left on Mazatzal Divide Trail. The North Peak USGS map shows Mazatzal Divide Trail passing Horse Camp Seep, but the current route of the trail takes it east of the seep. There is a signed spur trail to the seep, and it's worth the short side trip to see the dramatic cliffs at the head of North Fork Deadman Creek. There are fine campsites near the seep. You can hike cross-country to a scenic overlook about 0.3 mile down the north fork, to the point where it drops into a deep canyon.

Mazatzal Divide Trail continues north to Rock Creek Trail. Hopi Spring is located a few yards east on the Rock Creek Trail. There are small campsites near the trail junction.

Stay left on Mazatzal Divide Trail and climb gradually up the broad forested basin at the head of the north fork, then swing west to cross a ridge above Maverick Basin. The trail swings north again and descends gradually. At The Park, a small pine flat at the head of Wet Bottom Creek (there is camping here but no water), turn left onto Willow Spring Trail and follow it southwest as it contours across the headwaters of Wet Bottom Creek. At a saddle, the trail works its way along the ridge dividing Wet

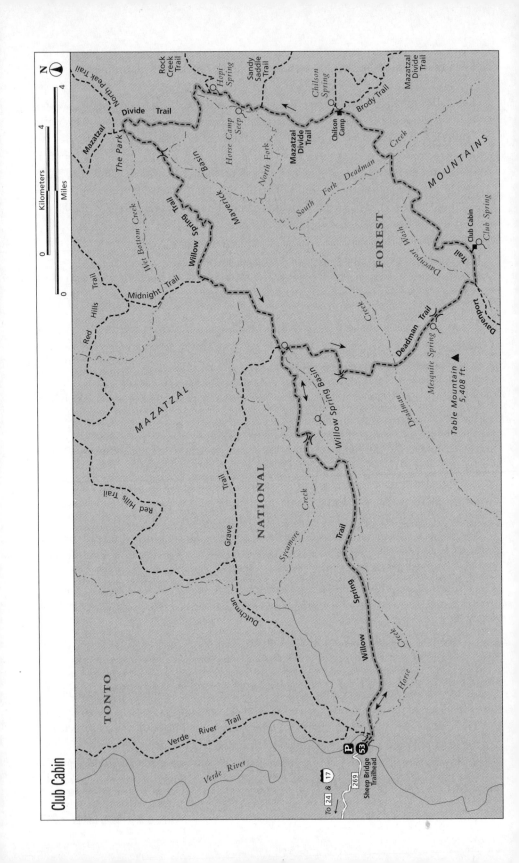

Club Cabin

Bottom Creek and Maverick Basin, then descends to cross an unnamed tributary of Wet Bottom Creek. There is a small campsite here.

At Midnight Trail, stay left on Willow Spring Trail. After contouring around the east end of Midnight Mesa, the Willow Spring Trail descends generally southwest to the Dutchman Grave Trail junction; stay left on Willow Spring Trail. At the Deadman Trail junction, stay right on Willow Spring Trail, closing the loop. Retrace your steps. At Verde River Trail, turn left and cross Sheep Bridge to reach Sheep Bridge Trailhead.

Option: From the pass east of Table Mountain, it's an easy climb up grassy slopes to the top of the mountain. From the 5,408-foot summit of this sloping mesa, you can see much of the western Mazatzal Mountains, as well as the rugged country west of the Verde River. This is one of the wildest and loneliest spots in Arizona, and it's only 50 miles, as the crow flies, from metropolitan Phoenix!

Miles and Directions

0.0 From the Sheep Bridge Trailhead, cross Sheep Bridge and start on Verde River Trail.

0.4 Turn right onto Willow Spring Trail.

9.9 Turn right onto Deadman Trail.

13.1 Cross Deadman Creek.

14.5 Cross the unnamed pass east of Table Mountain.

15.6 Turn left onto Davenport Trail.

16.2 Pass the short spur trail to Club Cabin.

19.9 Cross South Fork Deadman Creek.

21.9 Arrive at Chilson Camp and turn left onto Brody Trail.

22.0 Turn left onto Mazatzal Divide Trail (Arizona Trail).

23.9 At the Sandy Saddle Trail trail junction, stay left on Mazatzal Divide Trail.

25.2 At the Rock Creek Trail junction, stay left on Mazatzal Divide Trail.

28.4 Turn left onto Willow Spring Trail.

32.8 At the Midnight Trail junction, stay left on Willow Spring Trail.

35.6 At the Dutchmans Grave Trail junction; stay left on Willow Spring Trail.

35.7 At the Deadman Trail junction, stay right on Willow Spring Trail.

45.2 Turn left onto Verde River Trail.

45.6 Arrive back at the Sheep Bridge Trailhead.

54 Davenport Wash

This nice backpacking loop in the southwestern Sonoran Desert foothills of the Mazatzal Wilderness is relatively low in elevation. It's a good hike to do when the high country is snowy or muddy.

Start: Horseshoe Dam parking lot or Sears Trailhead (with a high-clearance vehicle)
Distance: 26.5-mile lollipop
Hiking time: About 3 days
Difficulty: Strenuous due to distance and elevation change
Best seasons: Oct–Apr
Trail surface: Dirt roads, dirt trails
Land status: Tonto National Forest, Mazatzal Wilderness
Nearest town: Carefree
Other users: Horses
Water availability: Seasonal at Andrea Spring, Midway Spring, Dog Spring, Davenport Wash, Round Spring, Sheep Creek, Lizard Spring,

Davenport Spring
Canine compatibility: Leashed dogs permitted
Fees and permits: None
Schedule: Year-round, 24 hours per day
Maps: USGS Horseshoe Dam AZ, Chalk Mountain AZ, Table Mountain AZ, Lion Mountain AZ; National Geographic/Trails Illustrated Mazatzal and Pine Mountain Wilderness Areas map; USFS Mazatzal Wilderness map; Tonto National Forest map
Trail contact: Cave Creek Ranger District, Tonto National Forest, 40202 N. Cave Creek Rd., Scottsdale, AZ 85262; (480) 595-3300; www.fs.usda.gov/tonto

Finding the trailhead: From Carefree, go about 5 miles north on Cave Creek Road, then turn right onto Bartlett Dam Road. Continue 6.3 miles, then turn left on Horseshoe Dam Road (FR 205). Go 10.3 miles, then turn right on the Horseshoe Dam Vista Road. In another 0.5 mile, the road ends at a parking area below the dam. GPS: N33 58.89' / W111 42.71'

High-clearance vehicles may be able to ford the Verde River during low water to reach the actual trailhead. Use caution and check the water depth before crossing. The ford is reached via an unmarked turnoff where the Horseshoe Dam Road first meets the river, about 7.2 miles from Bartlett Dam Road. Once across the river, go 1.1 miles, around KA Ranch (please respect all private property and signs), then turn right onto Chalk Mountain Road (FR 479). Continue 0.7 mile, then turn right onto the Davenport Road and park at Sears Trailhead. GPS: N33 58.63' / W111 40.60'

The Hike

The trails on this route are little used and can be difficult to find, so you should have both the USGS maps and the USFS wilderness map, as well as skill in route finding, before attempting this hike. Because the former road crossing at Horseshoe Dam is now closed to the public, most hikers will have to start this hike from the Horseshoe Dam parking area.

Cross the dam via the walkway under the spillway lip, which can be quite dramatic when the water is spilling over. Follow Chalk Mountain Road (FR 479) as

The western boundary of the Mazatzal Wilderness runs through classic Sonoran Desert east of the Verde River. The Mazatzal high country beckons in the distance.

it descends a hill, then skirts the north side of the KA Ranch. Stay left at each road intersection until you reach Davenport Road (FR 477); turn right and hike to Sears Trailhead.

Start the loop on Davenport Trail, an old jeep trail that climbs onto the broad ridge north of Davenport Wash and follows it northeast. When the jeep trail ends, a spur trail forks right to Andrea Spring, a scenic spot in Davenport Wash.

After visiting the spring, continue northeast on the Davenport Trail, now a foot trail, as it skirts south of a hill and then climbs over a saddle. The trail, which can be difficult to find in spots, stays north of Davenport Wash as it works its way through the complex foothills. After passing Midway Spring, which is in an unnamed tributary of

Davenport Wash

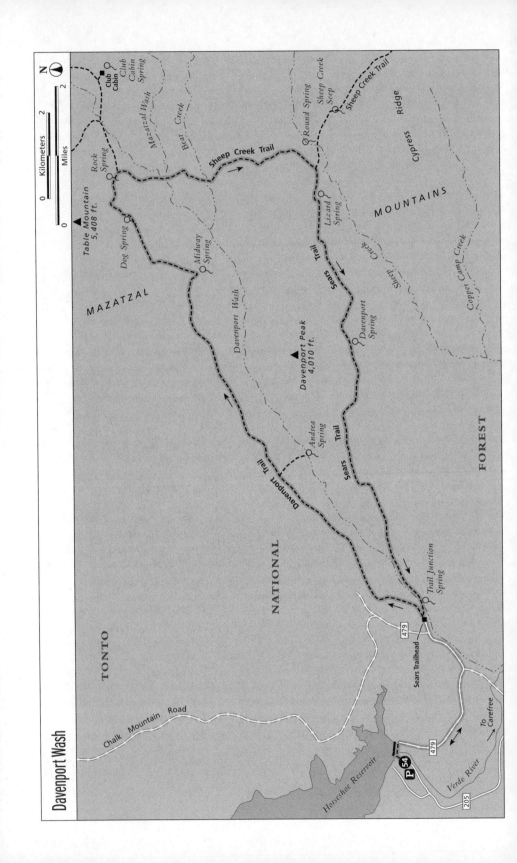

Davenport Wash, the trail climbs onto the south slopes of Table Mountain and passes Dog Spring before meeting Sheep Creek Trail.

Turn right onto Sheep Creek Trail and follow it south across Davenport Wash, where there may be seasonal water. A short climb leads south to a saddle, and an equally short descent to cross Bear Creek. A longer climb takes you to the high point of the trip, a saddle just north of Sheep Creek. It is a short descent to Sheep Creek and Sears Trail. Round Spring and the creek have seasonal water, and there are small campsites in the area.

Turn right onto Sears Trail and follow it west across the hills and ridges north of Sheep Creek. The trail passes Lizard Spring, climbs over a ridge, then drops into an unnamed tributary of Davenport Wash and passes south of Davenport Peak. Several unnamed, seasonal springs are located along this tributary. The trail, now a former jeep road, works its way west through the foothills, and eventually descends to Davenport Wash, closing the loop. Turn right onto FR 477, and follow it to Sears Trailhead. Retrace your steps on FR 477 and FR 479 to return to Horseshoe Dam and your vehicle.

Miles and Directions

0.0 From the Horseshoe Dam Parking Area, hike across the dam and follow Chalk Mountain Road (FR 479).

2.3 Where the road to the Verde River ford goes right, stay left on FR 479.

3.0 Stay right onto FR 477.

3.3 Arrive at the Sears Trailhead. Begin on Davenport Trail (FR 477 is the return route).

6.4 Pass the spur trail breaking right to Andrea Spring.

9.9 Pass Midway Spring.

10.9 Pass Dog Spring.

12.3 Turn right onto Sheep Creek Trail.

13.1 Cross Davenport Wash.

13.8 Cross Bear Creek.

15.4 Turn right onto Sears Trail.

17.4 Pass Lizard Spring, which is in the drainage south of the trail.

18.8 Pass unnamed springs south of Davenport Peak.

22.7 Turn right onto FR 477.

23.2 Arrive back at the Sears Trailhead; stay left on FR 477.

23.5 Turn left onto FR 479.

24.1 Stay right on FR 479.

26.5 Arrive back at the Horseshoe Dam Parking Area.

All wilderness water should be purified before using it for drinking or cooking. Here, water is being filtered through a paper coffee filter before being treated with a chemical purifier.

Wilderness

Aldo Leopold of the USDA Forest Service began to promote the idea of preserving wild country within the national forests in the 1920s. Under his influence and that of other like-minded employees, the agency soon began designating wilderness areas. Roads and other permanent man-made structures were excluded from such areas, although trails and activities considered compatible at the time, such as hunting, fishing, grazing, and limited mining, were allowed. Most of the land within the national park system was also managed as wilderness. This protection was under the control of the land management agencies, which could rescind the wilderness designation at any time. After a long campaign, conservationists succeeded in convincing Congress to take the wilderness concept further in 1964, when it passed the Wilderness Act. This landmark law established the National Wilderness Preservation System. Most of the existing designated Wilderness and Primitive Areas in the national forests were included in the system. Since then, Congress has added many deserving areas to the national wilderness system.

When I started hiking in Arizona in the 1960s, there were only a few protected wilderness areas. Interests such as ranching, mining, and even tourism fought to prevent any wilderness protection. As time passed, more people began to appreciate wild country as a priceless asset to the state. Now Arizona is a leader in wilderness protection. In recent years, Congress has protected many additional wild areas in Arizona as national wilderness areas, administered by the USDA Forest Service or the US Bureau of Land Management (BLM). Other wilderness areas have been protected as national monuments, administered by the National Park Service and the BLM. Private organizations such as The Nature Conservancy have also become managers of wild areas on private trust lands.

We owe this change to the dedication of the hardworking people in the conservation groups, government agencies, and the US Congress who believe in protecting what remains of the American wilderness.

While protecting existing roadless areas is vital, the protection of intact ecosystems is an even larger and more important issue. As we learn more about plant and animal habitats, we find that survival of individual species is linked to the health of other plants and animals, as well as the quality of the air and water over entire regions. Instead of protecting a few isolated wild areas and ignoring the consequences of unrestricted human activities on the rest of the land, we have to consider entire watersheds and entire forests, and how proposed activities will affect them. In Arizona, there is a growing movement to expand wilderness areas to protect entire ecosystems.

You can help by joining and supporting a conservation organization and by always hiking and camping responsively. Refer to the backcountry safety section of this book for detailed tips on equipment and technique that will let you enjoy this desert wilderness while leaving it unchanged for future generations.

Hike Index

About the Author

Bruce Grubbs is an avid hiker, mountain biker, paddler, and cross-country skier who has been exploring the American West for several decades. He has used high-technology gear in the backcountry in his work as a professional pilot, an amateur radio operator, and a mountain rescue team member. Bruce holds Airline Transport Pilot and Instrument Flight Instructor certificates. He lives in Flagstaff, Arizona, and is the author of more than thirty-five books.

Other books by the author:

- *Grand Canyon National Park Pocket Guide*
- *Hiking Arizona,* 3rd edition
- *Hiking Northern Arizona,* 3rd edition
- *Best Easy Day Hikes Flagstaff,* 2nd edition
- *Best Easy Day Hikes Sedona,* 2nd edition
- *Mountain Biking Phoenix*
- *Mountain Biking Flagstaff and Sedona*
- *Backpacker Magazine: Using a GPS*
- *Desert Hiking Tips*

For more information, check the author's website at brucegrubbs.com.